SPOKEN AND WRITTEN HINDI

# Spoken and Written Hindi

By GORDON H. FAIRBANKS

and BAL GOVIND MISRA

CORNELL UNIVERSITY

## Cornell University Press

ITHACA AND LONDON

First published 1966 by Cornell University Press
Fourth printing 1974


Published in the United Kingdom
by Cornell University Press Ltd.,
2-4 Brook Street, London W1Y 1AA




International Standard Book Number 0-8014-0123-2
Library of Congress Card Catalog Number 66-13345

Printed in the United States of America
by Valley Offset, Inc.
Bound by Vail-Ballou Press, Inc.

# PREFACE

This book is intended for those beginning the
study of Hindi.

Hindi is the major language of the states of Bihar,
Madhya Pradesh, Panjab, Rajasthan and Uttar Pradesh.
According to the census of 1961, out of a population of
approximately 440,000,000 for the whole of India, about
130,000,000 have indicated Hindi as their native
language, and close to another 9,000,000 have indicated
Hindi as a second language.

Hindi is similar to Urdu, another language spoken
in India. The two languages differ in writing system,
Urdu using the Arabic script, and Hindi using the
Devanagari script. They also differ in their inclina-
tions for borrowing learned words, Urdu borrowing more
from Persian and Arabic, and Hindi borrowing more from
Sanskrit. In their basic structure, however, the
languages are essentially identical, and hence their
spoken forms, if not too literary, are mutually in-
telligible. According to the 1961 census, almost
25,000,000 listed Urdu as their native language.

Hindi belongs to a group of related languages in
north India usually called the Indo-Aryan languages.
Besides Hindi, this group includes Assamese, Bengali,
Oriya, Marathi, Gujarati, Rajasthani, Panjabi,
Kashmiri, and Sindhi, as well as Sinhalese, which is
spoken in Ceylon. This group of languages is a sub-
group of the Indo-European family of languages, which
means that Hindi is ultimately related to such
languages as English and Russian. The relationship is,
however, too distant to aid the student in learning
Hindi. In addition to the languages mentioned above,
there are four major languages spoken in south India:
Telugu, Tamil, Malayalam, and Kannada. These are members
of a language family called Dravidian and are unrelated
to the Indo-Aryan languages.

The text is composed of twenty-four lessons plus
six review lessons. Each lesson is composed of three
sections: conversation, grammar, and drills. The
conversation should be drilled until it can be said at
normal speed and with a pronunciation that is acceptable
to a native speaker of Hindi. Each lesson introduces
from thirty to forty new vocabulary items, enough to
give the student practice in familiarizing himself with
new forms, but not so many that vocabulary learning be-
comes a burden. The grammar of each lesson presents the
forms and syntax of the material in the conversational

v

section. It is meant to enable the student to make the
analogies that are necessary in order to construct new
sentences in Hindi, and should be read and studied not
as an end in itself but as the means for making these
analogies. The drill section requires the student to
construct new sentences on the analogy of those he has
learned in the conversational section. This practice
will develop fluency in the manipulation of the forms
and syntax of Hindi within the vocabulary introduced
in the text.

The main body of the text is preceded by a section
on pronunciation. It is recommended that the student
start immediately with Lesson I rather than with the
pronunciation section. During the course of studying
the first six lessons, he should spend five to ten
minutes per day going over the words in the pronunciation section in order to overcome particular difficul-
ties that he may have.

In the early lessons, all the Hindi material is
presented in a phonemic transcription. The student
is not expected to learn to write this transcription.
Since all the work is to be done orally, the transcription is meant to give the student something to
look at which will draw his attention to distinctions
in the spoken language that he might otherwise overlook.
Beginning with Lesson V, the Hindi writing system is
gradually introduced. Once the script is introduced
the student should spend a few minutes per day practic-
ing writing, and the drill sections will give him some
practice at reading the script. In Lessons IX, X, XI,
and XII, the texts of all the conversational sections
are presented in Hindi script at the rate of three
texts per lesson. From Lesson XIII on, all new material
is presented in the Hindi script, and the student
should be prepared to do all his reading and writing
in this script. All work should be done orally only,
and the student should not be required to do any
writing until he has learned the Hindi script, that is,
until after Lesson XII. From then on most of the time
should still be devoted to oral work, but part of the
time should be spent on reading and writing the Hindi
script. It is recommended that, after doing all the
exercises of a particular lesson orally, one or two of
the exercises be assigned for writing practice.

An appendix gives the inflected forms of Hindi for
ready reference. Following this there is a Hindi-
English and an English-Hindi glossary of the words that
occur in the text. The Hindi is presented only in
Hindi script, since presumably the glossary will be
more useful and necessary in the latter part of the
course than in the earlier part.

The text has been used in mimeographed form for the last three years by our students at Cornell, and our thanks are due to them for helping to suggest improvements and corrections which have been incorporated into this version.  We owe special thanks to Mrs. Ruth Sønderhousen for typing the English parts of the text for photographing.

G. H. Fairbanks
B. G. Misra

Ithaca, New York
October, 1965

# TABLE OF CONTENTS

xviii

xxi

# PRONUNCIATION

## Vowels

There are 10 vowels in Hindi which are represented in this text by the following transcription: a aa i ii u uu ee oo ai au.

1. The vowel a is a mid, central, unrounded vowel. similar to the u in English but:

| | |
|---|---|
| ab | now |
| kab | when |
| das | ten |
| bas | bus |
| taraf | to |
| darjan | dozen |

There is one consistent exception to this pronunciation, namely, when a is followed by h plus another consonant, then it is pronounced like e in English bet.

| | |
|---|---|
| kahnaa | to say |
| rahnaa | to stay, live |

2. The vowel aa is a low, central, unrounded vowel, similar to the a in English father:

| | |
|---|---|
| kaa | of |
| naam | name |
| kyaa | what |
| jaanaa | to go |
| daam | price |

3. The vowel i is a rather high, front, unrounded vowel, similar to the i in English bit:

| | |
|---|---|
| mil | get |
| kitnaa | how much |
| likhnaa | to write |

4. The vowel ii is a high, front, unrounded vowel, similar to the ee in English meet, but without the off-glide that occurs in English.

| | |
|---|---|
| miil | mile |
| kii | of |
| tiin | three |
| xariidnaa | to buy |
| kamiiz | shirt |
| jaldii | soon |

5. The vowel u is a rather high, back, rounded vowel, similar to the u in English put:

| | |
|---|---|
| tum | you |
| dukaan | shop |
| ruknaa | to stop |
| sunnaa | to hear |

6. The vowel uu is a high, back, rounded vowel, similar to the oo in boot but without the off-glide that occurs in English.

| | |
|---|---|
| duur | far |
| naagpuur | Nagpur |
| mašhuur | famous |

7. The vowel ee is a high-mid, front, unrounded vowel, similar to the ai in English bait but without the final off-glide:

| | |
|---|---|
| kee | of |
| leenaa | to take |
| leetee | take! |
| santaree | oranges |
| yee | this, these |
| aaiyee | come! |

8. The vowel oo is a high-mid, back, rounded vowel, similar to the oa in English boat but without the final off-glide:

| | |
|---|---|
| doo | two |
| karoo | do! |
| jaaoo | go! |
| hooTal | hotel |
| woo | this |
| hoonaa | to be |
| moozaa | sock |

9. The vowel ai is a low, front, unrounded vowel, similar to the a in English bat. This is the pronunciation of the western Hindi-speaking area. In other areas it may have a diphthongal pronunciation approaching the pronunciation of the i in English bite. Imitate your teacher.

| | |
|---|---|
| hai | is |
| chai | six |
| kaisaa | how |
| paisaa | pice |

10. The vowel au is a low, back, rounded vowel in the

western Hindi-speaking area like the <u>ou</u> in English
<u>bought</u>. In the eastern area it may have a diphthongal
pronunciation approaching that of the <u>ow</u> of English
<u>now</u>. Imitate your teacher.

| | |
|---|---|
| nau | nine |
| kaun | who, which |
| aur | and |
| sau | hundred |

11. The above vowels may be subdivided into two
groups, one group of long vowels (each represented by
two letters), <u>aa</u> <u>ii</u> <u>uu</u> <u>ee</u> <u>oo</u> <u>ai</u> <u>au</u>, and one
group of short vowels (each represented by one letter),
<u>a</u> <u>i</u> <u>u</u>. The long vowels may all occur with nasali-
zation, represented by writing a tilde (~) over the
vowel.

11.1 Of these nasalized vowels, while <u>ee</u> is similar
to the <u>ai</u> of English <u>bait</u>, the <u>ēē</u> is more similar to
the <u>e</u> of English <u>bet</u>, but with nasalization.

| | |
|---|---|
| mēē | in |
| dukaanēē | shops |
| basēē | buses |
| kamiizēē | shirts |
| jaaēē | may go |
| karēē | may do |

11.2 The other nasalized vowels are pronounced as they
are when not nasalized but with nasalization.

| | | |
|---|---|---|
| ãã | jii hãã | yes |
| | yahãã | there |
| | kahãã | where |
| | pããc | five |
| | patniyãã | wives |
| ĩĩ | daaĩĩ | right |
| | jaatĩĩ | go |
| | wahĩĩ | right there |
| | yahĩĩ | right here |
| | nahĩĩ | not |
| ũũ | hũũ | am |
| | jaaũũ | I may go |
| | karũũ | I may do |
| | dũũgaa | I will give |
| õõ | hooTalõõ | hotels (oblique) |
| | dukaanõõ | shops (oblique) |
| | santarõõ | oranges (oblique) |
| | doonõõ | both |

| ãĩ | mãĩ | I |
|----|-----|---|
|    | hãĩ | are |
|    | pãĩNT | pants |

| ãũ | cãũtiis | thirty-four |
|----|---------|-------------|

## Consonants

1.    Hindi has a set of voiceless, unaspirated consonants, p t T k c, which are similar to the English
p t k ch in pin, tin, kin and chin. There is one major
difference: in English these consonants are pronounced
with a release of breath, called aspiration, but in
Hindi there is no puff of breath.

1.1    p is similar to English p in pin, but with no
aspiration:

| aap | you |
|-----|-----|
| pããc | five |
| patnii | wife |
| paisaa | pice |
| par | on, at |

1.2    t is similar to English t in tin, but with two
differences.  English t is pronounced with the tip of
the tongue against the ridge behind the upper teeth,
but the Hindi t is pronounced with the tongue against
the upper teeth.  Also there is no aspiration.

| taraf | towards |
|-------|---------|
| tum | you |
| jaataa | go |
| tiin | three |
| saat | seven |

1.3    T is similar to English t in tin, but with two
differences.  English t is pronounced as mentioned
above, but in Hindi T is pronounced with the tongue-
tip bent back and touching the roof of the mouth
slightly farther back than in English.  Also there is
no aspiration in Hindi.  Hindi speakers hear the
English t as closer to Hindi T than to Hindi t.

| hooTal | hotel |
|--------|-------|
| isTaap | stop |
| TikaT | stamp |
| chuuTnaa | to leave |
| chooTaa | small |

1.4    k is similar to English k in kin, but with no
aspiration:

```
dukaan      shop
kaun        who
kaa         of
kahãã       where
kaam        work
kamiiz      shirt
```

1.5  c is similar to English ch in chin, but with no
aspiration:

```
caahnaa     to want
caar        four
caahiyee    need
haalcaal    welfare
calnaa      to go
```

2.   Hindi has a set of voiceless, aspirated consonants, ph th Th kh ch, parallel to the previous set,
but these are all pronounced with the same aspiration
that occurs in English.  This means that ph kh ch are
the same as p k ch in English pin, kin, chin. Hindi th,
like t, is pronounced with the tongue against the
teeth, but with aspiration.  Hindi Th, like T, is
pronounced with the tongue retracted, but with aspiration.

```
ph      phal        fruit
        phir        again

th      naath       Nath (name)
        keesaath    with
        cauthaa     fourth
        thaa        was
        thooRaa     little

Th      miiThee     sweet
        aaTh        eight
        Thahrnaa    to wait
        Thiik       good
        aThaaraa    eighteen

kh      deekh       see
        likh        write
        khaa        eat
        khulaa      open
        siikh       learn

ch      chai        six
        kuch        something
        chuuTnaa    to leave
        chooTaa     small
        pichlaa     last
```

3.    Hindi has a set of voiced, unaspirated stops
paralleling the two previous sets, b d D j g.  Of these
b j and g are pronounced like English b j and g in
bet, jet and get.  The d is pronounced like English
d in do, but with the tongue tip against the upper
teeth, and D is pronounced with the tongue tip farther
back in the mouth than for English d

| b | bas | bus |
| | ab | now |
| | sab | all |
| | baahar | outside |
| | baaraa | twelve |
| | | |
| d | deenaa | to give |
| | deekhnaa | to see |
| | dukaan | shop |
| | daam | price |
| | duur | far |
| | | |
| D | kaarD | card |
| | maniaarDar | money order |
| | DaakTar | doctor |
| | Dikšnarii | dictionary |
| | ThaNDaa | cold |
| | | |
| j | jaanaa | to go |
| | kiijiyee | do! |
| | jii | particle of respect |
| | bajaa | o'clock |
| | darjaa | class |
| | | |
| g | aglaa | next |
| | aagraa | Agra |
| | gaa | future particle |
| | gyaaraa | eleven |
| | nagar | city |

4.    Hindi has a set of voiced, aspirated consonants
paralleling the previous sets, bh dh Dh jh gh. English
has nothing similar to these.  They are all pronounced
like the previous voiced set but with the release of
breath called aspiration.

| bh | abhii | right away |
| | sabhii | all |
| | bhii | also |
| | bhaaii | brother |
| | | |
| dh | dhoobii | washerman |
| | suvidhaa | convenience |
| | dhanyavaad | thanks |
| | andheeraa | darkness |

xxx

| Dh | Dhaaii | two and a half |
|----|--------|----------------|

| jh | mujhee | to me |
|----|--------|-------|
|    | samajhnaa | to understand |
|    | samjhaa | understood |

| gh | ghaNTaa | hour |
|----|---------|------|
|    | ghar | house |
|    | jaghaa | place |
|    | ghuumnaa | to walk |
|    | durghaTnaa | accident |

5.    Hindi has a series of nasal consonants, m̲ n̲ N̲
and n̪. The m̲ is pronounced like English m̲ in m̲e̲t̲.
The n̲ is pronounced like English n̲ in n̲e̲t̲, but with the
tongue against the upper teeth. The N̲ is pronounced
with the tongue pulled back as for T̲ T̲h̲ D̲ and D̲h̲,
but it is produced by a quick flap of the tongue when
not followed by another consonant. The n̪ is pronounced
like English n̲g̲ in s̲i̲n̲g̲, but it is relatively rare.

| m | naam | name |
|---|------|------|
|   | ham | we |
|   | mãĩ | I |
|   | daam | price |
|   | moozaa | sock |

| n | naam | name |
|---|------|------|
|   | jaanaa | to go |
|   | karnaa | to do |
|   | tiin | three |
|   | nau | nine |

| N | ghaNTaa | hour |
|---|---------|------|
|   | kaaraN | reason |
|   | ThaNDaa | cold |

| ŋ | aŋgreezii | English |
|---|-----------|---------|
|   | maaŋnaa | to ask |

6.    Hindi has a series of semi-consonants, y̲ r̲ l̲ w̲.
The y̲ is pronounced like y̲ in English y̲e̲t̲. The w̲ is
like v̲ in English v̲a̲t̲ but with less friction, which
may make it sound like English w̲ in w̲e̲t̲ sometimes,
although the back of the tongue is not retracted as in
English. The r̲ is a tongue trill unlike any sound in
English. The l̲ is like English l̲ in l̲e̲t̲, not like
English l̲l̲ in a̲l̲l̲.

| y | yee | this |
|---|-----|------|
|   | yahãã | here |
|   | aayaa | came |

|   |                 |            |
|---|-----------------|------------|
|   | deekhiyee       | see!       |
|   | nayaa           | new        |
| r | taraf           | towards    |
|   | duur            | far        |
|   | baaraa          | twelve     |
|   | rooz            | day        |
|   | par             | on         |
| l | leenaa          | to take    |
|   | phal            | fruit      |
|   | miil            | mile       |
|   | xaalii          | vacant     |
|   | laanaa          | to bring   |
| w | woo             | he         |
|   | wahãã           | there      |
|   | waxt            | time       |
|   | pariwaar        | family     |
|   | dawaa           | medicine   |

7.    Hindi has two sibilant sounds, s and š. The s is pronounced like English s in sin, and the š like English sh in shin.

|   |            |             |
|---|------------|-------------|
| s | see        | from        |
|   | kaisaa     | how         |
|   | das        | ten         |
|   | saahab     | sir         |
|   | saknaa     | to be able  |
| š | mašhuur    | famous      |
|   | isTeešan   | station     |
|   | šaam       | evening     |
|   | aašaa      | hope        |
|   | koošiš     | attempt     |

8.    Hindi has three spirants, f z and x. The f is pronounced like English f in fat and the z like English z in zinc. The x is pronounced like the German ch in ach or Scottish ch in loch. It does not occur in English. These sounds occur mainly in words borrowed from English, Persian and Arabic, and many speakers of Hindi substitute ph for f, j for z, and kh for x in these words.

|   |            |             |
|---|------------|-------------|
| f | lifaafaa   | envelope    |
|   | afsoos     | sorrow      |
|   | daftar     | office      |
|   | Teeliifoon | telephone   |
|   | haftaa     | week        |
| z | bazaar     | bazaar      |

```
moozaa          sock
kamiiz          shirt
rooz            day
zaruur          certain

x     xariidnaa       to buy
      xaalii          vacant
      buxaar          fever
      xušii           pleasure
```

9.    Hindi has a glottal spirant, <u>h</u>, pronounced like
English <u>h</u> in <u>hat</u>.

```
h     kahãã           where
      hooTal          hotel
      pahlaa          first
      caahnaa         to want
      caahiyee        need
```

10.   Hindi has two types of flaps, represented by <u>R</u>
and <u>Rh</u>, unlike anything that occurs in English.  The
<u>R</u> is produced by a flap of the tongue against the roof
of the mouth touching the same position that is used
in pronouncing <u>T</u> <u>Th</u> <u>D</u> and <u>Dh</u>.  The <u>Rh</u> is pronounced
the same way but with the release of breath called
aspiration.

```
R     kapRaa          cloth
      baRaa           big
      thooRaa         little
      gaaRii          train
      khiRkii         window
      laRkaa          boy

Rh    paRhnaa         to read
      paRhaa          read
      saaRhee         plus one half
      DeeRh           one and a half
      paRhaaii        study
```

## Exercises in contrast

1.    Hindi has a series of voiceless, unaspirated
consonants <u>p t T k c</u>, which contrast with a series of
voiceless, aspirated consonants, <u>ph th Th kh ch</u>.
Remember not to aspirate the first series.

```
p  ph  par        on          phal       fruit

t  th  tiin       three       thii       was
       jaataa     go          cauthaa    fourth
```

|   |   | saat | seven | saath | along |
|---|---|------|-------|-------|-------|
| T | Th | TikaT | stamp | Thiik | fine |
|   |   | chooTaa | small | miiThaa | sweet |
|   |   | chuuT | leave | aaTh | eight |
| k | kh | kaa | of | khaa | eat |
|   |   | tak | until | siikh | learn |
|   |   | dukaan | shop | deekhaa | saw |
| c | ch | caar | four | chai | six |
|   |   | bacnaa | to be saved | pichlaa | last |
|   |   | caahaa | wanted | chooTaa | small |

2.     Hindi has a series of voiced, unaspirated consonants, b d D g j R, which contrast with a series of
voiced, aspirated consonants, bh dh Dh gh jh Rh.  Imitate your teacher to get the aspirated consonants
right.

| b | bh | ab | now | abhii | rightaway |
|---|----|----|-----|-------|-----------|
|   |    | baaraa | twelve | bhaaii | brother |
|   |    | beecnaa | to buy | bheejnaa | to send |
| d | dh | doo | two | dhoobii | washerman |
|   |    | andar | in | andheeraa | darkness |
|   |    | dukaandaar | shopkeeper | suwidhaa | convenience |
| D | Dh | DaakTar | doctor | Dhaaii | two and a half |
| g | gh | gaa | future particle | ghar | house |
|   |    | nagar | city | jaghaa | place |
|   |    | guru | teacher | ghuumnaa | to walk |
| j | jh | darjaa | class | samjhaa | understood |
|   |    | bajaa | o'clock | mujhee | to me |
|   |    | aaj | today | samajh | understand |
| R | Rh | paRaa | had to | paRhaa | read |
|   |    | paRnaa | to have to | paRhnaa | to read |
|   |    | gaaRii | train | saaRhee | plus one half |

3.     Hindi has a series of dental consonants pronounced with the tongue touching the upper teeth, t th
d dh n, which contrast with a retroflex series pronounced with the tip of the tongue bent back and
touching the roof of the mouth, T Th D Dh N.  Remember
to put your tongue against the upper teeth for the
first series.

| | | | | | |
|---|---|---|---|---|---|
| t | T | hootaa | be | hooTal | hotel |
| | | tak | until | TikaT | stamp |
| | | saat | seven | chuuT | leave |
| th | Th | saath | along | aaTh | eight |
| | | thii | was | Thiik | fine |
| | | cauthaa | fourth | miiThaa | sweet |
| d | D | daam | price | DaakTar | doctor |
| | | andar | in | ThaNDaa | cold |
| | | baad | after | rooD | road |
| dh | Dh | dhoobii | washerman | Dhaaii | two and a half |
| n | N | andar | in | ThaNDaa | cold |
| | | jaantaa | know | ghaNTaa | hour |
| | | moohan | Mohan | kaaraN | reason |

# LESSON I

## Conversation -- Asking Directions

### JOHN

| | |
|---|---|
| suniyee | please listen |
| mãĩ | I |
| hooTal | hotel |
| janaa | to go |
| caahtaa hũũ | (I) want |
| hũũ | (I) am |
| suniyee, mãĩ hooTal jaanaa caahtaa hũũ. | Pardon me, I want to go to a hotel. |
| kahãã | where |
| hai | is |
| hooTal kahãã hai? | Where is the hotel? |

### RAM NATH

| | |
|---|---|
| aap | you (polite) |
| yahãã | here |
| see | from |
| siidhee | straight |
| jaaiyee | please go |
| aap yahãã see siidhee jaaiyee, | Go straight ahead from here, |
| aur | and |
| phir | then |
| daaĩĩ | right |
| taraf | direction |
| daaĩĩ taraf | to the right |

1

| aur phir daaîî taraf. | and then to the right. |
| wahîî | there (emphatic) |
| eek | one |
| wahîî eek hooTal hai. | There is a hotel there. |

JOHN

| kaa | of |
| naam | name |
| kyaa | what |
| hooTal kaa naam kyaa hai? | What's the name of the hotel? |

RAM NATH

| ajmeerii hooTal | Ajmer Hotel |
| hooTal kaa naam ajmeerii hooTal hai. | The hotel's name is Ajmer Hotel. |

JOHN

| kyaa | (interrogative particle) |
| yee | this |
| acchaa | good |
| kyaa yee hooTal acchaa hai? | Is it a good hotel? |

RAM NATH

| jii hãã | yes |
| bahut | very |
| mašhuur | famous |
| jii hãã, yee hooTal bahut mašhuur hai. | Yes, sir, it's a very famous hotel. |

JOHN

| dhanyawaad | thanks |
| bahut acchaa, dhanyawaad. | Very well, thanks. |

2

# GRAMMAR

## 1. Article

Hindi has no equivalent of the English definite article "the."

hooTal kahãã hai?        Where is the hotel?

hooTal kaa naam kyaa hai?   What is the name of the hotel?

Normally Hindi does not make use of any equivalent of the English indefinite article "a" or "an," although occasionally the Hindi numeral eek, "one," is used this way.

mãĩ hooTal jaanaa        I want to go to a hotel.
  caahtaa hũũ.

wahĩĩ eek hooTal hai.     There is a hotel there.

## 2. Word Order

In Hindi the verb or the verbal phrase usually occurs at the end of the construction to which it belongs.

hooTal kahãã <u>hai</u>?      Where <u>is</u> the hotel?

mãĩ hooTal jaanaa     I <u>want</u> to go to the hotel.
  <u>caahtaa hũũ</u>.

An interrogative word such as "who," "where," "why," or "what" will occur immediately before the verbal phrase.

hooTal <u>kahãã</u> hai?     <u>Where</u> is the hotel?

hooTal kaa naam <u>kyaa</u> hai?  <u>What</u> is the name of the hotel?

## 3. Interrogative Particle, kyaa, "what"

The Hindi form <u>kyaa</u>, "what," has two different usages.

It may be the equivalent of the English interrogative particle "what," in which case it occurs immediately before the verbal phrase:

hooTal kaa naam <u>kyaa</u> hai?  <u>What</u> is the name of the hotel?

3

It is also used as an interrogative particle where a sentence has no other interrogative word to indicate that it is interrogative. Such sentences are the equivalent of English interrogative sentences that have no interrogative word in them. In this usage, the form kyaa will occur at the beginning of the sentence.

kyaa yee hooTal acchaa     Is this hotel a good one?
hai?

## 4. Postpositions

In English, prepositions are used with nouns or pronouns. Equivalent constructions in Hindi are expressed by postpositions with nouns or pronouns. The Hindi forms are called postpositions because they occur after the noun or pronoun instead of before, as in English. The postpositions you have had so far are the following:

| see | from | yahãã see | from here |
|-----|------|-----------|-----------|
| kaa | of | hooTal kaa naam | the name of the hotel |

### EXERCISES

A. Substitute orally in the sentences below the Hindi equivalent of the English given:

1. mãĩ _____ jaanaa caahtaa hũũ.

   hotel                  to the right

   famous hotel           straight ahead

   there                  where

2. _____ kahãã hai?

   hotel                  Ajmer Hotel

   famous hotel           this hotel

   good hotel

3. aap _____ see siidhee jaaiyee.

   here                   hotel

   there                  Ajmer Hotel

4

4. _____ kaa naam kyaa hai?

               hotel

               famous hotel

5. wahíí eek _____ hai.

   hotel             good hotel

   famous hotel     good and famous hotel

6. kyaa yee hooTal _____ hai?

   good             there

   famous          to the right

   here             straight ahead

7. yee hooTal _____ hai.

   famous          here

   good            there

   very good       to the right

   very famous     straight ahead

8. yee hooTal bahut _____ hai.

   famous          good and famous

   good            famous and good

B. Transform the following sentences into interrogative sentences according to the model given:

yee hooTal acchaa hai ....... kyaa yee hooTal acchaa
                              hai?

1. yee hooTal bahut acchaa hai.

2. yee hooTal bahut mašhuur hai.

3. yee hooTal acchaa aur mašhuur hai.

4. yee hooTal mašhuur hai.

5. yee hooTal yahãã hai.

6. yee hooTal wahíí hai.

5

7. yee hooTal daaîî taraf hai.

8. yee hooTal siidhee hai.

C.  Say in Hindi:

1. Pardon me, I want to go to a hotel.

2. Where is a hotel?

3. Go to the right from here.

4. And then go straight ahead.

5. There is a good hotel there.

6. Is this a good hotel?

7. Yes, it's a good hotel.

8. What's the name of the hotel?

9. The hotel's name is Ajmer Hotel.

10. Is Ajmer Hotel a good hotel?

11. Yes, it is a very good and well-known hotel.

12. Very well, thanks.

# LESSON II

## Conversation -- Asking for a Fruit Store

### JOHN

| | |
|---|---|
| kuch | some |
| phal | fruit |
| xariidnaa | to buy |
| suniyee, mãĩ kuch phal xariidnaa caahtaa hũũ | Pardon me, I want to buy some fruit |
| kii | of |
| dukaan | store, shop |
| phal kii dukaan kahãã hai? | Where's a fruit store? |

### RAM LAL

| | |
|---|---|
| bazaar | bazaar |
| sadar bazaar | Sadar Bazaar |
| mẽẽ | in |
| sadar bazaar mẽẽ. | In the Sadar Bazaar. |

### JOHN

| | |
|---|---|
| woo | he, she, it |
| kitnii | how much |
| duur | far |
| woo yahãã see kitnii duur hai? | How far is it from here? |

### RAM LAL

| | |
|---|---|
| nahĩĩ | not |
| bahut duur nahĩĩ. | Not very far. |
| miil | mile |
| eek miil hai. | It is one mile. |

| | |
|---|---|
| paidal | on foot |
| caahtee hãĩ | (you) want |
| hãĩ | are |
| kyaa aap paidal jaanaa caahtee hãĩ? | Do you want to go on foot? |

JOHN

| | |
|---|---|
| jii nahĩĩ | no |
| bas | bus |
| see | by |
| jii nahĩĩ, bas see. | No, by bus. |
| miltii | (is) available |
| bas kahãã miltii hai? | Where do I get a bus? |

RAM LAL

| | |
|---|---|
| aap yahãã see siidhee jaaiyee. | Go straight ahead from here. |
| baaĩĩ | left |
| aur phir baaĩĩ taraf. | And then to the left. |
| bas-isTaap | bus stop |
| wahĩĩ bas-isTaap hai. | There's a bus stop there. |

JOHN

| | |
|---|---|
| bahut acchaa, dhanyawaad | O.K., thanks. |

GRAMMAR

1.  Personal Pronouns

    Hindi has the following personal pronouns:

| | Singular | | Plural | |
|---|---|---|---|---|
| 1st Per. | mãĩ | I | ham | we |
| 2nd Per. | – | – | tum, aap | you |

8

|          | Singular |              | Plural |        |
|----------|----------|--------------|--------|--------|
| 3rd Per. | woo      | he, she, it  | wee    | they   |

The pronoun aap, "you," is a polite or honorific form and should be used under most conditions. The form tum, "you," implies either that you are extremely well acquainted with the person you are talking to or that you are assigning him a lower status. Note that tum, "you," and aap, "you," may be used when speaking to one person or more than one.

## 2. Demonstratives

Hindi has the following demonstratives:

| Singular | | Plural | |
|----------|------|--------|-------|
| yee | this | yee | these |
| woo | that | wee | those |

As in English, these demonstratives may be used either as pronouns (i.e., without a following dependent noun) or as adjectives (i.e., with a following dependent noun).

| yee hooTal acchaa hai. | This hotel is a good one. |
|------------------------|---------------------------|
| yee kyaa hai? | What is this? |
| woo kyaa hai? | What is that? |

## 3. Verbs

## 3.1. Verb hoonaa, "to be"

The verb hoonaa, "to be," in Hindi has the following simple present forms. These may be used as a main verb or as an auxiliary verb:

|          | Singular | Plural |
|----------|----------|--------|
| 1st Per. | hũũ      | hãĩ    |
| 2nd Per. | -        | hoo    |
| 3rd Per. | hai      | hãĩ    |

For this verb, as for all others, the form listed as second person is always to be understood as the verb form to be used with the pronoun tum, "you"; this form is always in the second person plural. The form

9

used with the pronoun aap, "you," is always in the 3rd person plural, regardless of whether tum or aap refers to one person or more than one.

## 3.2. Infinitive and Verb Stem

Hindi verbs have an infinitive form which always ends in -naa. The form obtained by dropping this ending from the infinitive form will be referred to as the verb stem. The infinitives and stems of the verbs that you have met so far are:

| Infinitive | | Verb Stem |
|---|---|---|
| hoonaa | to be | hoo |
| jaanaa | to go | jaa |
| caahnaa | to want | caah |
| sunnaa | to listen, hear | sun |
| xariidnaa | to buy | xariid |
| milnaa | to be available, get | mil |

The infinitive is used with any inflected form of the verb caahnaa, "to want," and other similar verbs, as in English. Note that the infinitive precedes the inflected verb, whereas in English it follows.

mãĩ bas see jaanaa    I want to go by a bus.
caahtaa hũũ

## 3.3. Imperfect Form

Hindi has an imperfect form that is formed by adding -taa to the verb stem. This form is inflected for gender (masculine and feminine) and for number (singular and plural).

| Masc. Sg. | caahtaa | jaataa | hootaa |
|---|---|---|---|
| Masc. Pl. | caahtee | jaatee | hootee |
| Fem. Sg. | caahtii | jaatii | hootii |
| Fem. Pl. | caahtĩĩ | jaatĩĩ | hootĩĩ |

## 3.4. Present Imperfect

In Hindi the present imperfect tense of a verb is

10

formed by using the imperfect form of the verb, fol-
owed by the simple present tense form of the verb "to
be" used as an auxiliary.  Note that the auxiliary will
agree with the subject in number and person whereas
the imperfect form will agree with the subject in number and gender, with the special limitation that, if
plural number is indicated elsewhere in the verbal
phrase, the feminine form of the imperfect will not
indicate plurality.  The practical effect of this ·
limitation is that for the present imperfect tense
forms, the form caahtĩĩ is never used but, where the
agreement is feminine, whether singular or plural,
only caahtii is used.  However, in the first person
plural, i.e., with the pronoun ham, "we," some women
will use the masculine plural form of the imperfect
form, i.e., they will say: ham jaatee hãĩ, "we go,"
instead of ham jaatii hãĩ, "we go."

| mãĩ caahtaa hũũ | I (masc.) want |
| mãĩ caahtii hũũ | I (fem.) want |
| woo caahtaa hai | he or it wants |
| woo caahtii hai | she or it wants |
| ham caahtee hãĩ | we (masc.) want |
| ham caahtii hãĩ | we (fem.) want |
| tum caahtee hoo | you (familiar, masc.) want |
| tum caahtii hoo | you (familiar, fem.) want |
| aap caahtee hãĩ | you (polite, masc.) want |
| aap caahtii hãĩ | you (polite, fem.) want |
| wee caahtee hãĩ | they (masc.) want |
| wee caahtii hãĩ | they (fem.) want |

4.  Postpositions

    In this lesson there is a new postposition mẽẽ,
"in" or "at," and the postposition see, which occurs
in the first lesson meaning "from," occurs in this
lesson meaning "by" or "by means of."


                        EXERCISES

A.  Substitute orally in the sentences below the Hindi
equivalent of the English given:

1. woo _____ see kitnii duur hai?

   here            store

   there           bus stop

   hotel           bazaar

2. woo yahãã see _____ hai.

   far             to the left

   how far         to the right

   very far        straight ahead

   one mile

3. _____ yahãã see kitnii duur hai?

   the store                the bus stop

   the fruit store          that hotel

   that store               that bus stop

   that fruit store         the Sadar Bazaar

   the hotel

4. wahîî eek _____ hai.

   store           bazaar

   hotel           famous store

   fruit store     famous bazaar

   bus stop

5. _____ kahãã hai?

   the store                the bus stop

   the fruit store          the bazaar

   that fruit store         that bazaar

   the hotel                that bus stop

   that hotel               that store

12

6. mãĩ _____ xariidnaa caahtaa hũũ.

fruit                     that fruit

hotel                     that bus

bus                       that hotel

store                     that store

B. Transform the following sentences according to the model given:

kyaa aap paidal jaanaa  ..... mãĩ paidal jaanaa
  caahtee hãĩ?                 caahtaa hũũ

1. kyaa aap phal xariidnaa caahtee hãĩ?

2. kyaa aap kuch phal xariidnaa caahtee hãĩ?

3. kyaa aap hooTal jaatee hãĩ?

4. kyaa aap baaĩĩ taraf jaanaa caahtee hãĩ?

5. kyaa aap siidhee jaanaa caahtii hãĩ?

6. kyaa aap kuch phal xariidtee hãĩ?

7. kyaa aap sadar bazaar jaatee hãĩ?

8. kyaa aap daaĩĩ taraf jaanaa caahtee hãĩ?

C. Translate orally:

1. I (masc.) want to go to the bazaar.

2. They (fem.) want to go to the bazaar.

3. You (masc., polite) want to go to the bazaar.

4. She wants to go to the bazaar.

5. We (masc.) want to go to the bazaar.

6. You (fem., familiar) want to go to the bazaar.

7. They (masc.) want to go to the bazaar.

8. You (fem., polite) want to go to the bazaar

9. I (fem.) want to go to the bazaar.

10. He wants to go to the bazaar.

13

11. You (masc., familiar) want to go to the bazaar.

12. We (fem.) want to go to the bazaar.

D.  Translate orally:

1. Pardon me, I want to buy some fruit.

2. Where is a fruit store?

3. It's in the Sadar Bazaar.

4. How far is the Sadar Bazaar from here?

5. It is not very far.

6. It is one mile from here.

7. Go straight ahead from here.

8. And then go to the right.

9. The Sadar Bazaar is right there.


10. I want to go to the Ajmer Hotel.

11. Where is it?

12. It is in the Sadar Bazaar.

13. How far is the Sadar Bazaar from here?

14. It's far from here.

15. Go straight ahead from here.

16. And then to the left.

17. There is a bus stop over there.

18. It's one mile from the bus stop.

19. Go by bus from there.

20. Very well, thanks.

# LESSON III

## Conversation -- Buying Fruit

### JOHN

| | |
|---|---|
| sunoo | listen |
| tumhaaree | your |
| paas | with, near |
| sunoo, kyaa tumhaaree paas phal hãĩ? | Excuse me. Have you (some) fruit? |

### STOREKEEPER

| | |
|---|---|
| koo | to |
| kaun | which |
| see | sort of, kind of |
| caahiyee | are wanted, are needed |
| jii hãã, aap koo kaun see phal caahiyee? | Yes, sir, what kind of fruit do you want? |

### JOHN

| | |
|---|---|
| santaree | oranges |
| leenaa | to take |
| mãĩ kuch santaree leenaa caahtaa hũũ. | I want to buy some oranges. |
| acchee | good |
| kyaa tumhaaree paas acchee santaree hãĩ? | Do you have good oranges? |

### STOREKEEPER

| | |
|---|---|
| deekhiyee | please see |
| jii hãã, yee santaree deekhiyee. | Yes, sir, please look at these oranges. |
| naagpurii | from Nagpur |

15

yee naagpurii santaree          These are Nagpur oranges.
  hãĩ.

  hootee hãĩ.                    are

kyaa naagpurii santaree         Are Nagpur oranges good?
  acchee hootee hãĩ?

  miiThee                        sweet

jii hãã, naagpurii              Yes, sir, Nagpur oranges
  santaree bahut miiThee          are very sweet.
  hootee hãĩ.

  in                             these

  in kaa                         their

  daam                           price

acchaa, in kaa daam             O.K., what's their price?
  kyaa hai?

  tiin                           three

  rupaee                         rupees

  darjan                         dozen

tiin rupaee darjan.             three rupees a dozen.

  doo                            give

  dee doo                        give

  mujhee                         to me

acchaa, mujhee eek darjan  O.K., give me a dozen.
  dee doo.

  liijiyee                       please take

yee liijiyee eek darjan     Here's a dozen oranges.
  santaree.

    loo                         take

yee loo tiin rupaee.        Here are three rupees.

bahut acchaa.               Very well.

## GRAMMAR

### 1. Nouns

Nouns in Hindi are classified as either masculine
or feminine.  Nouns show an inflection for two numbers,
singular and plural, and also an inflection for two
cases, nominative and oblique, which will be discussed
later.

### 1.1. Gender of Nouns

The gender of the nouns you have met so far is as
follows:

| Masc. | | Fem. | |
|---|---|---|---|
| hooTal | hotel | dukaan | ship |
| naam | name | bas | bus |
| phal | fruit | duur | distance |
| bazaar | bazaar | | |
| miil | mile | | |
| santaraa | orange | | |
| daam | price | | |
| rupayaa | rupee | | |
| darjan | dozen | | |
| bas-isTaap | bus stop | | |

17

## 1.2. Plural of Nouns

Most masculine nouns ending in -aa form the plural by replacing -aa with -ee.

| Sg. | | Pl. |
|---|---|---|
| santaraa | orange | santaree |
| rupayaa | rupee | rupaee |

Other masculine nouns have identical singular and plural forms:

| Sg. | | Pl. |
|---|---|---|
| hooTal | hotel | hooTal |
| naam | name | naam |
| phal | fruit | phal |
| bazaar | bazaar | bazaar |
| miil | mile | miil |
| bas-isTaap | bus stop | bas-isTaap |
| daam | price | daam |
| darjan | dozen | darjan |

The feminine nouns you have met so far form the plural by adding -ẽẽ to the singular:

| Sg. | | Pl. |
|---|---|---|
| dukaan | shop | dukaanẽẽ |
| bas | bus | basẽẽ |
| duur | distance | (no pl.) |
| taraf | direction | (no pl.) |

## 2. New Verbs

The following new verbs occur in this lesson:

| | |
|---|---|
| deekhnaa | to see |
| leenaa | to take |
| deenaa | to give |

## 3. Verb hoonaa, "to be"

In Lesson II'3 the simple present forms of the verb hoonaa, "to be," were given, and the present imperfect forms of verbs in general were discussed. In this lesson there is an example of the present imperfect of hoonaa. This is the only verb in Hindi that has both simple present forms and present imperfect forms; all other verbs have only the present imperfect forms. The present imperfect of hoonaa is used to make a general statement or to state a condition that is generally valid (e.g., grass is green). The simple present form of hoonaa is used in all other situations.

| | |
|---|---|
| naagpurii santaree miiThee hootee hãĩ. | Nagpur oranges are sweet (are generally sweet). |
| yee santaree miiThee hãĩ. | These oranges are sweet. |

## 4. Imperatives

Hindi has an imperative form made by adding the ending -oo to the verb stem. This form of the imperative will be referred to as the familiar imperative; it is used in situations where the pronoun tum, "you," is appropriate.

| Infinitive | | Verb Stem | Imperative |
|---|---|---|---|
| jaanaa | to go | jaa | jaaoo |
| sunnaa | to listen, hear | sun | sunoo |
| xariidnaa | to buy | xariid | xariidoo |
| milnaa | to be available, to get | mil | miloo |
| deekhnaa | to see | deekh | deekhoo |

The two verbs leenaa, "to take," and deenaa, "to give," are irregular in that the -ee of the verb stem is dropped when the imperative ending -oo is added.

| Infinitive | | Verb Stem | Imperative |
|---|---|---|---|
| deenaa | to give | dee | doo |
| leenaa | to take | lee | loo |

Hindi has another imperative form made by adding the ending -iyee to the verb stem. This will be referred to as the polite imperative; it is used in sit-

19

uations where the pronoun <u>aap</u>, "you," is appropriate.

| Infinitive | | Verb Stem | Imperative |
|---|---|---|---|
| jaanaa | to go | jaa | jaaiyee |
| sunnaa | to listen, to hear | sun | suniyee |
| xariidnaa | to buy | xariid | xariidiyee |
| milnaa | to be available, to get | mil | miliyee |
| deekhnaa | to see | deekh | deekhiyee |

The verbs <u>leenaa</u>, "to take," and <u>deenaa</u>, "to give,"
use irregular stems <u>liij</u> and <u>diij</u>, to which the ending
<u>-iyee</u> is added.

| Infinitive | | Verb Stem | Imperative |
|---|---|---|---|
| deenaa | to give | dee | diijiyee |
| leenaa | to take | lee | liijiyee |

Note that at the beginning of the conversation in
Lesson II, when John is addressing an Indian friend,
he starts the conversation with the polite form
<u>suniyee</u>, "please listen," but in the conversation in
Lesson III, where John is talking to a storekeeper,
he uses the familiar form <u>sunoo</u>, "listen." Also in
Lesson III the storekeeper in offering John some
oranges uses the polite form <u>liijiyee</u>, but John in
offering the money for the oranges uses the familiar
form <u>loo</u>.

The expression <u>dee doo</u>, "give," which occurs in
this lesson is an alternative of the form <u>doo</u>, "give,"
and is composed of the verb stem <u>dee</u> followed by the
familiar imperative <u>doo</u>. This type of construction
will be discussed later.

5. <u>Adjectives</u>

Adjectives in Hindi that end in -<u>aa</u> show inflection
for gender and number and agree in number and gender
with the noun they are dependent upon. The form ending in -<u>aa</u> is used with the masculine singular noun.
If the noun is masculine plural, the ending -<u>aa</u> is
replaced by -<u>ee</u>. If the noun is feminine, either
singular or plural, the ending -<u>aa</u> is replaced by -<u>ii</u>.
The adjectives of this type that you have met so far
are:

20

| Masc. Sg. | | Masc.Pl. | Fem. |
|---|---|---|---|
| acchaa | good | acchee | acchii |
| miiThaa | sweet | miiThee | miiThii |
| kitnaa | how much, how many | kitnee | kitnii |

Other adjectives in Hindi do not change their form under any conditions.

| | |
|---|---|
| yee santaraa acchaa hai. | This orange is good |
| yee santaree acchee hãĩ. | These oranges are good. |
| yee dukaan acchii hai. | This shop is good. |
| yee dukaanẽẽ acchii hãĩ. | These shops are good. |
| yee hooTal mašhuur hãĩ. | This hotel is famous. |
| yee hooTal mašhuur hãĩ. | These hotels are famous. |
| yee dukaan mašhuur hai. | This shop is famous. |
| yee dukaanẽẽ mašhuur hãĩ. | These shops are famous. |

## EXERCISES

A. Substitute orally in the sentences below the Hindi equivalent of the English given:

1. kyaa tumhaaree paas _____ hãĩ.

| | |
|---|---|
| oranges | good fruit (pl.) |
| fruit | three rupees |
| rupees | one dozen oranges |
| some oranges | Nagpur oranges |
| some rupees | some good oranges. |
| sweet oranges | |

2. mãĩ kuch santaree _____ caahtaa hũũ.

| | |
|---|---|
| to take | to give (away) |
| to buy | to see |

21

3. mãĩ _____ xariidnaa caahtaa hũũ.

some oranges     some good oranges

good oranges     some sweet oranges

sweet oranges     these sweet oranges

three oranges     those good oranges

one dozen oranges   those three oranges

Nagpur oranges

4. yee santaree _____.

(please) see     (please) buy

(please) take     (please) give (away)

5. yee phal _____.

give (away)     take

buy         see

6. yee liijiyee _____.

one orange     one dozen good oranges

oranges       one dozen sweet oranges

these oranges     these three oranges

one dozen oranges   those dozen oranges

7. yee santaree _____ hãĩ.

good        one dozen

sweet        three

good and sweet    three dozen

how many

B. Transform the following sentences according to the model given:

mujhee eek darjan santaree ... mujhee eek darjan
 diijiyee        santaree doo.

 1. yee phal deekhiyee.

2. tiin rupaee liijiyee.

3. baaĩ̃ taraf jaaiyee.

4. miiThee santaree xariidiyee.

5. kuch rupaee dee diijiyee.

6. suniyee.

C. Transform the following sentences according to the model given:

mãĩ bazaar jaataa hũũ.  ..... mãĩ bazaar jaanaa caahtaa hũũ.

1. mãĩ kuch phal leetaa hũũ.

2. mãĩ tiin rupaee deetaa hũũ

3. mãĩ acchee santaree deekhtaa hũũ.

4. mãĩ eek darjan santaree xariidtaa hũũ.

5. mãĩ suntaa hũũ.

D. Transform the following sentences according to the model given:

woo suntaa hai.        ..... woo sunnaa caahtaa hai.

1. woo kuch santaree xariidtaa hai.

2. woo ajmeerii hooTal jaataa hai.

3. woo tiin repaee deetaa hai.

4. woo miiThee santaree deekhtaa hai.

5. woo kuch acchee phal leetaa hai.

E.  Translate orally

1. I (masc.) buy some oranges.

2. He buys some oranges.

3. You (masc., familiar) buy some oranges.

4. She buys some oranges.

5. We (masc.) buy some oranges.

6. They (fem.) buy some oranges.

7. You (fem., polite) buy some oranges.

8. I (fem.) buy some oranges.

9. They (masc.) buy some oranges.

10. You (masc., polite) buy some oranges.

11. We (fem.) buy some oranges.

12. You (fem. familiar) buy some oranges.

F. Translate orally:

1. I (fem.) see the hotel.

2. They (masc.) see the hotel.

3. You (masc., polite) see the hotel.

4. She sees the hotel.

5. I (masc.) see the hotel.

6. You (fem., familiar) see the hotel.

7. We (masc.) see the hotel.

8. They (fem.) see the hotel.

9. You (masc., familiar) see the hotel.

10. We (fem.) see the hotel.

G. Translate orally:

1. Have you some good oranges?

2. Yes, sir, these oranges from Nagpur are very good.

3. How much are they?

4. Three rupees a dozen.

5. Give me a dozen.

6. Here, sir, have these dozen oranges.

7. O.K., have three rupees.

8. Have you some fruit?

9. No, sir, not here.

10. Go to the shop on the right.

11. All right.


12. I want to buy some fruit.

13. What kind of fruit do you want, sir.

14. I want some good and sweet oranges.

15. Here are some good oranges.

16. See these oranges from Nagpur.

17. How many do you want?

18. One dozen.

19. Have a dozen oranges, sir.

20. Here are three rupees.

# LESSON IV

## Conversation -- Talking to the Dhobee

### JOHN

| | |
|---|---|
| kaun hai? | Who is there? |

### WASHERMAN

| | |
|---|---|
| dhobii | washerman, dhobee |
| saahab | sir |
| dhoobii hai, saahab. | It's the washerman, sir. |

### JOHN

| | |
|---|---|
| andar | in, inside |
| aa jaaoo | come |
| andar aa jaaoo. | Come in. |
| tumhĩĩ | you (emphatic) |
| is | this |
| kee | of |
| kyaa tumhĩĩ is hooTal kee dhoobii hoo? | Are you the washerman of this hotel? |

### WASHERMAN

| | |
|---|---|
| hii | (emphatic particle) |
| kaam | work |
| karnaa | to do |
| jii hãã, mãĩ hii yahãã kaa kaam kartaa hũũ. | Yes, sir, I work here. |

### JOHN

| | |
|---|---|
| doo | two |
| minaT | minute |
| ruknaa | to stop, wait |

| | |
|---|---|
| acchaa, doo minaT rukoo. | All right, wait a minute. |
| abhii | right away, right now |
| kapRee | clothes |
| abhii kapRee deetaa hũũ. | I'll give you the clothes right away. |
| rahee | are |
| loo, yee rahee kapRee. | Here, these are the clothes. |

WASHERMAN

| | |
|---|---|
| likhnaa | to write |
| likh liijiyee | write, write down |
| acchaa saahab, likh liijiyee. | All right, sir, please write (them) down. |
| caar | four |
| pãĩNT | trousers |
| caar pãĩNT. | Four pairs of trousers. |
| chai | six |
| kamiiz | shirt |
| chai kamiiz. | Six shirts. |
| saat | seven |
| baniyaain | undershirt |
| saat baniyaain. | Seven undershirts. |
| pããc | five |
| jooRee | pairs |
| moozee | socks |
| pããc jooRee moozee. | Five pairs of socks. |
| nau | nine |
| rumaal | handkerchiefs |
| aur nau rumaal. | And nine handkerchiefs. |

27

### JOHN

| | |
|---|---|
| Thiik | right |
| jaldii | soon |
| Thiik hai, mujhee yee kapRee jaldii caahiyee. | That's right. I want these clothes back soon. |

### WASHERMAN

| | |
|---|---|
| bahut acchaa, saahab. | All right, sir. |

## NUMERALS

| | |
|---|---|
| eek | one |
| doo | two |
| tiin | three |
| caar | four |
| pããc | five |
| chai | six |
| saaT | seven |
| aaTh | eight |
| nau | nine |
| das | ten |

## GRAMMAR

1. **New Nouns**

In this lesson the following new masculine nouns with a singular in -**aa** and a plural in -**ee** occur:

| Sg. | | Pl. | |
|---|---|---|---|
| moozaa | sock | moozee | socks |
| kapRaa | cloth | kapRee | clothes |

Note the meaning of kapRaa, "cloth," kapRee, "clothes."

The following masculine nouns with unchanged plurals

occur in this lesson:

| | |
|---|---|
| dhoobii | dhobee |
| saahab | sir |
| kaam | work |
| pãĩNT | trousers |
| rumaal | handkerchief |

In Hindi, some borrowed items vary in gender from region to region, from person to person within the same region, and even in the speech of the same person. This is true of the items pãĩNT, "trouser," and rumaal, "handkerchief," both of which are sometimes also used as feminine.

The following new feminine nouns occur:

| Sg. | | Pl. | |
|---|---|---|---|
| kamiiz | shirt | kamiizẽẽ | shirts |
| baniyaain | undershirt | baniyaainẽẽ | undershirts |

2. New Verbs

The following new verbs occur in this lesson:

| | |
|---|---|
| aanaa | to come |
| karnaa | to do |
| ruknaa | to stop, wait |
| likhnaa | to write |

The present imperfect forms of these verbs are regular according to the rules discussed in Lesson II. The imperative forms of all except karnaa, "to do," are regular. Thus:

| Infinitive | | Imperative (familiar) | Imperative (polite) |
|---|---|---|---|
| aanaa | to come | aaoo | aaiyee |
| ruknaa | to stop, wait | rukoo | rukiyee |
| likhnaa | to write | likhoo | likhiyee |

29

The familiar imperative of <u>karnaa</u> is regular, but the polite imperative has an irregular form similar to the polite imperative forms of <u>deenaa</u>, "to give," and <u>leenaa</u>, "to take."

| Infinitive | | Imperative (familiar) | Imperative (polite) |
|---|---|---|---|
| karnaa | to do | karoo | kiijiyee |

3.  caahiyee, "<u>to want</u>"

The polite imperative form of the verb <u>caahnaa</u>, "to want," frequently equates with the English "to want" or "to need" as follows:

aap koo kaun see phal
  caahiyee?

- What kind of fruit do you want?
- What kind of fruit do you need?

mujhee yee kapRee jaldii
  caahiyee.

- I want these clothes back soon.
- I need these clothes back soon.

4.  <u>Compound Verbs</u>

There are two main types of compound verbs in Hindi --a verbal compound and a nonverbal compound.

4.1.  <u>Verbal Compounds</u>

The main type of verbal compound in Hindi is com- posed of one verb in the stem form followed by a second verb in any of the possible inflected forms. The meaning of the compound form is usually the same as the meaning of the first verb. The inflected verb, therefore, does not have its own basic meaning but acts as a sort of auxiliary, to which the inflection is added. The number of verbs that can be used as the first member of a compound is thus very large, but only a very limited number of verbs may be used as the second verb in a compound. The verbs so far used as a second member of the compound are <u>jaanaa</u>, "to go," <u>deenaa</u>, "to give," and <u>leenaa</u>, "to take." The compounds of this type that you have met so far are the following:

| dee | doo | give |
|---|---|---|
| aa | jaaoo | come |

likh    liijiyee    write down, write

Note that, although in all these expressions the inflected verb is in the imperative, doo. jaaoo,
liijiyee, it is possible for it to be in any other
inflected form.

Yee dhoobii kapRee        This dhobee gives the
  jaldii dee deetaa hai.    clothes back soon.

Compound verbs of this type will be called Type I.

## 4.2. Nonverbal Compound Verbs

A second type of compound is one in which the first
element is a noun, adjective or adverb and the second
is a verb form, usually hoonaa, "to be" or karnaa,
"to do." This type of form is strictly speaking not
really a compound but is classified here as a compound
because it is likely to be translated into English by
a single verbal form. Such forms will be referred to
in the future as Type II.

The only verb of this type you have met so far is
kaam karnaa, "to work."

## 5. Postposition kaa, "of"

The postposition kaa, "of," is inflected like an
adjective and has the following forms:

masc. sg.:  kaa

masc. pl.:  kee

fem.    :  kii

It will agree with the noun following.  Examples are:

hooTal kaa naam kyaa      What is the name of the
  hai?                      hotel?

mãĩ yahãã kaa kaam        I work here.
  kartaa hũũ.

dhoobii kee kapRee        The washerman's clothes
  yahãã hai?                are here.

phal kii dukaan          Where is a fruit store?
  kahãã hai?

The nouns naam, "name," and kaam, "work," are masculine singular; hence the masculine singular form kaa
is used.  But kapRee, "clothes," is masculine plural;

31

hence the masculine plural form <u>kee</u> is used.  And <u>dukaan</u>, "store," is feminine; hence the feminine form <u>kii</u> is used.

Note the difference in meaning between the following pairs of sentences:

| | |
|---|---|
| mãĩ hooTal mẽẽ kaam kartaa hũũ. | I work in the hotel. |
| mãĩ hooTal kaa kaam kartaa hũũ. | I do the work of the hotel (i.e., I work for the hotel). |

Note that in equational sentences of the type "are you such-and-such a person," whether in Hindi a pronoun is <u>tum</u> or <u>aap</u>, the form for "such-and-such a person" will be in the plural.

| | |
|---|---|
| Kyaa tumhĩĩ is hooTal kee dhoobii hoo? | Are you the washerman of this hotel? |

## 6. <u>Emphatic Particle</u> hii

In Hindi there is an emphatic particle <u>hii</u>, sometimes occurring in the form hĩĩ, which is generally used to emphasize the form preceding it.  Sometimes it is joined with the preceding item as a single word and sometimes it is separated.

| Simple | | Emphatic | |
|---|---|---|---|
| wahãã | there | wahĩĩ | |
| yahãã | here | yahĩĩ | |
| tum | you | tumhĩĩ | |
| mãĩ | I | mãĩ hii | |
| ab | now | abhii | right away |

## 7. <u>Numerals</u>

In counting and enumerating, it is common to use a numeral with a noun in the singular, as in <u>chai kamiiz</u>, "six shirts," but the plural may also be used, as in <u>pããc jooRee moozee</u>, "five pairs of socks."  In situations other than counting or listing, the plural of the noun is likely to be used with numerals above one.

yahãã chai kamiizẽẽ hãĩ. There are six shirts here.

32

# EXERCISES

A. Substitute orally in the sentences below the Hindi equivalent of the English given:

1. _____ aa jaaoo.

   inside              in the store

   here               in the famous store

   in the hotel       in the famous hotel

2. mãî _____ kaam kartaa hũũ.

   here               of the store

   there              of the Ajmer Hotel

   of the hotel       of the bazaar

3. mãî abhii _____ deetaa hũũ.

   clothes            one dozen oranges

   fruit              seven oranges

   oranges            five rupees

   rupees             handkerchiefs

   some fruit         two pairs of socks

   five oranges       nine handkerchiefs

   ten rupees         some clothes

4. _____ minaT rukoo.

   two                eight

   five               three

   seven              nine

   ten                one

   four

5. yee rahee _____.

   clothes            two handkerchiefs

|                            |                  |
|----------------------------|------------------|
| oranges                    | some fruit (pl.) |
| five rupees                | some oranges     |
| four pairs of trousers     | some clothes     |
| seven pairs of socks       | some rupees      |

6.  mujhee _____ jaldii caahiyee.

|                  |                          |
|------------------|--------------------------|
| clothes          | those oranges            |
| these clothes    | this dozen oranges       |
| those clothes    | this dozen sweet oranges |
| these oranges    |                          |

B.  Substitute orally in the sentences below the Hindi
equivalent of the English given, making other changes
if necessary.

1.  _____ yahãã kaa kaam kartaa hũũ.

|             |               |
|-------------|---------------|
| I (masc.)   | they (masc.)  |
| he          | they (fem.)   |
| she         | I (fem.)      |
| we (fem.)   | we (masc.)    |

2.  _____ abhii kapRee deetaa hũũ.

|             |               |
|-------------|---------------|
| I (masc.)   | they (masc.)  |
| we (fem.)   | I (fem.)      |
| he          | we (masc.)    |
| she         | they (fem.)   |

3.  _____ bahut acchaa hai.

these pairs of trousers

these shirts

those undershirts

those pairs of socks

34

these handkerchiefs

those oranges

these clothes

C. Transform the following sentences according to the model given:

baaîî taraf jaaoo ....... baaîî taraf jaaiyee.

1. kuch phal xariidoo.

2. yee santaree loo.

3. kapRee likhoo

4. dhoobhii kee kapRee likh loo.

5. sunoo.

6. naagpurii santaree deekhoo.

7. andar aaoo.

8. eek minaT rukoo.

9. hooTal kaa kaam karoo.

10. mujhee pããc rupaee doo.

D. Transform the following sentences according to the model given:

woo bazaar jaanaa caahtaa ....... woo bazaar jaataa
   hai.                               hai.

1. woo kuch phal xariidnaa caahtaa hai.

2. woo santaree leenaa caahtaa hai.

3. woo kapRee likhnaa caahtaa hai.

4. woo mujhee phal deena caahtaa hai.

5. woo hooTal mẽẽ ruknaa caahtaa hai.

6. woo yahãã kaam karnaa caahtaa hai.

7. woo andar aanaa caahtaa hai.

8. woo naagpurii santaree deekhnaa caahtaa hai.

E.  Translate orally:

    1.  I work here.

    2.  I work in the hotel.

    3.  I work in the store.

    4.  I work in the fruit store.

    5.  I work in the Ajmer Hotel.

    6.  Where do you work?

    7.  I need these clothes back soon.

    8.  I need these trousers back soon.

    9.  I need these undershirts back soon.

   10.  I need these shirts back soon.

   11.  I need these handkerchiefs back soon.

   12.  I need these oranges.

   13.  I want to write.

   14.  I want to go to the market.

   15.  He is the washerman of this hotel.

F.  Translate orally:

    1.  I (masc.) work here.

    2.  He works here.

    3.  They (fem.) work here.

    4.  We (masc.) work here.

    5.  She works here.

    6.  They (masc.) work here.

    7.  We (fem.) work here.

    8.  I (fem.) work here.

    9.  Do you (masc., familiar) work here?

   10.  Do you (fem., familiar) work here?

11. Do you (masc., polite) work here?

12. Do you (fem., polite) work here?

G. Translate orally:

1. I (fem.) want to write.

2. They (masc.) want to write.

3. She wants to write.

4. We (masc.) want to write.

5. I (masc.) want to write.

6. They (fem.) want to write.

7. We (fem.) want to write.

8. He wants to write.

9. Do you (fem., polite) want to write?

10. Do you (masc., familiar) want to write?

11. Do you (fem., familiar) want to write?

12. Do you (masc., polite) want to write?

## REVIEW I

A. Substitute orally in the sentences below the Hindi equivalent of the English given:

1. woo _____ caahtaa hai.

| | |
|---|---|
| to go | to stop |
| to come | to write |
| to buy | to listen |
| to take | to see |
| to give | to work |

2. yee phal _____.

| | |
|---|---|
| please buy | buy |
| please see | take |

```
        please take          give (away)

        please give (away)   see
```

3.  mujhee _____ jaldii caahiyee.

```
        the clothes          those shirts

        these clothes        these handkerchiefs

        those clothes        this undershirt

        these oranges        this pair of trousers

        these sweet oranges  some oranges

        those good oranges   one dozen oranges
```

4.  kyaa yee hooTal _____ hai?

```
        good                 to the left

        very good            to the right

        famous               straight ahead

        very famous          far

        famous and good      very far

        here                 one mile

        there                ten miles
```

5.  yee dukaan _____ kitnii duur hai.

```
        from here            from the bazaar

        from there           from the Sadar Bazaar

        from the hotel       from the Ajmer Hotel

        from the bus stop
```

6.  _____ kaa naam kyaa hai?

```
        the hotel            the washerman

        the store            the famous hotel

        the fruit store      the famous store

        the bazaar           the famous bazaar
```

7. woo _____ kaam kartaa hai.

> here                     in the store
>
> there                    in the fruit store
>
> in the hotel             in the famous bazaar
>
> in the bazaar            in the Ajmer Hotel
>
> in the famous hotel

8. in kaa daam _____ hai?

> two rupees               eight rupees
>
> five rupees              three rupees
>
> ten rupees               nine rupees
>
> seven rupees             six rupees
>
> four rupees

9. yee santaree _____ hãĩ.

> sweet                    ten
>
> good                     one dozen
>
> famous                   how many
>
> very sweet               very good and very sweet
>
> very good

10. _____ kahãã miltee hãĩ?

> oranges                  socks
>
> fruit                    trousers
>
> these oranges            sweet oranges
>
> these clothes            good oranges
>
> Nagpur oranges           good clothes
>
> handkerchiefs

11. yee liijiyee _____.

> the oranges              the sweet oranges

39

|                     |                     |
|---------------------|---------------------|
| one dozen oranges   | the clothes         |
| the Nagpur oranges  | the undershirts     |
| the handkerchiefs   | the shirts          |
| the trousers        | the sweet fruit     |

12. mãĩ _____ xariidnaa caahtaa hũũ.

|                     |                         |
|---------------------|-------------------------|
| fruit               | some good trousers      |
| some fruit          | ten handkerchiefs       |
| some good fruit     | two handkerchiefs       |
| some oranges        | five shirts             |
| one dozen oranges   | eight pairs of socks    |
| some clothes        | some good shirts        |
| some trousers       | one dozen shirts        |

13. mãĩ abhii _____ deetaa hũũ.

|                     |                              |
|---------------------|------------------------------|
| the clothes         | the fruit                    |
| the trousers        | ten rupees                   |
| the shirts          | some oranges                 |
| the undershirts     | some clothes                 |
| the socks           | some sweet oranges           |
| the handkerchief    | one dozen shirts             |
| the oranges         | one dozen pairs of trousers  |

14. _____ yahãã see kitnii duur hai?

|                     |                     |
|---------------------|---------------------|
| the bazaar          | that bazaar         |
| the hotel           | this bazaar         |
| the famous hotel    | this store          |
| the Ajmer Hotel     | this fruit store    |
| the Nagpur Hotel    | that fruit store    |
| the bus stop        | that store          |

the store

15. wee _____ kahãã hãĩ?

shirts                          good handkerchiefs

one dozen shirts   five handkerchiefs

good shirts              oranges

handkerchiefs          good oranges

B.  Substitute orally in the sentences below the Hindi
equivalent of the English given, making other changes,
if necessary.

1. _____ bahut mašhuur hai.

this hotel               those fruit stores

these hotels           those markets

this market            that hotel

this store              those hotels

these markets        this store

those stores           these stores

2. _____ bahut miiThaa hai.

this orange            this fruit

these oranges        that fruit

those oranges

3. _____ bazaar jaanaa caahtaa hũũ.

he                          the washerman

she                        we (masc.)

I (masc.)                I (fem.)

we (fem.)               they (fem.)

they (masc.)          Ram Nath

John

4. in kaa daam _____ rupayaa hai.

41

| | |
|---|---|
| one | three |
| two | seven |
| five | nine |
| seven | four |
| ten | eight |

5. kyaa _____ bazaar jaanaa caahtee hãĩ?

       you (masc. polite)

       you (fem. familiar)

       you (masc. familiar)

       you (fem. polite)

C. Transform the following sentences according to the model given:

bas yahãã miltii hai. ....... kyaa bas yahãã miltii
                                 hai?

  1. bas-isTaap bahut duur hai.

  2. yee dhoobhii yahãã kaa kaam kartaa hai.

  3. ajmeerii hooTal bahut acchaa hooTal hai.

  4. wahĩĩ eek hooTal hai.

  5. yee phal kii dukaan hai.

  6. in kaa daam tiin tupaee hai.

  7. bazaar yahãã see eek miil duur hai.

  8. woo yee kapRee jaldii caahtaa hai.

  9. naagpurii santaree bahut miiThee hootee hai.

10. yee aap kii dukaan hai.

11. aap kii dukaan acchii hai.

12. yee hooTal mašhuur hai.

13. bas-isTaap yahãã see baaĩĩ taraf hai.

14. hooTal kaa naam ajmeerii hooTal hai.

15. woo santaree xariidnaa caahtaa hai.

D. Transform the following sentences according to the model given:

sunoo.       ....... suniyee.

1. sadar bazaar jaaoo.

2. naagpurii santaree xariidoo.

3. miiThee phal loo.

4. kapRee likhoo.

5. yee phal deekhoo.

6. mujhee kuch rupaee doo.

7. yahãã doo minaT rukoo.

8. hooTal kaa kaam karoo.

9. andar aaoo.

10. mujhee eek darjan santaree dee doo.

E. Transform the following sentences according to the model given:

woo phal xariidtii hai.  ....... woo phal xariidnaa
                                 caahtii hai.

1. woo sadar bazaar jaatii hai.

2. woo kuch phal leetii hai.

3. woo pããc rupaee deetii hai.

4. woo dhoobhii kee kapRee likhtii hai.

5. woo suntii hai.

6. woo andar aatii hai.

7. woo das kamiizẽẽ xariidtii hai.

8. woo naagpurii santaree deekhtii hai.

9. woo bas-isTaap mẽẽ ruktii hai.

10. woo hooTal mẽẽ kaam kartii hai.

43

F. Transform the following sentences according to the model given:

yee santaraa acchaa hai. ..... yee santaree acchee hãĩ.

1. yee bas acchii hai.

2. yee bazaar mašhuur hai.

3. yee hooTal acchaa hai.

4. yee kamiiz acchii hai.

5. yee rumaal acchaa hai.

6. yee dukaan acchii hai.

7. yee hooTal mašhuur hai.

8. yee pãĩNT acchaa hai.

9. yee phal miiThaa hai.

10. yee bazaar bahut acchaa hai.

11. yee baniyaain acchii hai.

12. yee dukaan mašhuur hai.

13. yee santaraa miiThaa hai.

14. yee moozaa acchaa hai.

15. yee phal acchaa hai.

G. Translate orally:

1. He writes.

2. We (masc.) write.

3. You (fem., familiar) write.

4. I (masc.) write.

5. They (fem.) write.

6. You (masc., polite) write.

7. I (fem.) write.

8. She writes.

9. You (fem., polite) write.

44

10. We (fem.) write.

11. They (masc.) write.

12. You (masc., familiar) write.

H.  Translate orally:

1. He takes (buys) some oranges from the store.

2. I (masc.) take (buy) some oranges from the store.

3. They (fem.) take (buy) some oranges from the store.

4. We (masc.) take (buy) some oranges from the store.

5. She takes (buys) some oranges from the store.

6. You (masc., familiar) take (buy) some oranges from the store.

7. They (masc.) take (buy) some oranges from the store.

8. You (fem., familiar) take (buy) some oranges from the store.

9. I (fem.) take (buy) some oranges from the store.

10. You (masc., polite) take (buy) some oranges from the store.

11. We (fem.) take (buy) some oranges from the store.

12. You (fem., polite) take (buy) some oranges from the store.

I.  Translate orally:

1. I (masc.) wait here.

2. She waits here.

3. You (masc., familiar) wait here.

4. They (fem.) wait here.

5. We (masc.) wait here.

6. You (fem., polite) wait here.

7. He waits here.

8. I (fem.) wait here.

9. You (masc., polite) wait here.

10. They (masc.) wait here.

11. We (fem.) wait here.

12. You (fem., familiar) wait here.

J.  Translate orally:

1. The washerman comes in.

2. They (fem.) come in.

3. I (masc.) come in.

4. You (fem., polite) come in.

5. We (masc.) come in.

6. They (masc.) come in.

7. I (fem.) come in.

8. You (masc., familiar) come in.

9. She comes in.

10. You (masc., polite) come in.

11. We (fem.) come in.

12. You (fem., familiar) come in.

K.  Conversation

1.  A wants to go to the bazaar.  He stops B on the
    street and asks him where the bazaar is.  B tells
    him that the bazaar isn't very far.  A asks how
    far it is.  B tells him that it's one mile.  B
    asks if A wants to go to the bazaar by bus.  A
    replies in the affirmative.  B directs him to the
    bus stop asking him to go to the left and then
    straight ahead.  A thanks B.

2.  The washerman knocks at A's door in the hotel.  A
    asks who it is.  The washerman tells him it's the
    washerman.  A asks him to come in.  A asks him if
    he is the washerman of that hotel.  The washerman
    replies that he is the one who works there.  A
    gives his clothes to the washerman.  The washerman
    requests A to write them down and enumerates them.

46

After writing them down, A tells the washerman that he wants the clothes back soon.

3.  A wants to buy some oranges and enters a fruit store. A asks the storekeeper if he has some oranges. The storekeeper asks him what kind of oranges he needs. A tells him that he wants to buy Nagpur oranges. The storekeeper shows him the Nagpur oranges and tells him that they are very good and sweet. A asks their price. The storekeeper says that their price is two rupees a dozen. A asks him to give him five dozen oranges. The storekeeper gives him five dozen oranges. A gives ten rupees to the storekeeper.

4.  A asks to go to a hotel. He stops B on the road and asks him where a hotel is. B tells him about the Ajmer Hotel. A asks him if it is a good hotel. B tells him that it is very good. A asks B where the Ajmer Hotel is. B tells him that it is in the Sadar Bazaar. A asks directions to go there. B tells him to go to the right and then straight ahead. He says that the Ajmer Hotel is right there. A thanks B and leaves.

5.  A enters a store and tells the storekeeper that he wants to buy some shirts. The storekeeper brings some shirts and shows them to A. A asks their price. The storekeeper says that they are three rupees each. A asks the storekeeper to give him three shirts. The storekeeper gives A three shirts. A pays him nine rupees and leaves.

# LESSON V

## Conversation -- Talking to a Hotel Manager

### HOTEL MANAGER

| | |
|---|---|
| namastee | hello |
| kahnaa | to say |
| kee liyee | for |
| saknaa | to be able |

namastee, kahiyee, kyaa mãĩ aap kee liyee kuch kar saktaa hũũ?

Hello. Can I do something for you?

### JOHN

| | |
|---|---|
| kee paas | at |
| kooii | any, some |
| kamraa | room |
| xaalii | vacant |

kyaa aap kee paas kooii kamraa xaalii hai?

Do you have a vacant room?

### HOTEL MANAGER

| | |
|---|---|
| kaisaa | what kind |
| siŋgil | single |
| yaa | or |
| Dabal | double |

aap koo kaisaa kamraa caahiyee--siŋgil yaa Dabal?

What kind of room do you want--single or double?

### JOHN

| | |
|---|---|
| meeree | my |
| saath | with |
| meerii | my |

48

| patnii | wife |
|---|---|
| bhii | also |

Dabal, meeree saath meerii patnii bhii hãĩ. — Double, my wife is with me too.

## HOTEL MANAGER

| deekh leenaa | to take a look |
|---|---|

acchaa, aaiyee, kamraa deekh liijiyee. — All right, come and take a look at the room.

| sabhii | all |
|---|---|
| suwidhaa* | convenience |

is kamree mẽẽ sabhii suwidhaaẽẽ hãĩ. — This room has all the con-veniences.

| pasand | pleasing |
|---|---|

kahiyee, aap koo pasand hai? — Do you like it?

## JOHN

Thiik hai, mujhee pasand hai. — It's fine. I like it.

| kiraayaa | rent |
|---|---|
| kitnaa | how much |

is-kaa kiraayaa kitnaa hai? — How much is it?

## HOTEL MANAGER

| keewal | only |
|---|---|
| das | ten |
| rooz | day |

aap kee liyee keewal das rupaee rooz. — For you it's only ten rupees a day.

----------

* This expression in Hindi means that the room is likely to include chairs, sofa, and writing table. It may or may not imply that there is a separate bathroom.

JOHN

| | |
|---|---|
| tab | then |
| tab too | then |
| isee | it |
| lee lũũgaa | (I) will take |
| tab too Thiik hai, mãĩ isee lee lũũgaa. | Then it's all right. I'll take it. |

GRAMMAR

1. New Nouns

| Masc. | | Fem. | |
|---|---|---|---|
| kamraa | room | patnii | wife |
| kiraayaa | rent | suwidhaa | convenience |
| rooz | day | | |

2. New Verbs

| | |
|---|---|
| kahnaa | to say, tell |
| saknaa | to be able |

The forms of these verbs are regular.

2.1. New Compound Verbs

Type I

| | |
|---|---|
| deekh leenaa | to take a look |
| lee leenaa | to take |

3. New Adjectives in -aa

| | |
|---|---|
| kaisaa | what kind |

4. Oblique Case

Nouns in Hindi, besides being inflected for number, are inflected for two cases--nominative and oblique. Hindi nouns may be subdivided into four classes on the basis of their inflection. These classes will be referred to as Masc. I, Masc. II, Fem. I, and Fem. II.

50

## Masculine I

The nouns of this class are characterized by having a nominative singular form ending in -aa.  The other forms of this class are as follows:

|      | Sg.     | Pl.     |
|------|---------|---------|
| Nom. | kamraa  | kamree  |
| Obl. | kamree  | kamrõõ  |

Note that for nouns of this class the nominative plural and the oblique singular forms are identical.

## Masculine II

The nouns of this class are those masculine nouns which do not end in -aa.  The forms are:

|      | Sg.     | Pl.       |
|------|---------|-----------|
| Nom. | hooTal  | hooTal    |
| Obl. | hooTal  | hooTalõõ  |

Note that for nouns of this class the nominative singular, the oblique singular, and the nominative plural forms are all identical.

## Feminine I

Nouns of this class are characterized by having a nominative singular form ending in -ii.  The other forms are:

|      | Sg.     | Pl.       |
|------|---------|-----------|
| Nom. | patnii  | patniyãã  |
| Obl. | patnii  | patniyõõ  |

## Feminine II

The nouns of this class are those feminine nouns which do not end in -ii.  The forms are:

|      | Sg.     | Pl.       |
|------|---------|-----------|
| Nom. | dukaan  | dukaanẽẽ  |
| Obl. | dukaan  | dukaanõõ  |

51

There are a limited number of nouns which do not
fit the classifications above.  They will be called
irregular nouns, and their forms will be given when
they occur.

## 4.1.  Use of the Cases

The oblique case of a noun is used in Hindi when-
ever the noun is followed by a postposition.

| | |
|---|---|
| kamraa xaalii hai. | The room is vacant. |
| kamree mẽẽ sabhii suwidhaaẽẽ hã̃ĩ. | All the conveniences are in the room. |
| santaree acchee hã̃ĩ. | The oranges are good. |
| santarõ̃õ̃ kaa daam kyaa hai? | What's the price of the oranges? |

## 5.  Verb saknaa, "to be able"

When a second verb is used dependent upon the verb
saknaa, "to be able," the dependent verb is used in the
verb-stem form.

| | |
|---|---|
| kyaa mã̃ĩ aap kee liyee kuch kar saktaa hũ̃ũ? | Can I do something for you? |
| kyaa woo kamraa deekh saktaa hai? | Can he see the room? |

Note the contrast between saknaa, "to be able,"
which takes a dependent verb in the verb-stem form,
and the verb caahnaa, "to want," which takes a dependent
verb in the infinitive form.

| | |
|---|---|
| mã̃ĩ jaa saktaa hũ̃ũ. | I can go. |
| mã̃ĩ jaanaa caahtaa hũ̃ũ. | I want to go. |

## 6.  kyaa

In an interrogative sentence in which kyaa may be
used as an interrogative particle (but not when used
meaning "what"), the form kyaa may often be omitted,
e.g.

| | |
|---|---|
| kyaa aap koo yee kamraa pasand hai? | |
| aap koo yee kamraa pasand hai? | Do you like this room? |

## 7. Writing System

The Hindi writing system is called Devanagari
(deevanaagrii). Under most conditions the writing of
a consonant symbol will assume that there is a following short vowel -a after the consonant. The first
letters you should learn are the following:

| | | | |
|------|------|------|------|
| pa | प | ma | म |
| ta | त | na | न |
| ba | ब | ka | क |
| da | द | sa | स |

When these symbols occur at the end of a word,
however, they represent a consonant sound only; i.e.,
there is no following -a, as for example:

| | |
|-----|-----|
| bas | बस |
| das | दस |
| tab | तब |

To indicate the long vowel -aa after a consonant a
vertical stroke T is used after the consonant symbol:

| | | | |
|------|------|------|------|
| paa | पा | maa | मा |
| taa | ता | naa | ना |
| baa | बा | kaa | का |
| daa | दा | saa | सा |

### EXERCISES

A. Substitute orally in the sentences below the Hindi
equivalent of the English given:

1. kyaa woo _____?

| | |
|------------|------------|
| can write | can take |
| can come | can see |
| can wait | can buy |
| can go | can say |
| can listen | can work |

2. kyaa aap kee paas _____ hai?

      a room               a shirt

      a single room       a handkerchief

      a double room      an undershirt

      a good room        a rupee

3. _____ sabhii suwidhaaẽẽ hãĩ.

      in the room        in the single room

      in the hotel        in the double room

      in the rooms        in the single rooms

      in the hotels       in the double rooms

4. is kaa kiraayaa _____ hai?

      how much          ten rupees

      very much         five rupees

5. _____ deekh liijiyee.

      a room              the single room

      the room           the double room

      the rooms          the good room

      the fruit           the good rooms

      some oranges       the sweet oranges

6. mujhee yee _____ pasand hai.

      room                store

      hotel               market

      bus                 work

      washerman

7. _____ kaa naam kyaa hai?

      the hotel           the wife

      the store           the washerman

the bazaar

8. aap koo _____ kamraa caahiyee?

   what kind of        single

   good                double

9. aap koo _____ caahiyee?

   what kind of rooms        what kind of socks

   what kind of fruit        what kind of handker-
                               chiefs
   what kind of oranges
                             what kind of undershirts
   what kind of room
                             what kind of stores
   what kind of shirts

10. mujhee _____ pasand hãĩ.

    these rooms              these socks

    those oranges            those undershirts

    those rooms              these handkerchiefs

    these hotels             those shirts

    those hotels             those socks

    these oranges            these undershirts

    these shirts             these stores

    those handkerchiefs      those stores

B. Substitute orally in the sentence below the Hindi
equivalent of the English given, making other changes
if necessary.

1. kyaa _____ aap kee liyee kuch kar saktaa hũũ.

   I (masc.)           they (fem.)

   John                the washerman

   she                 the wife

   they (masc.)        he

   I (fem.)

55

C. Transform the following sentences according to the model given:

woo phal xariidtaa hai ..... woo phal xariid sakta hai.

1. woo kamree deekhtaa hai.

2. woo phal leetaa hai.

3. woo hooTal jaataa hai.

4. woo kyaa kartaa hai?

5. woo bazaar see aataa hai.

6. woo kapRee likhtaa hai.

7. woo mujhee pãāc rupaee deetaa hai.

8. woo hooTal mẽẽ ruktaa hai.

9. woo dukaan mẽẽ kaam kartaa hai.

10. woo suntaa hai.

D. Transform the following sentences according to the model given:

ham phal xariidnaa caahtee ... ham phal xariid saktee
  hãĩ.                               hãĩ.

1. ham kuch kamree deekhnaa caahtee hãĩ.

2. ham hooTal mẽẽ kaam karnaa caahtee hãĩ.

3. ham sunnaa caahtee hãĩ.

4. ham pãāc rupaee leenaa caahtee hãĩ.

5. ham hooTal mẽẽ ruknaa caahtee hãĩ.

6. ham dhoobii koo kapRee deenaa caahtee hãĩ.

7. ham andar aanaa caahtee hãĩ.

8. ham bazaar jaanaa caahtee hãĩ.

9. ham yee kamiizẽẽ likhnaa caahtee hãĩ.

10. ham bas-isTaap mẽẽ ruknaa caahtee hãĩ.

E. Translate orally:

1. Can I do something for you?

56

2. Do you have a vacant room?

3. Do you want a single room?

4. No, I want a double room.

5. Do you have a double room?

6. Yes, do you want to see the room?

7. Come with me and see the room.

8. This room has all the conveniences in it.

9. How much is it?

10. Ten rupees a day.

11. It's all right. I'll take it.

12. They want to buy some clothes from the store.

13. The market isn't very far from here.

14. Do you want to come in?

15. She looks at these oranges.

16. These oranges are (generally) sweet.

17. What kind of fruit do you need?

18. Do you want to buy some socks?

19. Here's a dozen oranges.

20. Please write down these clothes.

21. I want to buy six pairs of trousers.

22. There is a fruit store right there.

23. What is the name of the bazaar?

24. Is it a good fruit store?

25. What's their price?

F. Read the following:

| काम | दस | सात | तब |
|-----|-----|-----|-----|
| बस | नाम | पास | दाम |

## Conversation -- In the Post Office

### CLERK

| | |
|---|---|
| kahiyee, aap koo kyaa caahiyee? | Hello.  What do you want? |

### JOHN

| | |
|---|---|
| kaarD | card, postcard |
| lifaafaa | envelope |
| aadi | et cetera |
| mãĩ kuch kaarD lifaafee aadi leenaa caahtaa hũũ | I want to buy some postcards, envelopes, etc. |

### CLERK

| | |
|---|---|
| aglaa | next |
| khiRkii | window |
| par | at, on, to |
| tab aglii khiRkii par jaaiyee. | Then go to the next window. |
| maniaarDar | money order |
| liyee jaatee hãĩ. | are taken, are accepted |
| yahãã maniaarDar liyee jaatee hãĩ. | Money orders are accepted here. |

(at the next window)

### JOHN

| | |
|---|---|
| poosT kaarD | postcard |
| baaraa | twelve |
| mujhee das poosT kaarD aur baaraa lifaafee dee diijiyee. | Please give me ten postcards and twelve envelopes. |

aur kuch            something else

yee liijiyee, aur kuch    Here, sir.  Do you want
    caahiyee.                    anything else?

## JOHN

pandraa              fifteen

nayaa                new

paisaa             pice

nayaa paisaa*        new pice (Indian coin)

waalaa             of

tiis                 thirty

TikaT               stamp

jii hãã, pandree naee    Yes, please give (me) thirty
    paisee waalee tiis TikaT   fifteen-new-pice stamps
    bhii dee diijiyee.        too.

patr                 letter

antardeešiiy patr**     inland letter

kyaa aap kee paas       Do you have inland letters
    antardeešiiy patr bhii hãĩ?   also?

## CLERK

jii hãã, kitnee caahiyee?   Yes, how many do you need?

----------

\*   In the present-day Indian coinage system, introduced
in 1957, one hundred new pice are equal to one rupee.
Under the old coinage system four pice (paisaa)
equals one anna (Hindi - aanaa), and sixteen annas
equals one rupee.  In some places in India the old
terms may still be used.

\*\* In India there are two types of air letters:
antardeešiiy patr, "inland letter," which costs ten
new pice and is good only within India; and hawaaii
patr, "air letter," which is used for destinations
outside the country and costs fifty-five new pice.

## JOHN

| | |
|---|---|
| hawaaii patr | air letter |
| saat. | Seven. |
| saath hii das hawaaii patr bhii dee diijiyee. | Give me ten air letters also. |

## CLERK

| | |
|---|---|
| liijiyee, yee rahee aap kee TikaT, antardeešiiy patr aur hawaaii patr. | Here are your stamps, inland letters and air letters. |

## JOHN

| | |
|---|---|
| huee | became |
| kitnee paisee huee? | How much is it? |

## CLERK

| | |
|---|---|
| kul | in all |
| teeraa | thirteen |
| kul teeraa rupaee. | Thirteen rupees in all. |

## JOHN

| | |
|---|---|
| yee liijiyee teeraa rupaee. | Here are thirteen rupees. |

## NUMERALS

| | |
|---|---|
| gyaaraa | eleven |
| baaraa | twelve |
| teeraa | thirteen |
| caudaa | fourteen |
| pandraa | fifteen |
| soolaa | sixteen |
| satraa | seventeen |
| aThaaraa | eighteen |

| unniis | nineteen |
|--------|----------|
| biis   | twenty   |

## GRAMMAR

1. ### New Nouns

   **Masc. I**           **Fem. I**

   | lifaafaa | envelope | khiRkii | window |
   |----------|----------|---------|--------|
   | paisaa   | pice     |         |        |

   **Masc. II**

   | kaarD      | card        |
   |------------|-------------|
   | maniaarDar | money order |
   | TikaT      | stamp       |
   | patr       | letter      |

2. ### New Adjectives in -aa

   | aglaa  | next |
   |--------|------|
   | waalaa | of   |

3. ### New Postpositions

   | par       | on, at, to |
   |-----------|------------|
   | kee paas  | at         |
   | kee liyee | for        |

   The last two postpositions are compound postpositions which are best learned as single items.

4. ### Pronouns

   Personal pronouns in Hindi, besides having nominative and oblique case forms, also have a dative case form.

   4.1. ### Personal Pronouns

   The forms of the personal pronouns are:

61

|        | 1st Per. | 3rd Per. | 3rd Per. | 2nd Per. |
|--------|----------|----------|----------|----------|
|        | Sg.      | Sg.      | Sg.      | Familiar |
| Nom.   | mãĩ      | woo      | yee      | tum      |
| Dat.   | mujhee   | usee     | isee     | tumhẽẽ   |
| Obl.   | mujh     | us       | is       | tum      |
|        | Pl.      | Pl.      | Pl.      | Polite   |
| Nom.   | ham      | wee      | yee      | aap      |
| Dat.   | hamẽẽ    | unhẽẽ    | inhẽẽ    | -        |
| Obl.   | ham      | un       | in       | aap      |

These pronouns that have a dative form different from the oblique form may replace this special dative with the oblique followed by the postposition koo, "to." Thus mujh koo, us koo, is koo, tum koo, ham koo, un koo, in koo, and aap koo may be used. The pronoun aap, "you" (polite), has only the form aap koo as an equivalent to the dative of the other pronouns.

## 4.2. Interrogative Pronoun kaun, "who"

The forms of the interrogative pronoun kaun, "who," are:

|        | Sg.    | Pl.     |
|--------|--------|---------|
| Nom.   | kaun   | kaun    |
| Dat.   | kisee  | kinhẽẽ  |
| Obl.   | kis    | kin     |

Like the personal pronouns, the dative form kisee may be replaced by kis koo, and kinhẽẽ by kin koo.

## 5. Indefinite Adjectives kooii, kuch

The forms of kooii, "some," and kuch, "some," are:

|        | Sg.    | Pl.    |
|--------|--------|--------|
| Nom.   | kooii  | kuch   |
| Dat.   | kisii  | kuch   |
| Obl.   | kis    | kuch   |

The form <u>kuch</u> is generally used only with plural nouns and <u>kooii</u> with singular nouns, although both may be used with nouns that refer to objects which are not countable, such as sugar, cloth etc., in which case <u>kuch</u> refers to "some quantity" and <u>kooii</u> to "some kind."

| | |
|---|---|
| kyaa aap koo kooii kamraa caahiyee? | Do you want a room (some room or other)? |
| kyaa aap koo kuch santaree caahiyee? | Do you want some oranges? |
| kyaa aap koo kooii kapRaa caahiyee? | Do you want some cloth or other? |
| kyaa aap koo kuch kapRaa caahiyee? | Do you want some cloth? |

6. <u>Use of Dative Case and Postposition</u> koo, "<u>to, for</u>"

One of the main uses of the dative case of pronouns is as the indirect object of a verb.

| | |
|---|---|
| mujhee baaraa lifaafee dee diijiyee. | Please give me twelve envelopes. |
| usee doo rupaee dee diijiyee. | Please give him two rupees. |

Nouns do not have a dative case form but express the indirect object by the use of the postposition <u>koo</u>, "to," "for," preceded by the noun in the oblique case form. As mentioned earlier, those pronouns which do have a dative case may use the <u>koo</u> form instead of the dative case.

| | |
|---|---|
| dhoobii koo eek rupayaa dee diijiyee. | Please give one rupee to the washerman. |
| raam koo lifaafee dee diijiyee. | Please give envelopes to Ram. |
| mujh koo baaraa lifaafee dee diijiyee. | Please give me twelve envelopes. |

As noted previously, the form <u>caahiyee</u> equates with the English verb "want," "need." The person involved in the construction with <u>caahiyee</u> is in the dative case. Thus <u>mujhee caahiyee</u>, "I need," "I want," means literally "to me is necessary."

| | |
|---|---|
| aap koo kaun see phal caahiyee? | What kind of fruit do you need? |

```
raam koo kapRee           Ram needs clothes.
   caahiyee.
```

The expression <u>pasand hoonaa</u> is literally "to be
pleasing," but is used where English would use the
verb "to like." The person who likes something will
in Hindi be in the dative case.

```
kyaa aap koo yee kamraa   Do you like this room?
   pasand hai?               (Lit.: Is this room
                              pleasing to you?)

jii hãã, mujhee pasand    Yes, I like it.
   hãĩ.

raam koo yee naee         Ram likes these new clothes.
   kapRee pasand hãĩ.
```

Note that since the Hindi construction of the last
sentence is literally "these new clothes are pleasing
to Ram," the verb <u>hãĩ</u>, "are," is in the plural, agreeing with <u>yee naee kapRee</u>, "these new clothes."

## 7. <u>Use of the Oblique Case of Pronouns</u>

The oblique case of pronouns is, like the oblique
case of nouns, the form used with postpositions.

```
is mẽẽ sabhii suwidhaaẽẽ  All conveniences are there
   hãĩ.                      (in it).

is taraf jaaiyee.         Please go to this side.

mujh see yee santaree     Please buy these oranges
   liijiyee.                 from me.
```

## 8. <u>Oblique Case of Adjectives</u>

An adjective modifying a noun that is in the
oblique case must also be in the oblique case. The
forms of the adjective with a nominative masculine
singular in -<u>aa</u> are as follows:

|          | Masc.  | Fem.   |
|----------|--------|--------|
| Nom. Sg. | acchaa | acchii |
| Obl. Sg. | acchee | acchii |
| Nom. Pl. | acchee | acchii |
| Obl. Pl. | acchee | acchii |

Note that for the masculine forms, it is only the

nominative singular that does not end in -ee. The
feminine adjectives do not have different forms for
the oblique, either singular or plural. Also adjectives which do not end in -aa, like mašhuur, "famous,"
do not undergo any change in form for number, gender,
or case.

| | |
|---|---|
| acchaa kamraa | a good room |
| acchee kamree mẽẽ | in a good room |

In the second phrase above, the adjective is in the
oblique form, agreeing with the noun, which in turn is
in the oblique form because it is used with the postposition mẽẽ, "in."

| | |
|---|---|
| acchee kamree | good rooms |
| acchee kamrõõ mẽẽ | in good rooms |

The postposition kaa, "of," has the same forms as
adjectives of this type. Compare the following phrases
with those above:

| | |
|---|---|
| raam kaa kamraa | Ram's room |
| raam kee kamree mẽẽ | in Ram's room |
| raam kee kamree | Ram's rooms |
| raam kee kamrõõ mẽẽ | in Ram's rooms |

9. Demonstrative Adjectives

The forms yee, "this," and woo, "that," like their
English equivalents are used both as pronouns (i.e.,
used without a following noun) and as adjectives (i.e.,
used with a following noun).

| | | |
|---|---|---|
| Pronoun | yee kyaa hai? | What's this? |
| Adjective | yee kamraa acchaa hai. | This room is good. |
| Pronoun | woo kyaa hai? | What's that? |
| Adjective | woo hooTal mašhuur hai. | That hotel is famous. |

When these forms are used as adjectives modifying
a following noun in the oblique case, the demonstrative has the oblique form: is, us, in, un.

is kamree mẽẽ sabhii     All conveniences are in

65

suwidhaaẽ̃ hãĩ.                    this room.

in dukaanõ̃ mẽ̃ phal            Fruit is available in
miltee hãĩ.                         these stores.

us dhoobii koo kapRee          Give the clothes to that
dee doo.                            washerman.

un santarõ̃ kaa daaw          What is the price of those
kyaa hai?                           oranges?

10.   Emphatic Particles, hii and bhii

     The emphatic particle hii has an exclusive meaning,
whereas bhii has an additive meaning.

mãĩ hii yahãã kaa kaam        I am the one who does the
kartaa hũũ.                         work here (excluding all
                                         others).

mãĩ bhii yahãã kaa kaam      I also work here (in
kartaa hũũ.                         addition to others).

11.   Writing System

     Some other consonant symbols are:

|       |       |       |       |
|-------|-------|-------|-------|
| pha   | फ     | ja    | ज     |
| tha   | थ     | bha   | भ     |
| ca    | च     | ra    | र     |
| Ta    | ट     | la    | ल     |
| Tha   | ठ     | ha    | ह     |

A short -i following a consonant is written with the
symbol ि preceding the consonant symbol, e.g.,

| pi | पि | ri | रि |
|----|----|----|----|
| ti | ति | ki | कि |

A long ii following a consonant is written with the
symbol ी following the consonant symbol, e.g.,

| dii  | दी  | kii | की |
|------|-----|-----|----|
| thii | थी  | lii | ली |

A short -u following a consonant is written with the
symbol ु underneath the consonant symbol, e.g.,

66

| | | | | |
|---|---|---|---|---|
| ju | जु | | mu | मु |
| bhu | भु | | bu | बु |

A long -uu following a consonant is written with the
symbol ॒ underneath the consonant symbol, e.g.,

| | | | | |
|---|---|---|---|---|
| nuu | नू | | huu | हू |
| suu | सू | | Tuu | टू |

Note that a short -u and a long -uu after the consonant
r are written differently, as follows:

| | | | | |
|---|---|---|---|---|
| ru | रु | | ruu | रू |

## EXERCISES

A.  Substitute orally in the sentences below the Hindi
equivalent of the English given:

1. _____ yee kapRee jaldii caahiyee.

| | |
|---|---|
| I | Ram |
| you (familiar) | washerman |
| he | she |
| we | you (polite) |
| they | John |

2. _____ kaa kiraayaa kitnaa hai?

| | |
|---|---|
| this room | that fruit store |
| those rooms | this famous store |
| these rooms | this single room |
| these good rooms | these single rooms |
| this good room | this double room |
| that store | those good single rooms |
| that famous store | these good double rooms |

3. _____ daam kyaa hai?

of these oranges    of these seventeen stamps

of these shirts     of those good oranges

of these air     of fifteen postcards
   letters

of this envelope     of these seven handkerchiefs

of these twelve     of those undershirts
   inland letters

of those good shirts

4. _____ kuch lifaafee dee diijiyee.

| | |
|---|---|
| me | them |
| him | her |
| John | the washerman |
| us | Ram |

5. mã̂i _____ kuch rupaee deetaa hũ̂u.

| | |
|---|---|
| him | her |
| you (polite) | Ram |
| them | you (familiar) |

6. kyaa aap kee paas _____ hã̂i?

| | |
|---|---|
| inland letters | some new clothes |
| some air letters | some new pice |
| ten postcards | twenty rupees |
| fifteen envelopes | thirty new pice |

B. Substitute orally in the sentences below the Hindi equivalent of the English given, making other changes, if necessary:

1. _____ kuch antardeešiiy patr leenaa caahtaa hũ̂u.

| | |
|---|---|
| I (masc.) | you (fem., polite) |
| he | we (masc.) |
| you (fem., familiar) | they (fem.) |
| they (masc.) | you (masc., polite) |

68

```
                she                     we (fem.)

        I (fem.)                you (masc., familiar)

2.  _____ yee kamraa lee saktaa hũũ.

        I (masc.)               you (fem., familiar)

        we (fem.)               we (masc.)

        John                    she

        you (fem., polite)      you (masc., polite)

        they (masc.)            they (fem.)

        I (fem.)                you (masc., familiar)
```

C. Transform the following sentences according to the model given:

```
woo bazaar jaa saktaa hai .... woo bazaar jaanaa
                                    caahtaa hai.
```

  1. woo kuch lifaafee xariid saktaa hai.

  2. woo yee kamraa lee saktaa hai.

  3. woo yee kapRee likh saktaa hai.

  4. woo kyaa kar saktaa hai?

  5. woo hooTal mẽẽ aa saktaa hai.

  6. woo yee siŋgil kamraa deekh saktaa hai.

  7. woo yahãã kaam kar saktaa hai.

  8. woo mujhee kuch poosT kaarD dee saktaa hai.

  9. woo sun saktaa hai.

  10. woo bas-isTaap mẽẽ ruk saktaa hai.

D. Transform the following sentences according to the model given:

```
mujhee kuch lifaafee caahiyee ... mãĩ kuch lifaafee
                                       caahtaa hũũ.
```

  1. mujhee das poosT kaarD caahiyee.

  2. mujhee pããc kamiizẽẽ caahiyee.

3. mujhee yee kapRee jaldii caahiyee.

4. mujhee kuch miiThee santaree caahiyee.

5. mujhee yee rupaee caahiyee.

6. mujhee pandraa hawaaii patr caahiyee.

7. mujhee sabhii suwidhaaẽẽ caahiyee.

8. mujhee eek siŋgil kamraa caahiyee.

9. mujhee baaraa antardeešiiy patr caahiyee.

10. mujhee tumhaaree kapRee caahiyee.

E.  Translate orally:

1. I want to buy some envelopes, air letters, etc.

2. Please go to the next window.

3. Do you want anything else?

4. Money orders are accepted here.

5. Give me fifteen five-new-pice stamps.

6. Do you have inland letters as well.

7. How many inland letters do you need?

8. How much does this cost?

9. It costs thirty rupees.

10. He can go to the next store.

11. These are ten-new-pice stamps.

12. Can I buy some shirts in this store?

13. My wife can wait here.

14. Can he come in this room?

15. Do you want these clothes back soon?

16. What is the rent of this single room?

17. Can he go to the bazaar?

18. Its rent is ten rupees a day.

19. Please write down these trousers, shirts, undershirts, etc.

20. Can I buy some clothes from this store.

F. Read the following:

| | | |
|---|---|---|
| सदर | साथ | सभी |
| बहुत | जाना | भी |
| तीन | जी | साहब |
| दूर | दुकान | टिकट |
| रूमाल | ठीक | मिनट |
| तीस | फिर | बीस |
| पर | की | ही |
| कुल | चार | मील |
| तुम | हम | मीठा |
| जाता | मीठी | जाती |

# LESSON VII

## Conversation -- At the Bus Station

### BILL

| | |
|---|---|
| bataanaa | to tell |
| ki | that (conjunction) |
| aagraa | Agra |
| mileegii | will be available |

suniyee, kyaa aap bataa
saktee hãĩ ki aagree kee
liyee bas kahãã mileegii?

Pardon me. Can you tell me
where I will get a bus
for Agra?

### CLERK

jii, yahĩĩ mileegii.  Yes, right here.

### BILL

| | |
|---|---|
| deer | delay, duration |
| jaaeegii | will go |

kitnii deer mẽẽ jaaeegii?  When will it leave?

### CLERK

| | |
|---|---|
| ghaNTaa | hour |
| eek ghaNTee mẽẽ. | In an hour. |
| bajaa | o'clock |
| chuuTeegii | will leave |

Thiik aaTh bajee
chuuTeegii.

It will leave at eight
o'clock sharp.

| | |
|---|---|
| nambar | number |
| pleeTfaarm | platform |
| calee jaanaa | to go away |

aap pããc nambar kee
pleeTfaarm par calee
jaaiyee.

Please go to platform No.5.

72

| | |
|---|---|
| taiyaar | ready |
| wahãã bas taiyaar mileegii. | You'll find the bus ready there. |
| TikaT | ticket |
| kyaa aap kee paas TikaT hai? | Do you have a ticket? |

BILL

| | |
|---|---|
| abhii nahĩĩ, TikaT kahãã miltee hãĩ. | Not yet.  Where do I get the tickets? |

CLERK

| | |
|---|---|
| na | aren't they |
| aagree kee liyee na? | They're for Agra, aren't they? |
| kee saamnee | in front of |
| saamnee čaar nambar kii khiRkii par. | At window No. 4, in front of you. |

BILL

| | |
|---|---|
| kiraayaa | fare |
| aagree kaa kiraayaa kyaa hai? | What's the fare to Agra? |

CLERK

| | |
|---|---|
| kis | which |
| darjaa | class |
| pahlaa | first |
| duusraa | second |
| kis darjee kaa, pahlee yaa duusree? | Which class, first or second? |

BILL

| | |
|---|---|
| pahlee darjee kaa. | First class. |

CLERK

| | |
|---|---|
| zaraa | a little |

73

| | |
|---|---|
| Thahrnaa | to wait, stay |
| zaraa Thahriyee, abhii bataataa hũũ. | Please wait a little. I'll tell you in a moment. |
| lagbhag | approximately, nearly, about |
| lagẽẽgee | will cost |
| lagbhag tiin rupaee lagẽẽgee. | It will cost (you) about three rupees. |

BILL

| | |
|---|---|
| bahut acchaa, dhanyawaad | All right, thank you. |

ADDITIONAL VOCABULARY

| | |
|---|---|
| samai | time |
| waxt | time |

GRAMMAR

1. New Nouns

   Masc. I                          Fem. I

   | aagraa | Agra | deer (no plural) delay, duration |
   |---|---|---|
   | ghaNTaa | hour | |
   | bajaa | o'clock | |
   | darjaa | class | |

   Masc. II

   | nambar | number |
   |---|---|
   | pleeTfaarm | platform |
   | samai (no plural) | time |
   | waxt (no plural) | time |

2. New Verbs

   | bataanaa | to tell |
   |---|---|
   | chuuTnaa | to leave |
   | Thahrnaa | to wait, stay |

74

lagnaa          to cost

3. New Adjectives in -aa

pahlaa          first

duusraa         second

4. Pronominal Adjectives

The Hindi equivalents of the English "my," "your" (familiar), and "our" are respectively meeraa, tumhaaraa, and hamaaraa.

These forms in Hindi have the same inflection as any adjective in -aa (e.g., meeraa, meeree, meerii), and the forms are used the same as adjectives.

meeraa kamraa acchaa hai.      My room is good.

meeree kapRee acchee hãĩ.      My clothes are good.

meerii dukaan mašhuur hai.     My store is a famous
                               one.

meeree kamree mẽẽ sabhii       My room has all the
  suwidhaaẽẽ hãĩ.              conveniences.

These are the only personal pronouns that have a special adjective form.

Adjective forms for other pronouns and also for nouns are formed by using the postposition kaa, "of."

meeraa naam raam naath hai. My name is Ram Nath.

us kaa naam raam naath hai. His name is Ram Nath.

kyaa aap kaa naam raam         Is your name Ram Nath?
  naath hai?

dhoobii kaa naam raam          The washerman's name
  naath hai.                   is Ram Nath.

5. Postpositions

Certain postpositions in Hindi are best considered as compound postpositions and learned in the compound form. So far you have met the following:

kee liyee               for

kee paas                at

| | |
|---|---|
| kee saamnee | in front of |
| kee saath | with |
| kee andar | in, inside |
| aagree kee liyee TikaT kahãã miltee hãĩ? | Where do you get the tickets for Agra? |
| hooTal kee saamnee bas miltii hai. | You can get the bus in front of the hotel. |

Since the forms meeraa, tumhaaraa, and hamaaraa are used where other forms employ the postposition kaa, "of," the oblique forms meeree, tumhaaree, and hamaaree are used along with the postposition but without the kee.

| | |
|---|---|
| raam kaa kamraa | Ram's room |
| us kaa kamraa | his room |
| meeraa kamraa | my room |
| | |
| raam kee saath | with Ram |
| us kee saath | with him |
| meeree saath | with me |

Other examples are:

| | |
|---|---|
| us kee liyee | for him |
| meeree liyee | for me |
| aap kee saamnee | in front of you (polite) |
| dhoobii kee saamnee | in front of the washer-man |
| tumharee sammnee | in front of you (familiar) |
| hamaaree saamnee | in front of us |
| meeree saath | with me |
| meerii patnii kee saath | with my wife |

The compound postposition kee paas is used in constructions where the English equivalent uses the verb "have."

kyaa aap kee paas     Do you have a ticket?
TikaT hai?

The Hindi construction is literally "Is there a
ticket at you?" This construction in Hindi is the
usual one that will equate with the English verb
"have" when referring to objects that are personally
owned or possessed.

meeree paas TikaT hãĩ.     I have the tickets.

kyaa tumhaaree paas phal  Do you have some fruit?
hãĩ?

meerii patnii kee paas    My wife has some good
kuch acchee kapRee hãĩ.   clothes.

Many of the compound postpositions may be used
without either the preceding kee or a preceding noun
or pronoun, and in this case they are likely to equate
with English adverbs. Cf. the above saamnee, saath,
andar and paas are used this way, where saamnee equates
with the English "in front," saath with "along," andar
with "in," "inside," and paas with "near," "nearby."

saamnee čaar nambar kii  At window No. 4, in front
khiRkii par.             (opposite).

andar aaiyee.            Come in.

saath hii kuch santaree  Give (me) some oranges as
bhii dee diijiyee.       well (along with other
                         things).

paas aaiyee.             Come near (or nearer).

## 6. Optative

Hindi has an optative form made from the stem of a
verb with the addition of endings for person and number
as follows:

|          | Sg.       | Pl.      |
|----------|-----------|----------|
| 1st Per. | deekhũũ   | deekhẽẽ  |
| 2nd Per. | --        | deekhoo  |
| 3rd Per. | deekhee   | deekhẽẽ  |

The verbs leenaa, "to take," and deenaa, "to give,"
are irregular in that the person-number endings are
added to the stem l- and d- instead of the regular stem
lee and dee.

77

|         | Sg.   | Pl.   | Sg.   | Pl.   |
|---------|-------|-------|-------|-------|
| 1st Per. | dũũ  | dẽẽ   | lũũ  | dẽẽ   |
| 2nd Per. | -     | doo   | -     | doo   |
| 3rd Per. | dee   | dẽẽ   | lee   | dẽẽ   |

The verb <u>hoonaa</u>, "to be," has irregular forms as follows:

|         | Sg.          | Pl.   |
|---------|--------------|-------|
| 1st Per. | hũũ, hooũũ  | hõõ   |
| 2nd Per. | --           | hoo   |
| 3rd Per. | hoo          | hõõ   |

One of the main uses of the optative is in the formation of the future tense of the verbs.

## 7. Future Tense

The future in Hindi is formed by adding the particle -<u>gaa</u>, -<u>gee</u>, or -<u>gii</u> to the optative form. The particle -<u>gaa</u> agrees with the subject in number and gender in the same way that an imperfect form like <u>deekhtaa</u> agrees with the subject.

|         | Masc. Sg.    | Masc. Pl.    |
|---------|--------------|--------------|
| 1st Per. | deekhũũgaa  | deekhẽẽgee   |
| 2nd Per. | --           | deekhoogee   |
| 3rd Per. | deekheegaa   | deekhẽẽgee   |

|         | Fem. Sg.     | Fem. Pl.     |
|---------|--------------|--------------|
| 1st Per. | deekhũũgii   | deekhẽẽgii   |
| 2nd Per. | --           | dekhoogii    |
| 3rd Per. | deekheegii   | deekhẽẽgii   |

mãĩ saat bajee bazaar jaaũũgaa.  —  I (masc.) will go to the bazaar at seven o'clock.

tum bazaar jaaoogee.  —  You (masc.) will go to the bazaar.

ham phal xariidẽẽgee.  —  We (masc.) will buy (some) fruit.

78

| bas kahãã mileegii? | Where will the bus be available? |
| Thiik aaTh bajee chuuTeegii. | It'll leave at eight o'clock sharp. |

## 8.  Telling Time

To ask time in Hindi, any of the following expressions may be used:

kyaa waxt hai?

waxt kyaa hai?

kyaa samai hai?

samai kyaa hai?          } What time is it?

kyaa bajaa hai?

kitnee bajee hãĩ?

The answer to this question is expressed by using the numerals one to twelve followed by the work bajaa in the nominative case.

| eek bajaa hai. | It's one o'clock. |
| doo bajee hãĩ. | It's two o'clock. |
| gyaaraa bajee hãĩ. | It's eleven o'clock. |

To state "at a certain time," the same expression, with bajaa in the oblique case, is used. The practical result of using the oblique case is that only the expression "one o'clock" is affected.

| eek bajee | at one o'clock |
| tiin bajee | at three o'clock |
| nau bajee | at nine o'clock |
| Thiik aaTh bajee | at eight o'clock sharp |

## 9.  Use of na

The negative particle na may be used at the end of any statement equating with the English "isn't it," "isn't he," "aren't you," "aren't they," etc.

| aagree kee liyee na? | They're for Agra, aren't they? |

79

aap jaatee hãĩ na?          You are going, aren't you?

wee yahĩĩ kaam kartee       They work here, don't they?
hãĩ na?

## 10. Interrogative kaun

The interrogative kaun, like yee and woo, can be
used as an adjective as well as a pronoun. When used
as an adjective, like yee and woo, the nominative form
is used with a noun in the nominative case and the
oblique form with a noun in the oblique case. Compare:

yee kamraa              this room

is kamree mẽẽ           in this room

kaun kamraa             which room

kis kamree mẽẽ          in which room

kis darjee kaa          of which class

As an adjective the form kaun means "which" or
"what."

## 11. Writing System

Other consonant symbols are:

| kha | ख | Dha | ढ |
| ga  | ग | dha | घ |
| gha | घ | ya  | य |
| cha | छ | wa  | व |
| jha | फ | ša  | श |
| Da  | ड |     |   |

The following consonants since they occur only in
borrowings, usually from Sanskrit, do not occur with as
high a frequency as the others you have learned:

Na      ण            ša      ष

In Hindi, the symbol given for ša ष is pronounced
the same as the earlier symbol ša श but is used in
writing certain words borrowed from Sanskrit, none of
which you have met yet.

The symbols for Ra and Rha are the same as the

80

symbols for Da and Dha except that they are written
with a dot underneath them.

      Ra   ड़                 Rha   ढ़

The symbols for fa, za, and xa are as follows:

      fa   फ़

      za   ज़

      xa   ख़

    Notice that these are the symbols for pha, ja, and
kha, respectively, except that they are written with a
dot underneath them. Frequently in Hindi the dot will
be omitted for fa, za, and xa, but not for Ra and Rha.

    The vowel -ee following the consonant is written
with the symbol  ैं  over the consonant symbol, e.g.,

      kee  के            see  से

      wee  वे           dee  दे

    The vowel -ai following the consonant is written
with the symbol  •  over the consonant symbol, e.g.,

      kai  कै            hai  है

      pai  पै            gai  गै

    The vowel -oo following the consonant is written
with the symbol  ो  after the consonant symbol, e.g.,

      koo  को            doo  दो

      loo  लो           khoo  खो

    The vowel -au following the consonant is written
with the symbol  ौ  after the consonant symbol, e.g.,

      dau  दौ            kau  कौ

      jau  जौ           Thau  ठौ

EXERCISES

A. Substitute orally in the sentences below, the Hindi
equivalent of the English given:

1. _____ bas kahãã mileegii?

for Agra                for the Nagpur Hotel

for the Sadar Bazaar    for the Ajmer Hotel

for the hotel           for the famous hotel

for the bazaar          for that hotel

2. bas _____ chuuTeegii.

   in an hour           at seven o'clock

   in about an hour     at eleven o'clock

   in about two hours   at four o'clock

   in about three hours at eight o'clock

   at six o'clock       at twelve o'clock

   at two o'clock       at ten o'clock

   at five o'clock      at three o'clock

   at nine o'clock      at one o'clock

3. kyaa _____ TikaT hai?

   you (polite)         you (familiar)

   she                  they

   John                 he

   Ram                  we

   I

4. woo yee kapRee _____.

   will write           can give

   will take            can take

   will give            can buy

   will buy             can see

   will see             can write

5. ham hooTal mẽẽ _____.

   will stop            will stay

```
will work              can work

can stay               can stop
```

6. _____ naam kyaa hai?

```
his                    the hotel's

your (polite)          the store's

her                    the fruit store's

the washerman's        of that hotel

your (familiar)        of that store
```

B. Substitute orally in the sentences below the Hindi equivalent of the English given, making other changes if necessary:

1. _____ aagree kee liyee eek TikaT xariidũũgaa.

```
I (masc.)                  we (masc.)

you (familiar, fem.)       you (fem., polite)

he                         they (masc.)

we (fem.)                  I (fem.)

you (masc., polite)        you (masc., familiar)

she                        they (masc.)
```

2. kyaa _____ mujhee kapRee dee saktaa hai?

```
he                         they (fem.)

you (fem., familiar)       John

they (masc.)               you (fem., polite)

she                        you (masc., familiar)

you (masc., polite)        the washerman
```

C. Transform the following sentences according to the model given:

kyaa tum dukaan mẽẽ kaam ... kyaa tum dukaan mẽẽ kaam
  kartee hoo?                 karoogee?

   1. kyaa tum bazaar jaatee hoo?

2. kyaa tum dhoobii koo kapRee deetee hoo?

3. kyaa tum dukaan see phal xariidtee hoo?

4. kyaa tum mujhee bataatee hoo?

5. kyaa tum suntee hoo?

6. kyaa tum pleeTfaarm par Thahrtee hoo?

7. kyaa tum yee kapRee jaldii caahtee hoo?

8. kyaa tum hooTal kee kamree deekhtee hoo?

9. kyaa tum kuch deer yahãã ruktee hoo?

10. kyaa tum abhii aatee hoo?

D. Transform the following sentences to sentences with caahiyee construction, according to the model given:

mãi kuch phal caahtaa hũũ ... mujhee kuch phal caahiyee.

1. woo kuch kapRee caahtaa hai.

2. tum kyaa caahtee hoo?

3. mãĩ pããc poosT kaarD caahtii hũũ.

4. kyaa raam pahlee darjee kaa TikaT caahtaa hai?

5. woo kuch santaree caahtii hai.

6. ham eek Dabal kamraa caahtee hãĩ.

7. kyaa aap yee kapRee caahtee hãĩ?

8. wee pandraa rupaee caahtee hãĩ.

9. ham aagree kee doo TikaT caahtii hãĩ.

10. wee kyaa caahtee hãĩ?

E. Transform the following sentences to future tense sentences according to the model given:

woo TikaT xariid saktaa ... woo TikaT xariid sakeegaa. hai.

1. tum kaarD, lifaafee aadi lee saktee hoo.

2. uskii patnii yahãã Thahr saktii hai.

84

3. kyaa aap bazaar jaa saktee hãĩ?

4. mãĩ aap koo antardeešiiy patr dee saktaa hũũ?

5. kyaa woo kapRee likh saktii hai?

6. ham kuch bataa saktii hãĩ.

7. kyaa mãĩ hooTal kaa kaam kar saktii hũũ?

8. tum yee kamraa lee saktii hoo.

9. ham is dukaan mẽẽ kapRaa deekh saktee hãĩ.

10. kyaa wee kuch kah saktee hãĩ?

F. Translate orally

1. The bus will leave at six o'clock sharp.

2. The fare to Agra is three rupees.

3. I want a first-class ticket for Agra.

4. The tickets are available at window No. 4, in front of you.

5. It'll cost (you) about eighteen rupees.

6. Please go to window No. 4, in front of you.

7. I can buy six shirts and five pairs of pants.

8. Please give me seventeen five-new-pice stamps.

9. How many inland letters do you want?

10. Do you have some postcards, envelopes, etc.

11. What is the fare to Nagpur?

12. Can you tell me where I'll get a bus to Ajmer?

13. The bus stops at platform No. 13.

14. This is a second-class ticket.

15. Can she tell me where the bus stop is?

G. Read the following:

| लिफ़ाफ़ा | तरफ़ | देना |
|---|---|---|
| नौ | छूटेगी | कुछ |

| | | |
|---|---|---|
| मुझे | ख़ाली | मेरी |
| फल | ख़रीदो | या |
| कैसा | लो | धोबी |
| डबल | कमीज़ | पैदल |
| के | मेरे | बताता |
| कहेगी | दोगे | दोगी |
| देर | सुनो | दो |
| देखो | होटल | लोगी |
| को | होना | सुविधा |
| है | रहे | लोगे |
| ख़रीदोगे | लिखोगे | किराया |
| से | लेना | जोड़ा |
| केवल | सीधे | मीठे |
| मोज़े | रोज़ | लिफ़ाफ़े |
| नया | बताना | पैसा |
| वाला | कि | बजा |
| मिलेगी | तैयार | न |
| किस | ज़रा | लगेगी |
| लिखेगा | होगी | मोज़ा |
| मेरा | जोड़ा | सकेगा |
| चाहेगी | करो | रुको |
| लिखो | कहेगा | छूटेगा |
| करेगा | लेगी | देगा |
| होगा | सकेगी | कहो |
| चाहेगा | ख़रीदेगा | रुकोगे |
| सकोगे | कहोगे | बजे |
| जोड़े | मेरा | हो |

# LESSON VIII

## Conversation -- Going for a walk

### BILL

| | |
|---|---|
| haalcaal | welfare |

namastee, kahiyee, kyaa haalcaal hai?     Hello, how are you?

### RAM NATH

| | |
|---|---|
| sab | all |
| kaisaa | how |

sab Thiik hai; aap kaisee hãĩ?     I'm fine; how are you?

### BILL

| | |
|---|---|
| acchaa hũũ | I'm fine. |
| jaa rahee hãĩ | (you) are going |

aap kahãã jaa rahee hãĩ?     Where are you going?

### RAM NATH

| | |
|---|---|
| ghuumnaa | to walk |
| calnaa | to go |

ghuumnee jaa rahaa hũũ.     I'm going for a walk.

| | |
|---|---|
| cal rahee hãĩ | are going |

kyaa aap bhii ghuumnee cal rahee hãĩ?     Are you also going for a walk?

### BILL

| | |
|---|---|
| apnaa | my, one's |
| mitr | friend |
| milnaa | to meet, to see (a person) |

jii nahĩĩ, mãĩ is samai apnee eek mitr see     No, right now I'm going to meet a friend of mine.

milnee jaa rahaa hũũ.

| | |
|---|---|
| zaruurii | important |

| | |
|---|---|
| mujhee un see kuch zaruurii kaam hai. | I have some important work with him. |

| | |
|---|---|
| baad, kee baad | after |

| | |
|---|---|
| baahar | out, outside |

| | |
|---|---|
| aur eek ghaNTee baad hii wee baahar calee jaaẽẽgee. | And he is going out in an hour. |

| | |
|---|---|
| kidhar | which direction |

| | |
|---|---|
| aap kidhar jaa rahee hãĩ? | Which direction are you going? |

RAM NATH

| | |
|---|---|
| mãĩ neehruu paark tak jaaũũgaa. | I'm going to Nehru Park. |

| | |
|---|---|
| jaghaa | place |

| | |
|---|---|
| ghuumnee kee liyee woo jaghee acchii hai. | That's a good place for walking. |

| | |
|---|---|
| hameešaa | always |

| | |
|---|---|
| mãĩ hameešaa wahĩĩ jaataa hũũ. | I always go there. |

| | |
|---|---|
| thooRaa | little |

| | |
|---|---|
| saath deenaa | to accompany |

| | |
|---|---|
| tab Thiik hai, mãĩ thooRii duur tak aap kaa saath dũũgaa. | Then it's all right. I'll go a short distance with you. |

| | |
|---|---|
| ghar | house |

| | |
|---|---|
| usii | that (emphatic) |

| | |
|---|---|
| oor | direction |

| | |
|---|---|
| meeree mitr kaa ghar usii oor hai. | My friend's house is in that direction. |

RAM NATH

| | |
|---|---|
| calẽẽ | let's go |

bahut acchaa, caliyee,      O.K., let's go there.
   tab calẽẽ.


GRAMMAR

1.  New Nouns

    Masc. II

    mitr                        friend

    paark                       park

    ghar                        house

    saath (no plural)           company

    haalcaal (no plural)        welfare

The word mitr may agree as either a masculine or
feminine noun, but its inflection is always that of a
type II masculine noun.

    Fem. II

    oor (no plural)             direction

    Irregular

The noun jaghaa, "place," has the following irregular forms:

|        | Sg.                | Pl.     |
|--------|--------------------|---------|
| Nom.   | jaghaa,<br>jaghee  | jaghẽẽ  |
| Obl.   | jaghee             | jaghõõ  |

2.  New Verbs

    rahnaa                      to stay, to live

    ghuumnaa                    to walk

    milnaa                      to meet, to see (a per-
                                   son)

2.1.  New Compound Verbs

    Type II

    saath deenaa                to accompany

3. New Adjectives in -aa

|            |          |
|------------|----------|
| kaisaa     | how      |
| apnaa      | one's    |
| thooRaa    | little   |

4. New Postpositions

|                  |                      |
|------------------|----------------------|
| baad, kee baad   | after                |
| tak              | up to, as far as     |
| kee baahar       | outside              |

The postposition <u>kee baad</u>, "after," when used with expressions of time and distance may occur either as <u>kee baad</u> or as <u>baad</u> but in other expressions only as <u>kee baad</u>.

eek ghaNTee kee baad wee
   baahar calee jaaēēgee.

eek ghaNTee baad wee baahar
   calee jaaēēgee.

He'll go out in an hour.

aap see milnee kee baad mãĩ
   bazaar jaaũũgaa.

I'll go to the market after meeting you.

The form <u>kee baahar</u>, "outside," may be used as a postposition along with a noun or pronoun, and the form <u>baahar</u> by itself may be used as an adverb.

eek ghaNTee baad wee baahar
   calee jaaēēgee.

He will go out in an hour.

hooTal kee baahar hii
   bas-isTaap hai.

The bus-stop is right outside the hotel.

5. Present Progressive

Hindi has a present progressive tense that is made up of three parts. The first part is the stem of the verb and is the form that carries the basic meaning. The second part is the perfect form of the verb <u>rahnaa</u> "to stay," "to live." The perfect has the masculine singular form <u>rahaa</u> and is inflected for number and gender like the imperfect, i.e., <u>rahaa</u>, <u>rahee</u>, <u>rahii</u> and in this use it is simply an auxiliary imparting a progressive meaning to the construction. The third part is the simple present of the verb <u>hoonaa</u>, "to be," with its usual inflection. The Hindi present progres-

90

sive form is usually used where English uses its present progressive "am going," "is going," "are going."

**Masc.**

|         | Sg.           | Pl.            |
|---------|---------------|----------------|
| 1st Per. | jaa rahaa hũũ | jaa rahee hãĩ |
| 2nd Per. | --            | jaa rahee hoo  |
| 3rd Per. | jaa rahaa hai | jaa rahee hãĩ |

**Fem.**

|         | Sg.           | Pl.            |
|---------|---------------|----------------|
| 1st Per. | jaa rahii hũũ | jaa rahii hãĩ |
| 2nd Per. | --            | jaa rahii hoo  |
| 3rd Per. | jaa rahii hai | jaa rahii hãĩ |

aap kahãã jaa rahee hãĩ? Where are you going?

woo phal xariid rahaa hai. — He is buying fruit.

ham is kamree mẽẽ kaam kar rahee hãĩ. — We are working in this room.

mãĩ dhoobii koo kapRee dee rahii hũũ. — I'm giving the clothes to the washerman.

## 6. Infinitive

The infinitive in Hindi is often used as a noun and has a nominative form ending in -aa and an oblique form in -ee, e.g., jaanaa, jaanee.

The oblique form of the infinitive is used with postpositions:

ghuumnee kee liyee woo jaghee acchii hai. — That's a good place for walking.

mãĩ phal leenee kee liyee bazaar jaa rahaa hũũ. — I'm going to the bazaar to buy some fruit.

aap see milnee kee baad woo bazaar jaaeegii. — She'll go to the bazaar after meeting you.

The infinitive in the oblique form with the postposition kee liyee, "for," equates with the English

91

"to," "in order to" and is common with verbs of motion. In such expressions the infinitive may be used in the oblique form omitting the postposition kee liyee.

| | |
|---|---|
| mãĩ ghuumnee kee liyee jaa rahaa hũũ | I'm going for a walk (I'm going to take a walk). |
| mãĩ ghuumnee jaa rahaa hũũ. | |

## 7. The Verb milnaa

The verb milnaa may have the meaning "to see a person," or "to meet a person." In this use the person met will be expressed by using the postposition see.

| | |
|---|---|
| mãĩ is samai apnee eek mitr see milnee jaa rahaa hũũ. | Right now I'm going to meet a friend of mine (to see a friend of mine). |
| mãĩ aaTh bajee raam see milũũgaa. | I'll meet Ram at eight o'clock. |

The verb milnaa also has the meaning "to be available," "to get." In this use the thing that is available is the subject of the verb, i.e., it is in the nominative case and the verb agrees with it. The person who gets something is in the dative case.

| | |
|---|---|
| bas kohãã mileegii? | Where will the bus be available (where can I, or anybody, get a bus). |
| mujhee acchee santaree kohãã milẽẽgee? | Where can I get good oranges? |

## 8. "To have work"

Note the following sentence taken from the basic conversation in this lesson:

| | |
|---|---|
| mujhee un see kuch zaruurii kaam hai. | I have some important work with him. |

The subject of the English sentence is in the dative case in Hindi and the prepositional phrase introduced by "with" in English is expressed by a postpositional phrase using see in Hindi.

## 9. Emphatic Forms with hii

There are two more emphatic forms in this lesson.

92

| Non-emphatic | Emphatic |
|---|---|
| sab | sabhii |
| us | usii |

Some other pronouns have similar emphatic forms.

| Non-emphatic | Emphatic |
|---|---|
| is | isii |
| in | inhĩĩ |
| un | unhĩĩ |
| ham | hamĩĩ, hamhĩĩ |

## 10. Polite Forms

When referring to a single person as third person, it is a more polite usage to refer to the person in the plural than to refer to him or her in the singular.

eek ghaNTee baad wee
baahar calee jaaẽẽgee.
(Polite)

} He will go out in an hour.

eek ghaNTee baad wee
baahar calaa jaaeegaa.

mujhee un see kuch
zaruurii kaam hai.
(Polite)

} I have some urgent work with him.

mujhee us see kuch
zaruurii kaam hai.

meeree saath meerii
patnii bhii hãĩ.
(Polite)

} My wife is also with me.

meeree saath meerii
patnii bhii hai.

## 11. Use of apnaa

The form apnaa is a reflexive adjectival form referring to the person who is the subject of the verb. This means that in the first person and the second person the form apnaa must be used instead of meeraa "my," hamaaraa "our," tumhaaraa "your" (familiar), and aap kaa "your" (polite) if the person referred to is the same person as the subject of the main verb.

93

mãĩ apnee ghar jaaũũgaa.    I'll go to my house.

           but

woo meeree ghar jaaeegaa.    He will go to my house.

In the third person there is a difference in meaning
between apnaa on the one hand and us kaa, un kaa, is kaa
in kaa on the other hand. apnaa refers to the same
person as the subject of the main verb whereas the
others refer to some other person.

woo apnee ghar jaataa          He goes to his house
   hai.                        (to his own house).

woo us kee ghar jaataa         He goes to his house
   hai.                        (somebody else's house).

## 12.  Use of Oblique

With verbs of going, the place to which one goes is
expressed in Hindi by the noun in the oblique case but
without the postposition koo, "to."

mãĩ us kee kamree jaa          I'm going to his room.
   rahaa hũũ.

woo bazaar jaanaa              He wants to go to the
   caahtaa hai.               market.

mãĩ aagree jaanaa caahtaa      I want to go to Agra.
   hũũ.

## 13.  Writing System

## 13.1.  Vowels

The vowel symbols previously discussed may only be
used for a vowel that immediately follows a consonant.
When a vowel occurs initially in a word or immediately
after another vowel, Devanagari uses the following
symbols:

| | | | |
|---|---|---|---|
| a | अ | ee | ए |
| aa | आ | ai | ऐ |
| i | इ | oo | ओ |
| ii | ई | au | औ |
| u | उ | | |
| uu | ऊ | | |

94

Examples:

| | | | |
|---|---|---|---|
| ab | अब | aur | और |
| aap | आप | jaaoo | जाओ |
| is | इस | jaaee | जाए |
| us | उस | kooii | कोई |
| eek | एक | rupaee | रुपए |
| oor | ओर | aaiyee | आइए |

## 13.2. Nasalization

Nasalization of long vowels in Hindi is indicated by using the normal writing for the vowel and a dot placed above the horizontal line for the nasalization as follows:

| | | | |
|---|---|---|---|
| mẽẽ | में | daaĩĩ | दाईं |
| mãĩ | मैं | lũũgaa | लूंगा |
| hũũ | हूं | kamiizõõ | कमीज़ों |
| hãã | हां | jaaũũgaa | जाऊंगा |
| nahĩĩ | नहीं | jaaẽẽgee | जाएंगे |
| kahãã | कहां | pããc | पांच |

In printed Hindi this dot is sometimes replaced by the symbol ँ although this symbol is not usually found on typewriters.

The same dot is used to indicate a nasal consonant after a short vowel and before another consonant. Note that in this case the dot is printed over the preceding consonant or vowel symbol.

| | | | |
|---|---|---|---|
| andar | अंदर | siŋgil | सिंगिल |
| pasand | पसंद | ghaNTaa | घंटा |

## 13.3. Consonant Clusters

When one consonant immediately follows another consonant in Hindi, the first one will be written with the normal consonant symbol even though there is no following -a in the spoken form. It is only in this position and in final position that the consonant does not imply a following vowel -a.

95

| | | | |
|---|---|---|---|
| ruktaa | रुकता | kapRaa | कपड़ा |
| kartaa | करता | karnaa | करना |
| itnaa | इतना | kitnaa | कितना |
| kamraa | कमरा | apnee | अपने |

Not all consonant combinations are written this way but other writings will be discussed later.

## EXERCISES

A. Substitute orally in the sentences below the Hindi equivalent of the English given:

1. _____ mitr kaa ghar usii oor hai.

| my | John's |
|---|---|
| his | their |
| our | her |
| your (familiar) | your (polite) |

2. mãĩ _____ jaa rahaa hũũ.

| to take a walk | to see the hotel |
|---|---|
| to see his friend | to buy some clothes |
| to buy some fruit | |

3. woo _____ milnaa caahtaa hai.

| my friend | John's friends |
|---|---|
| her friend | your friends (polite) |
| our friend | their friends |
| my friends | John's friend |
| your friends (familiar) | his own friends |
| her friends | their friend |
| our friends | his own friend |

4. yee jaghee _____ bahut acchii hai.

| to take a walk | to work |
|---|---|

to wait                to write a letter

to stop                to meet him

to buy clothes         to live

5. _____ wee baahar calee jaaẽẽgee.

   in an hour           after meeting me

   in two hours         after taking a walk in
                          the park
   after some time
                        after buying fruit

6. mãĩ _____ jaa rahaa kũũ.

   to Nehru Park        to the bus stop

   to the market        very far

   to the store         Agra

7. mujhee _____ kuch zaruurii kaam hai.

   with him             with his friend

   with you (familiar)  with your friends (familiar)

   with John            with their friends

   with them            with John's friends

   with you (polite)    with him and his wife

   with Ram             with the dhobi

B. Substitute orally in the sentences below the Hindi
equivalent of the English given, making other changes,
if necessary:

1. _____ paark mẽẽ ghuum rahaa hai.

   John                 we (masc.)

   she                  I (fem.)

   I (masc.)            you (masc., familiar)

   we (fem.)            they (fem.)

   they (masc.)         you (masc., polite)

   you (fem., familiar) he

2. _____ yahãã kitnii deer Thahreegii.

the bus                    your friend

you (masc., familiar)      his wife

they (fem.)                the washerman

you (masc., polite)        his friend

she                        your wife

they (masc.)               John

C. Transform the following sentences according to the model given:

woo kaam kartaa hai     ..... woo kaam kar rahaa hai.

1. woo paark mẽẽ ghuumtaa hai.

2. woo apnee kamree kaa kiraayaa deetaa hai.

3. woo bazaar mẽẽ kuch kapRee xariidtaa hai.

4. woo apnee mitr see miltaa hai.

5. woo kapRee likhtaa hai.

6. woo apnee kamree mẽẽ Thahrtaa hai.

7. woo mujhee kamree kaa kiraayaa bataataa hai.

8. woo kuch lifaafee aur poosT kaarD leetaa hai.

9. woo apnee mitr see milnee jaataa hai.

10. woo kyaa kahtaa hai?

D. Transform the following sentences according to the model given:

mãĩ bazaar jaataa hũũ ..... mãĩ bazaar jaaũũgaa.

1. mãĩ apnee mitr see miltaa hũũ.

2. mãĩ satraa antardeešiiy patr leetaa hũũ.

3. mãĩ kamree kaa kiraayaa deetaa hũũ.

4. mãĩ neehruu paark deekhtaa hũũ.

5. mãĩ apnee kamree mẽẽ ruktaa hũũ.

98

6. mãĩ kuch hawaaii patr xariidtaa hũũ.

7. mãĩ yahãã see baaĩĩ taraf jaataa hũũ.

8. mãĩ apnee ghar aataa hũũ.

9. mãĩ yee kaam kar saktaa hũũ.

10. mãĩ apnii patnii see kuch kahtaa hũũ.

E. Transform the following sentences from the <u>caahnaa</u> to the <u>saknaa</u> construction according to the model given:

woo likhnaa caahtaa hai  ..... woo likh saktaa hai.

1. mãĩ ghuumnee jaanaa caahtaa hũũ.

2. us kii patnii usee kuch rupaee deenaa caahtii hai.

3. raam apnee mitr see milnaa caahtaa hai.

4. aap mujhee kyaa bataanaa caahtee hãĩ?

5. tum kuch zaruurii kaam karnaa caahtii hoo.

6. wee yee mašhuur paark deekhnaa caahtee hãĩ.

7. meeraa mitr kuch patr aur lifaafee xariidnaa caahtaa hai.

8. ham is ghar mẽẽ rahnaa caahtee hãĩ.

9. kyaa tum yee kapRee likhnaa caahtee hoo?

10. mãĩ yee siŋgil kamraa leenaa caahtii hũũ.

11. kyaa us kii patnii yahãã Thahrnaa caahtii hai.

12. kyaa woo meeree ghar aanaa caahtaa hai?

13. wee aagree kaa TikaT leenaa caahtee hãĩ?

14. ham paark mẽẽ ghuumnaa caahtee hãĩ?

15. kyaa tumhaarii mitr yahãã ruknaa caahtii hai?

16. kyaa aap kuch sunnaa caahtee hãĩ?

17. dhoobii kapRee leenaa caahtaa hai.

18. ham pããc bajee aap see milnaa caahtee hãĩ.

19. mãĩ yahãã see pããc miil duur jaanaa caahtaa hũũ.

99

20. kyaa aap dhoobii koo kapRee deenaa caahtee h̃ãĩ?

F.   Translate orally

1. He has some important work with my friend.

2. Your friend will go to the hotel at five o'clock.

3. His wife likes to take a walk in this park.

4. I'll go with you a short distance.

5. Our hotel is in that direction.

6. I want to meet my friend in my house.

7. Let's go to the bazaar.

8. He'll go out after an hour.

9. Will you be there at nine o'clock?

10. I'll give you some envelopes, air letters and stamps.

G.   Read the following:

1.  वहीं एक होटल है ।

2.  फल की दुकान कहां है ?

3.  मैं घूमने जाना चाहता हूं ।

4.  अजमेरी होटल यहां से बहुत दूर नहीं है ।

5.  इनका दाम पांच रुपए है ।

6.  हम मीठे संतरे ख़रीदना चाहते हैं ।

7.  एक मिनट रुको ।

8.  अभी तुम को सात कमीजें, पांच बनियाइनें आदि देता हूं ।

9.  राम ही इस होटल का धोबी है ।

10.  बस यहीं मिलती है ।

11.  उसके पास कोई कमरा ख़ाली नहीं है ।

12.  राम कैसा कमरा चाहता है ?

13.  इन कमरों में सभी सुविधारं हैं ।

14.  इस कमरे का किराया केवल दस रुपए रोज़ है ।

15. मैं कुछ लिफ़ाफ़े ले रहा हूं ।

16. ये दस नए पैसे वाले टिकट हैं ।

17. राम नाथ थोड़ी देर बाद बाहर जाना चाहता है ।

18. आपको वहां बस तैयार मिलेगी ।

19. मैं राम के घर जा रही हूं ।

20. ये रहे आपके टिकट और लिफ़ाफ़े ।

## REVIEW II

A. Substitute orally in the sentences below the Hindi equivalent of the English given:

1. _____ kaa ghar usii oor hai.

| | |
|---|---|
| my friend | this washerman |
| his friends | Ram's wife |
| your (familiar) friends | their friends |
| their friend | his friend |
| the washerman | our friend's wife |
| your (polite) wife | John's wife |

2. kyaa _____ kuch rupaee hãĩ?

| | |
|---|---|
| he | your wife |
| the washerman | she |
| you (polite) | her friends |
| his friend | Ram's wife |
| you (familiar) | their wives |
| they | our friends |
| John | your friend |
| the washerman | this washerman |

3. gaaRii _____ chuuTeegii.

| | |
|---|---|
| at what time | at eleven o'clock |

| | |
|---|---|
| at ten o'clock | at three o'clock |
| at five o'clock | at nine o'clock |
| at twelve o'clock | at four o'clock |
| at seven o'clock | at eight o'clock |
| at two o'clock | at one o'clock |

4. meeree mitr _____ taiyaar hãĩ.

| | |
|---|---|
| to take a walk | to buy some clothes |
| to go to the bazaar | to see the houses |
| to stay in this hotel | to work in the fruitstore |
| to meet Ram | to tell me something |
| to write a letter | to live in this house |

5. _____ wee is hooTal mẽẽ aaẽẽgee.

| | |
|---|---|
| in an hour | in ten hours |
| in three hours | in two hours |
| in some time | in seven hours |
| in five hours | in four hours |

6. _____ daam kitnaa huaa?

| | |
|---|---|
| of these postcards | of a ticket to Agra |
| of one dozen inland letters | of these undershirts |
| of these shirts | of one dozen handker- chiefs |

7. tab _____ khiRkii par calee jaaiyee.

| | |
|---|---|
| next | to the left |
| first | to the right |
| second | |

8. _____ kuch rupaee dee diijiyee.

| | |
|---|---|
| me | my friend |
| him | my wife |

| us | her friend (masc.) |
| her | her friend (fem.) |
| them | John's washerman |
| the washerman | Ram's wife |
| John | our friend |
| his wife | our friends |

B. Substitute orally in the sentences below the Hindi equivalent of the English given, making other changes, if necessary:

1. yee _____ bahut acchii hai.

| store | socks |
| stores | shirts |
| handkerchief | house |
| trousers | handkerchiefs |
| shirt | houses |
| rooms | clothes |
| hotel | cloth |

2. _____ raam kii dukaan see kuch phal lee rahaa hai.

| he | I (masc.) |
| I (fem.) | you (fem., polite) |
| you (masc., polite) | they (fem.) |
| we (fem.) | my friend |
| they (masc.) | Ram's wife |
| you (fem., familiar) | my friend's wife |
| we (masc.) | |

C. Transform the following sentences from the saknaa construction to future tense sentences according to the model given:

xariidə̃ə̃gee.
ham kuch phal xariid saktee hai ... ham kuch phal

1. raam meeree ghar m\~e\~e kaam kar saktaa hai.

2. kyaa woo phal xariidnee jaa saktii hai?

3. aap unh\~e\~e eek patr likh saktee h\~a\~i?

4. kyaa ham is ghar m\~e\~e aa saktee h\~a\~i?

5. jaan apnii patnii see kuch rupaee lee saktaa hai.

6. kyaa woo neehruu paark tak ghuumnee jaa saktii
   hai?

7. woo phal xariidnee kee liyee bazaar jaa saktii
   hai.

8. ham eek bajee tak bas-isTaap m\~e\~e Thahr saktee
   h\~a\~i.

9. kyaa aap saat nambar kee pleeTfaarm par ruk
   saktee h\~a\~i?

10. aap nau nambar kii khiRkii par aagree kee liyee
    TikaT xariid saktee h\~a\~i.

11. meeraa mitr aap koo is kamree kaa kiraayaa bataa
    saktaa hai.

12. kyaa tum paark tak meeraa saath dee saktee hoo?

13. ham sun saktee h\~a\~i.

14. dhoobii aap kee liyee kyaa kar saktaa hai?

15. kyaa woo yee si\jgil kamraa deekh saktii hai?

16. m\~a\~i is hooTal m\~e\~e rah saktaa h\~u\~u.

D.   Transform the following present progressive tense
sentences to present imperfect tense sentences according to the model given:

raam paark m\~e\~e ghuum rahaa ... raam paark m\~e\~e ghuumtaa
   hai.                              hai.

1. uskii patnii phal xariid rahii hai.

2. m\~a\~i aagree kee liyee eek TikaT lee rahaa h\~u\~u.

3. kyaa woo patr likh rahaa hai?

4. uskaa mitr kah\~a\~a jaa rahaa hai?

5. jaan mujhee kaarD, lifaafee aadi dee rahaa hai.

104

6. wee hooTal mẽẽ kaam kar rahee hãĩ.

7. kyaa aap usee naagpur kaa kiraayaa bataa rahee
   hãĩ.

8. woo kyaa kah rahii hai?

9. kyaa jaan kii patnii bazaar jaa rahii hai.

10. mãĩ apnee mitr koo patr likh rahaa hũũ.

E. Transform the following sentences to present progressive tense sentences according to the model given:

woo baahar jaataa hai ..... woo baahar jaa rahaa hai.

1. raam andar aataa hai.

2. ham paark mẽẽ ghuumtee hãĩ.

3. woo aap hii kaa kaam kartii hai.

4. mãĩ yee Dabal kamraa leetaa hũũ.

5. tum dhoobii koo kuch rupaee deetee hoo.

6. kyaa aap pããc rupaee rooz kaa kamraa leetee hãĩ?

7. aap is dukaan see kyaa xariidtii hãĩ?

8. jaan kaa mitr aap koo kyaa bataataa hai?

9. us kii patnii kyaa kahtii hai?

10. wee mitrõõ koo patr likhtee hãĩ.

11. bas pããc nambar kee pleeTfaarm see chuuTtii hai.

12. ham neehruu paark jaatee hãĩ.

13. mãĩ hooTal mẽẽ kaam kartaa hũũ.

14. raam kii patnii mujhee kuch phal deetii hai.

15. kyaa tum paark mẽẽ ghuumtii hoo?

16. us kaa mitr kahãã rahtaa hai?

G. Translate orally:

1. I want to take a walk in Nehru Park.

2. Do you want to take a walk in Nehru Park?

3. My friend always takes a walk in Nehru Park.

4. Can he take a walk in Nehru Park?

5. She will always take a walk in this park.

6. John is taking a walk in this park.

7. They can take a walk in this park.

8. The hotel is not very far from here.

9. The hotel is very far from his house.

10. The hotel is about two miles from the bazaar.

11. He wants to buy a ticket.

12. I want to buy a ticket to Agra.

13. She wants to buy a first class ticket to Agra.

14. I'll buy a first class ticket to Agra.

15. Can he buy a first class ticket to Agra?

16. Is John buying a second class ticket to Agra?

17. He is going outside.

18. He is going outside in an hour.

19. She wants to go outside.

20. Does she want to go outside?

H.  Conversation

1.  A enters a post office and asks the clerk at the
    window to give him some air letters, postcards etc.
    The clerk directs him to another window.  A goes
    there and asks for some postcards, envelopes, air
    letters, inland letters and stamps.  The clerk
    gives them to A.  A asks how much he has to pay.
    The clerk calculates and says that the cost is
    seventeen rupees.  A pays the clerk and leaves
    the post office.

2.  A enters a hotel.  The manager seeing A coming
    says "hello," and asks him if he can do anything
    for him.  A asks him if he has a room vacant in
    his hotel.  The manager inquires about the kind of
    room A needs.  A tells him that he needs a single

room. The manager takes him and shows him a room.
He tells him that the room is a very good one and
has all the conveniences. A asks the price of the
room. The manager tells him that it is eight
rupees a day. A likes the room and takes it.

3. A meets his friend B on the street. After an exchange of formal greetings, A asks B as to where
he is going. B tells A that he is going for a
walk and asks where A is going. A tells B that he
is also going for a walk. B asks A to join him.
A tells him that he wants to go to Nehru Park,
which is a very good place for taking a walk, and
asks B if he would like to go there. B agrees to
go to Nehru Park and both of them walk off together.

4. A enters a bus station and approaches the clerk at
the information window. He asks the clerk about
the time and the place of the departure of the bus
to Agra. The clerk gives him the proper details.
A further asks him if he can give him a ticket to
Agra. The clerk tells him to go to another counter
where A buys a second class ticket to Agra and pays
the fare.

5. A is waiting for a city bus at the bus stop. A bus
comes along and A asks the conductor of the bus if
it'll take him to the main bazaar. The conductor
replies in the affirmative and A boards the bus.
A asks the fare and is told that it's ten new pice.
A pays the fare and asks the conductor to tell him
where to get off. When the bus reaches the bazaar,
the conductor tells him to get off. A thanks the
conductor and leaves the bus.

I. Read the following:

1. वे एक घंटे बाद बाहर चले जाएंगे ।

2. मैं इसी दुकान से रुमाल खरीदूंगा ।

3. आगरे के लिए बस आठ बजे छूटेगी ।

4. मुझे पांच नए पैसे वाले तीस टिकट दे दो ।

5. राम एक सिंगिल कमरा लेना चाहता है ।

6. सामने सात नंबर की खिड़की पर आगरे के टिकट मिलते हैं ।

7. मैं थोड़ी दूर तक आपका साथ दूंगा ।

8. आप कैसा कमरा चाहते हैं - सिंगिल या डबल ?

9. आपका हालचाल कैसा है ?

10. मैं भी आपके साथ घूमने चलूंगा ।

11. मुझे उनसे कुछ ज़रूरी काम है ।

12. हमें कुछ मीठे संतरे कहां मिल सकते हैं ?

13. इन कमरों में सभी सुविधाएं नहीं हैं ।

14. मैं ही इस होटल में काम करता हूं ।

15. राम नाथ कुछ कपड़े लेना चाहता है ।

16. मैं इस दुकान में कुछ कपड़ा खरीदूंगा ।

17. आप किधर जा रहे हैं ?

18. मुझे भी उसी ओर काम है ।

19. बस कितनी देर में छूटेगी ?

20. जान धोबी को दस रुपए दे सकता है ।

# LESSON IX

## Conversation -- Going to the Station

### JOHN

| | |
|---|---|
| namastee | Hello! |
| kahiyee, kahãã jaa rahee hãĩ? | Where are you going? |

### RAM PAL

| | |
|---|---|
| isTeešan | station |
| baRaa | big |
| bhaaii | brother |
| isTeešan. | To the station. |
| meeree baRee bhaaii aa rahee hãĩ. | My elder brother is coming. |
| unhẽẽ leenee isTeešan jaa rahaa hũũ. | I'm going to the station to get him. |

### JOHN

| | |
|---|---|
| wee kahãã see aa rahee hãĩ? | Where is he coming from? |

### RAM PAL

| | |
|---|---|
| kaanpuur | Kanpur |
| wyaapaar | business |
| kaanpuur see. | From Kanpur. |
| wahãã wee wyaapaar kartee hãĩ. | He has a business there. |

### JOHN

| | |
|---|---|
| aisaa | such, so |
| aisaa, wee kyaa wyaapaar kartee hãĩ? | Is that so?  What's his business? |

109

### RAM PAL

| | |
|---|---|
| kaanpuur m̃ẽẽ un kii kapRee kii dukaan hai. | He has a clothing store in Kanpur. |
| suutii | cotton, of cotton |
| uunii | woolen |
| reešmii | silk, of silk |
| tarah | kind |
| wee suutii, uunii reešmii --sabhii tarah kee kapRee kaa kaam kartee h̃ãĩ. | He deals in all kinds of cloth--cotton, woolen, silk etc. |

### JOHN

| | |
|---|---|
| akeelaa | alone |
| kyaa wee akeelee hii aa rahee h̃ãĩ? | Is he coming alone? |

### RAM PAL

| | |
|---|---|
| pariwaar | family |
| baccaa | child |
| naukar | servant |
| jii nahĩĩ, un kee saath un kaa pariwaar bhii hai--un kii patnii, un kee doo baccee aur un kaa naukar. | No, his family is with him --his wife, his two children and his servant. |

### JOHN

| | |
|---|---|
| acchaa, tab too aap koo jaldii jaanaa caahiyee. | O.K., then you should go right away. |
| gaaRii | train |
| hoonaa | to be, become |
| gaaRii kaa waxt hoo rahaa hai. | It's getting to be train time. |

### RAM PAL

| | |
|---|---|
| aagyaa | permission |

jii hãã, ab mujhee aagyaa   Yes, I must go now.
  diijiyee.

    namastee                   good-bye

## ADDITIONAL VOCABULARY

| | |
|---|---|
| chooTaa | little |
| bahin | sister |
| pati | husband |
| ammãã, mãã, maataa | mother |
| pitaa, baap | father |
| mããbaap, maataapitaa | parents |
| aadmii | man |
| aurat | woman |
| laRkaa | boy, son |
| laRkii | girl, daughter |

## GRAMMAR

1. <u>New Nouns</u>

| <u>Masc. I</u> | | <u>Fem. I</u> | |
|---|---|---|---|
| baccaa | child | gaaRii | train |
| laRkaa | boy, son | laRkii | girl, daughter |

| <u>Masc. II</u> | | <u>Fem. II</u> | |
|---|---|---|---|
| isTeešan | station | tarah | kind |
| bhaaii | brother | bahin | sister |
| kaanpuur (no pl.) | Kanpur | aagyaa | permission |
| | | maataa | mother |
| wyaapaar | business | | |
| | | mãã | mother |
| pariwaar | family | | |
| | | ammãã | mother |
| naukar | servant | | |
| | | aurat | woman |
| pitaa | father | | |

| | |
|---|---|
| baap | father |
| pati | husband |
| mãã-baap | parents |
| maataa-pitaa | parents |
| aadmii | man |

2. New Adjectives in -aa

| | | | |
|---|---|---|---|
| baRaa | big | aisaa | such, so |
| chooTaa | little | akeelaa | alone |

3. Vocabulary Notes

3.1. Brother and Sister

When referring to a brother or a sister, it is customary to specify whether it's an elder or a younger brother, an elder or younger sister.

| | |
|---|---|
| baRaa bhaaii | elder brother |
| chooTaa bhaaii | younger brother |
| baRii bahin | elder sister |
| chooTii bahin | younger sister |

When addressing or referring to an older brother or older sister, the polite form of agreement (i.e., agreement of adjective and verb in the plural form) is always used.

When addressing a younger brother or sister, the familiar form of agreement rather than the polite form will be used.

When referring to a younger brother or sister among reasonably close friends, the familiar form of agreement will be used whereas under other conditions the polite form of agreement may be used.

3.2. Mother and Father

The most common word for mother is mãã or ammãã. The alternative form maataa is used under formal conditions and on ceremonial occasions.

The form baap, "father," is generally considered

112

impolite and should be avoided in favor of pitaa, "father."

The compound form mãã-baap, "parents," is a customary familiar form whereas maataa-pitaa, "parents," is used on formal and ceremonial occasions. The agreement for mãã-baap, maataa-pitaa "parents," mãã "mother" and pitaa "father" is always plural.

## 3.3. Husband and Wife

The term pati, "husband," will always use plural agreement whereas patnii, "wife," may use singular agreement on informal occasions.

## 3.4. Family

The term pariwaar, "family," may sometimes, as in the conversation in this lesson, include the family servant or the domestic servant.

## 3.5. Greeting

The term namastee is a polite salutation either on meeting or leaving a person usually accompanied by a gesture involving the putting of the palms of the hands together and raising them slightly. The gesture may be domonstrated by the instructor in the class.

## 3.6. Leave-taking

The expression mujhee aagyaa diijiyee, literally "Please give me permission" is a formal expression of leave-taking and may be equated with the English "I must go now," "I have to leave" or some such similar expression.

## 3.7. jii

The word jii that you have met in expressions jii hãã and jii nahĩĩ is a particle of respect. These expressions may occur without jii in which case they are simply not as respectful as when used with jii.

When the words maataa, "mother," ammãã, "mother," and pitaa, "father," are used, it is customary in most situations to add this respectful particle, thus maataa jii, ammãã jii, pitaa jii. With the words bhaaii, bahin, mãã, baap, pati, patnii, and maataapitaa this particle jii is not normally used or, when used, has a special meaning.

113

## 4. The Verb "to have"

As noted earlier, the Hindi equivalent of the verb "to have" with possessable objects is a construction with <u>kee paas</u> and the verb <u>hoonaa</u>. When referring to persons the construction is a different one. The Hindi equivalent of "I have two brothers" is literally "my two brothers are."

| | |
|---|---|
| meeree doo bhaaii hãĩ. | I have two brothers. |
| meeree eek chooTii bahin hai. | I have a younger sister. |

With larger objects such as cars, houses, stores, farms etc. either construction may be used.

| | |
|---|---|
| un kii kapRee kii dukaan hai. | He has a clothing store. |
| un kee paas kapRee kii dukaan hai. | |

Note the effect of word order on the following constructions:

| | |
|---|---|
| aagree mẽẽ meeree doo bhaaii hãĩ. | I have two brothers in Agra. |
| meeree doo bhaaii aagree mẽẽ hãĩ. | My two brothers are in Agra. |
| kaanpuur mẽẽ un kii dukaan hai. | He has a store in Kanpur. |
| un kii dukaan kaanpuur mẽẽ hai. | His store is in Kanpur. |

## 5. caahiyee

As learnt in Lesson IV, 3., the form <u>caahiyee</u> may equate with English "to need, to want, need."

| | |
|---|---|
| mujhee phal caahiyee. | I need (want) fruit. |

The form <u>caahiyee</u> may also be used with a dependent infinitive, in which case it equates with English "should," "ought to." As in the preceding type of construction, the subject is in the dative case.

| | |
|---|---|
| mujhee bazaar jaanaa caahiyee. | I should (ought to) go to the bazaar. |

## 6. Writing System

The Hindi alphabet in its alphabetical order (reading from left to right) is as follows. The alphabet includes some symbols that have not been discussed yet.

| अ | आ | इ | ई | उ | ऊ |
|---|---|---|---|---|---|
| a | aa | i | ii | u | uu |

| | ए | ऐ | ओ | औ | |
|---|---|---|---|---|---|
| | ee | ai | oo | au | |

| | अं | अः | | | |
|---|---|---|---|---|---|
| | an | ah | | | |

| | क | ख | ग | घ | ङ· |
|---|---|---|---|---|---|
| | ka | kha | ga | gha | ṇa |

| | च | छ | ज | झ | ञ |
|---|---|---|---|---|---|
| | ca | cha | ja | jha | (na) |

| | ट | ठ | ड | ढ | ण |
|---|---|---|---|---|---|
| | Ta | Tha | Da | Dha | Na |

| | त | थ | द | ध | न |
|---|---|---|---|---|---|
| | ta | tha | da | dha | na |

| | प | फ | ब | भ | म |
|---|---|---|---|---|---|
| | pa | pha | ba | bha | ma |

| | य | र | ल | व | |
|---|---|---|---|---|---|
| | ya | ra | la | wa | |

| | श | ष | स | ह | |
|---|---|---|---|---|---|
| | ša | ša | sa | ha | |

## 6.1.  The Consonant r

The consonant r besides being written र appears in two other forms. When the consonant r occurs immediately after another consonant, it is sometimes written with the symbol ⟋ attached to the lower part of the vertical stroke, where possible, e.g.,

| | | | |
|---|---|---|---|
| pra | प्र | dra | द्र |
| gra | ग्र | dhra | ध्र |

The combinations <u>tra</u> and <u>Tra</u> are written in an irregular manner.

| | | | |
|---|---|---|---|
| tra | त्र | mitr | मित्र |
| Tra | ट्र | | |

When the consonant <u>r</u> occurs immediately before another consonant, it is sometimes written with the symbol ˆ attached above the consonant that follows:

| | | | |
|---|---|---|---|
| rka | र्क | paark | पार्क |
| rja | र्ज | darjan | दर्जन |
| rDa | र्ड | kaarD | कार्ड |
| rdha | र्ध | | |
| rma | र्म | | |

Note that this does not apply to all items where <u>r</u> immediately precedes or follows another consonant, e.g.,

| | | | |
|---|---|---|---|
| kamraa | कमरा | karnaa | करना |
| kartaa | करता | | |

## 6.2. Consonant Combinations

Sometimes when one consonant occurs immediately followed by another instead of each consonant being written separately they are written by a combination of the two symbols. Usually, the two symbols are joined to each other side by side, but in the case of some combinations the second consonant is added below the first consonant. If the first consonant of the combination is normally written with a vertical stroke, the vertical stroke is dropped when it is joined to the second consonant. At first these combinations may appear strange, but in most cases the particular combinations are reasonably obvious. Those that occur in the first three lessons (all of which join in the horizontal direction) are:

| | | | |
|---|---|---|---|
| kya | क्य | kyaa | क्या |
| ccha | च्छ | acchaa | अच्छा |

116

| nya | न्य | dhanyawaad | धन्यवाद |
| sTa | स्ट | bas-isTaap | बसस्टाप |
| mha | म्ह | tumhaaree | तुम्हारे |

## 5.3. Initial s Plus Consonant

Words which begin with consonant s plus another consonant in their written form are pronounced in Hindi with an i vowel in front of the s. These words are always borrowings from Sanskrit, English or other languages.

| stop | isTaap | स्टाप |
| station | isTeešan | स्टेशन |

## 6.4. Nasal Consonant Plus a Consonant

When a nasal consonant follows a short vowel and immediately precedes another consonant in many cases it may be written with a consonant combination made up of the nasal consonant symbol plus the following consonant symbol instead of being written with the super-imposed dot, as follows:

| santaraa | संतरा | or | सन्तरा |
| nambar | नंबर | or | नम्बर |
| pasand | पसंद | or | पसन्द |
| andar | अंदर | or | अन्दर |
| ghaNTaa | घंटा | or | घण्टा |

Some combinations of nasal consonant followed by another consonant are always written in the consonant combination.

| mha | म्ह | tumhaaree | तुम्हारे |
| ny | न्य | dhanyawaad | धन्यवाद |

## 6.5. The Combination -iyee

The combination -iyee is sometimes written with the consonant symbol य and sometimes without it. Thus

| liyee | लिए | or | लिये |
| diijiyee | दीजिए | or | दीजिये |

117

jaaiyee    जाइए    or    जाइये

## 6.6. The Demonstratives yee, woo

The nominative forms of the demonstratives yee, "this," and woo, "that," are not written in a manner consistent with their pronunciation.

|          | This       | That       |
|----------|------------|------------|
| Nom. Sg. | yee  यह    | woo  वह    |
| Nom. Pl. | yee  ये    | wee  वे    |

When reading Hindi, many people use the reading pronunciation yah, wah for the nominative singular forms.

## 6.7. Irregular Spellings

The word bazaar in Hindi is sometimes pronounced bazaar and sometimes baazaar but is always written as if it were baazaar.

बाजार        bazaar, baazaar

## 6.8. Hindi Numerals

The Hindi numerals are:

| 1 | १ | 6  | ६  |
|---|---|----|----|
| 2 | २ | 7  | ७  |
| 3 | ३ | 8  | ८  |
| 4 | ४ | 9  | ९  |
| 5 | ५ | 10 | १० |

The system is the same decimal system that is used in English, e.g.:

| 11 | ११ | 18 | १८ |
|----|----|----|----|
| 15 | १५ | 20 | २० |

### EXERCISES

A. Substitute orally in the sentences below the Hindi equivalent of the English given:

1. wee _____ wyaapaar kartee hãĩ.

118

of all kinds of cloth

of cotton cloth

of silk cloth

of woolen cloth

of cotton and woolen cloth

2. un kee saath _____ bhii hai.

| his family | his servant |
|---|---|
| his wife | his brother's family |
| his younger brother | his sister's family |
| his younger sister | his friend |
| his son | his daughter |

3. _____ kaa waxt hoo rahaa hai.

| the train | the train for Nagpur |
|---|---|
| the bus | the bus for Ajmer |
| the bus for Agra | the train for Agra |

4. tab too _____ jaldii jaanaa caahiyee.

| the servant | his father |
|---|---|
| my brother | her mother |
| his sister | this man |
| his younger sister | these men |
| their younger sister | this woman |
| her elder sister | these women |
| his elder brother | that man |
| your younger brother | those men |
| our families | that woman |
| our servants | those women |
| my friends | his parents |

| | |
|---|---|
| his sons | my daughter |
| your daughters | her son |

5. _____ kaa ghar kis oor hai?

| | |
|---|---|
| Ram | John's friend |
| his brother | this girl |
| your sister | that boy |
| his brother | this man |
| his younger si.ster | those women |
| his elder brother | those men |
| his father | that man |
| her mother | his son |
| his parents | her daughter |
| her husband | his daughters |
| his wife | his sons |
| Bill's father | his brother's friends |
| Ram's servant | your friend's servants |

6. mãĩ _____ jaanaa caahtaa hũũ.

| | |
|---|---|
| my house | my sister's house |
| his hotel | his brother's hotel |
| my friend's house | his father's store |
| his parents' house | my brother's house |
| their hotel | my elder brother's house |
| my store | his younger sister's hotel |
| your room | this boy's house |
| my brother's hotel | that girl's house |

B. Substitute orally in the sentences below the Hindi

120

equivalent of the English given, making other changes,
if necessary:

1. _____ aa rahee hãĩ.

| | |
|---|---|
| my parents | my elder brother |
| my son | my friend |
| his sons | my friend's parents |
| my wife | his friend's sons |
| my father | her friend's daughters |
| my mother | my friend's younger brother |
| our parents | my friend's wife |
| my younger brother | my servant |
| his elder sister | my servants |
| my daughters | my servant's family |
| my younger sister | my children |
| her husband | his children |
| her husband's friend | my brother's children |

2. kaanpuur mẽẽ un kii _____ hai.

| | |
|---|---|
| a store | some fruit stores |
| a clothing store | many stores |
| some clothing stores | many clothing stores |
| a fruit store | |

C. Transform the following present progressive tense
sentences to future tense sentences according to the
model given:

woo kyaa kar rahii hai? ..... woo kyaa kareegii?

   1. us kaa mitr kahãã jaa rahaa hai?

   2. ham usee is kamree kaa kiraayaa bataa rahee hãĩ.

   3. tum kahãã ruk rahee hoo?

   4. us kii patnii kyaa kah rahii hai?

121

5. jaan patr likh rahaa hai.

6. wee paark m̃ẽ̃ ghuum rahee h̃ãĩ.

7. m̃ãĩ yee siŋgil kamraa deekh rahii h̃ũũ.

8. raam kapRee dee rahaa hai.

9. meerii bahin p̃ãã̃c bajee kii gaaRii see aa rahii
   hai.

10. naukar ghar kaa kaam kar rahaa hai.

11. raam kee maataa-pitaa kah̃ãã rah rahee h̃ãĩ?

12. aap kah̃ãã see aa rahee h̃ãĩ?

D.  Transform the following sentences according to the
model given:

usee bazaar jaanaa caahiyee ... woo bazaar jaanaa
                                        caahtaa hai.

1. tumh̃ẽ̃ un see jaldii milnaa caahiyee.

2. mujhee raam koo patr likhnaa caahiyee.

3. meerii patnii koo ghar kaa kaam karnaa caahiyee.

4. ham̃ẽ̃ kuch phal xariidnaa caahiyee.

5. usee bas-isTaap par ruknaa caahiyee.

6. mujhee yee siŋgil kamraa leenaa caahiyee.

7. usee kamree kaa kiraayaa batanaa caahiyee.

8. raam koo meeree bhaaii see milnaa caahiyee.

9. ham̃ẽ̃ us hooTal m̃ẽ̃ eek kamraa deekhnaa caahiyee.

10. usee kah̃ãã jaanaa caahiyee?

11. laRkee koo hooTal m̃ẽ̃ rahnaa caahiyee.

12. us kee mitr koo mujhee kuch rupaee deenaa caahiyee.

E.  Transform the following simple present tense sentences to present progressive tense sentences according
to the model given:

woo bazaar jaataa hai  ..... woo bazaar jaa rahaa hai.

1. us kii patnii kyaa kahtii hai?

2. woo raam koo eek patr likhtaa hai.

3. bas yahĩĩ see chuuTtii hai.

4. meeree baRee bhaaii kuch kapRee xariidtee hãĩ.

5. woo kaanpuur mẽẽ wyaapaar kartaa hai.

6. kyaa raam kii bahin paark mẽẽ ghuumtii hai.

7. meeraa mitr kuch kapRee leetaa hai.

8. woo mujhee aagree kaa kiraayaa bataataa hai.

9. naukar ghar kaa kaam kartaa hai.

10. us kaa patiuuntii kapRaa xariidtaa hai.

11. aap kee maataa-pitaa kahãã rahtee hai?

12. laRkee aatee hãĩ?

F.   Translate orally:

1. I'm going to the station.

2. I'm going to the station to get him.

3. I'm going to the station to get him and his
   family.

4. Is he going to the station?

5. Is he coming alone?

6. He is coming alone.

7. He has a clothing store.

8. He has a clothing store in Kanpur.

9. He has a clothing store in Nagpur.

10. Has he a clothing store in Agra?

11. He deals in all kinds of cloth.

12. He deals in all kinds of cloth -- cotton, woolen
    and silk.

13. Does he deal in all kinds of cloth?

14. It's getting to be train time.

15. It's getting to be bus time.

16. Where's he coming from?

17. He is coming from Kanpur.

18. Is he coming from Kanpur?

19. His family is coming with him.

20. His wife and children are coming with him.

G. Read the following:

## Text of Lesson I

१ सुनिए, मैं होटल जाना चाहता हूं ।

२ होटल कहां है ?

३ आप यहां से सीधे जाइए ।

४ और फिर दाईं तरफ ।

५ वहीं एक होटल है ।

६ होटल का नाम क्या है ?

७ होटल का नाम अजमेरी होटल है ।

८ क्या यह होटल अच्छा है ?

९ जी हां, यह होटल बहुत मशहूर है ।

१० बहुत अच्छा, धन्यवाद ।

## Text of Lesson II

१ सुनिए, मैं कुछ फल ख़रीदना चाहता हूं ।

२ फल की दुकान कहां है ?

३ सदर बाज़ार में ।

४ वह यहां से कितनी दूर है ?

५ बहुत दूर नहीं ।

६ एक मील है ।

124

७ क्या आप पैदल जाना चाहते हैं ?

८ जी नहीं, बस से ।

९ बस कहां मिलती है ?

१० आप यहां से सीधे जाइए ।

११ और फिर बाईं तरफ ।

१२ वहीं बस स्टाप है ।

१३ बहुत अच्छा, घन्यवाद ।

## Text of Lesson III

१ सुनो, क्या तुम्हारे पास फल हैं ?

२ जी हां, आप को कौन से फल चाहिए ?

३ मैं कुछ संतरे लेना चाहता हूं ।

४ क्या तुम्हारे पास अच्छे संतरे हैं ?

५ जी हां, ये संतरे देखिए ।

६ ये नागपुरी संतरे हैं ।

७ क्या नागपुरी संतरे अच्छे होते हैं ?

८ जी हां, नागपुरी संतरे बहुत मीठे होते हैं ।

९ अच्छा, इनका दाम क्या है ?

१० तीन रुपए दर्जन ।

११ अच्छा, मुझे एक दर्जन दे दो ।

१२ ये लीजिए एक दर्जन संतरे ।

१३ ये लो तीन रुपए ।

१४ बहुत अच्छा ।

Conversation -- Asking for a Doctor

### JOHN

| | |
|---|---|
| paRoos | neighborhood, vicinity |
| DaakTar | doctor |

kyaa yahãã paRoos mẽẽ    Is there a good doctor here
   kooii acchaa DaakTar hai?   in the neighborhood?

### RAM PAL

| | |
|---|---|
| leekin | but |
| baat | thing, affair, conversation |

hãã, leekin baat kyaa hai? Yes, but what's the matter?

| | |
|---|---|
| biimaar | sick, ill |

kyaa aap kee yahãã kooii    Is someone sick in your
   biimaar hai?            house?

### JOHN

| | |
|---|---|
| kal | yesterday, tomorrow |
| raat | night |
| zukaam | cold |
| hoo gayaa hai | has become, has caught |

jii hãã, meerii chooTii    Yes, my younger daughter
   laRkii koo kal raat see   caught a cold last night.
   zukaam hoo gayaa hai.

| | |
|---|---|
| kaaraN | reason |
| buxaar | fever |

aur isii kaaraN see usee   And for this reason she
   kuch buxaar bhii hai.     has some fever too.

### RAM PAL

| | |
|---|---|
| aree | oh! |

126

| | |
|---|---|
| afsoos | sorrow |
| aree, yee too baRee afsoos kii baat hai. | Oh, that's too bad. |
| šarmaa | Sharma |
| dawaa | medicine |
| dawaaxaanaa | doctor's office |
| deekhiyee, yahãã see kuch hii duur par DaakTar šarmaa kaa dawaaxaanaa hai. | Dr. Sharma's office is nearby. |
| aap usee wahãã lee jaaẽẽ. | You might take her there. |

JOHN

| | |
|---|---|
| kyaa DaakTar šarmaa eek acchee DaakTar hãĩ? | Is Dr. Sharma a good doctor? |

RAM PAL

| | |
|---|---|
| yoogy | competent |
| catur | skillful |
| prasiddh | well known, famous |
| jii hãã, bahut yoogy catur aur prasiddh. | Yes, very competent, skillful and well known. |

JOHN

| | |
|---|---|
| khulaa | open |
| kyaa un kaa dawaaxaanaa is samai khulaa hoogaa? | Will his office be open at this time? |

RAM PAL

| | |
|---|---|
| subah | morning |
| doopahar | noon (roughly) |
| šaam | evening |
| khulaa rahnaa | to be open, to remain open |
| jii hãã, un kaa dawaaxaanaa subah saat | Yes, his office is open from 7 a.m. in the morning till |

127

| | |
|---|---|
| bajee see doopahar baraa bajee tak aur šaam pããc bajee see raat baraa bajee tak khulaa rahtaa hai. | 12 noon and from 5 p.m. in the evening till 12 midnight. |
| is samai wee dawaaxaanee mẽẽ hii hõõgee. | He will be in the office right now. |

JOHN

| | |
|---|---|
| nahĩĩ too | otherwise |
| Thiik hai, tab mãĩ calũũ, nahĩĩ too deer hoo jaaeegii. | All right, then I must go, otherwise it might get late. |

ADDITIONAL VOCABULARY

| | |
|---|---|
| aspataal | hospital |

GRAMMAR

1. **New Nouns**

   **Masc. I**                           **Fem. II**

| | | | |
|---|---|---|---|
| dawaaxaanaa | doctor's office | baat | thing, affair, conversation |

   **Masc. II**

| | | | |
|---|---|---|---|
| | | raat | night |
| aspataal | hospital | subah | morning |
| paRoos | neighborhood, vicinity | doopahar | noon |
| | | šaam | evening |
| DaakTar | doctor | dawaa | medicine |
| zukaam | cold | | |
| buxaar | fever | | |
| kaaraN | reason | | |
| afsoos | sorrow | | |

2. **New Compound Verbs**

   **Type I**

   lee jaanaa    to take

128

# 3. New Adjectives in -aa

khulaa        open

# 4. Vocabulary Notes

## 4.1. DaakTar

The Hindi term DaakTar, "doctor," is likely to imply a western trained medical practitioner.

## 4.2. dawaaxaanaa

The term dawaaxaanaa, literally "a place for dispensing medicine," is a term used for a doctor's office since the doctor's office in India will normally also dispense medicine.

The term dawaaxaanaa as well as aspataal may be used for a hospital.

## 4.3. Time Expressions

The term subah, "morning," refers roughly to the period from sunrise to about 10 a.m. The term doopahar refers to the hot part of the day, roughly 11 a.m. to 3 p.m. but varying somewhat with the season. The term šaam, "evening," refers roughly to the time from 5 p.m. to sunset, and raat, "night," to the time from sunset to sunrise.

Note the following Hindi-English equivalents:

| | |
|---|---|
| doopahar baaraa bajee | at noon |
| doopahar | roughly from 11 a.m. to 3 p.m. |
| doopahar eek bajee | at 1 p.m. in the afternoon |
| šaam saat bajee | at 7 in the evening |
| raat aath bajee | at 8 in the evening |

# 5. Optative

One common use of the optative in Hindi, particularly in questions, equates with English "to be to," "to be supposed to," "ought to," "should."

kyaa mãĩ bazaar jaaũũ

> Am I supposed to go to the market?
>
> Should I go to the market?

mãĩ kab aaũũ

> When should I come?
>
> When am I to come?

Note that where English will use the form "should" in either a question or a statement, Hindi uses the optative form in the question and uses <u>caahiyee</u> construction in the statement. Compare the following two sentences:

kyaa mãĩ bazaar jaaũũ?    Should I go to the bazaar?

mujhee bazaar jaanaa    I should go to the bazaar.
caahiyee.

Another use of the optative is to make a suggestion. In this usage, the optative form is used instead of an imperative as a more polite way of suggesting that somebody do something just as in English it is more polite to say by way of suggestion "you might read this book" instead of the rather abrupt imperative "read this book."

aap usee wahãã lee    You might take her there.
jaaẽẽ.

aap yahãã rukẽẽ, mãĩ    You might stay here, I'll
abhii aataa hũũ.    be back right away.

The expression <u>tab mãĩ calũũ</u> is a use of the optative similar to the one mentioned above inasmuch as it is a polite way of taking leave.

6. <u>Verb "to have"</u>

We have already learned two expressions in Hindi which equate with the English verb "to have." A third equivalent of the English verb "to have" which occurs in this lesson, is expressed by putting the person who possesses something in the dative case. Thus, where English uses "she has some fever," the Hindi equivalent is literally "some fever is to her."

isii kaaraN see usee kuch    For this reason he has
buxaar bhii hai.    some fever as well.

130

usee kal raat see zukaam    He has had a cold since
  hai.                        last night.

This construction for English "have" unlike the expressions learned earlier is used for abstract objects
that are possessed rather than concrete objects.

7.  "Since" or "for"

    Where English uses the form "has been," i.e.,
"has been since or for a certain time," Hindi uses
the simple present of the verb hoonaa, "to be."  In
similar sentences where English uses a verb form, such
as "has been living," "has been working" etc. "since
or for a certain time," Hindi uses the verb in the
present progressive.  Where English uses "since" or
"for" with the time expression, Hindi always uses see
with the time expression.

    kal raat see mãĩ yahãã    I have been here since
      hũũ.                      last night.

    kal raat see mãĩ          I have been sick since
      biimaar hũũ.             last night.

    doo ghaNTee see mãĩ       I have been here for two
      yahãã hũũ.               hours.

    woo aath bajee see kaam   He has been working since
      kar rahaa hai.           8 o'clock.

    woo kuch samai see        He has been living here
      yahãã rah rahaa hai.     for some time.

8.  Writing System

8.1.  Consonant Combinations

    The following new consonant combinations occur in
Lessons IV, V and VI:

| st | स्त | namastee | नमस्ते |
| tn | त्न | patnii | पत्नी |
| ld | ल्द | jaldii | जल्दी |
| gy | ग्य | gyaaraa | ग्यारह |
| nn | न्न | unniis | उन्नीस |

131

## 8.2. Irregular Spellings

The numerals eleven through eighteen are pronounced with a final -aa but written as if they had
-ah:

| | | | |
|---|---|---|---|
| gyaaraa | ग्यारह | pandraa | पन्द्रह |
| baaraa | बारह | soolaa | सोलह |
| teeraa | तेरह | satraa | सत्रह |
| caudaa | चौदह | aThaaraa | अठारह |

The numeral "six" is also written irregularly as
follows:

chai    छह    or    ६:

## EXERCISES

A. Substitute orally in the sentences below the Hindi
equivalent of the English given:

1. _____ kal raat see kuch buxaar hai.

| | |
|---|---|
| I | my younger son |
| he | my older daughter |
| this man | my friend's wife |
| this woman | Ram's elder brother |
| this girl | Bill's mother |
| my son | his younger daughter |
| my brother | my elder sister |
| his father | this boy |
| John's sister | that boy |
| her husband | that man |
| Ram's daughter | that woman |

2. un kaa dawaaxaanaa _____ khulaa rahtaa hai.

    from five o'clock to seven o'clock

    from one o'clock to ten o'clock

from three o'clock to twelve o'clock

from two o'clock to eight o'clock

from six o'clock to eleven o'clock

from four o'clock to nine o'clock

from eight o'clock to eleven o'clock

from seven o'clock to twelve o'clock

3. is samai wee _____ mε̃ε̃ hõõgee.

| | |
|---|---|
| the house | the room |
| the hospital | the fruit store |
| the doctor's office | Agra |
| the hotel | |

4. _____ kaa naam kyaa hai?

| | |
|---|---|
| this man | his friend's brother |
| this boy | his father |
| this girl | his mother |
| this woman | his son |
| this child | her daughter |
| the doctor | his younger sister |
| John's brother | his elder son |
| his elder sister | his younger daughter |
| his friend | |

5. wee kal _____ aaε̃ε̃gee.

| | |
|---|---|
| morning | noon |
| evening | at one o'clock in the afternoon |
| night | |
| | at what time |

6. kyaa _____ kooii acchaa DaakTar hai?

here                          in Agra

| | |
|---|---|
| there | in Kanpur |
| here in the vicinity | in this hospital |

B. Substitute orally in the sentences below the Hindi equivalent of the English given, making changes, if necessary:

1. kyaa is samai _____ khulaa hoogaa?

| | |
|---|---|
| the bazaar | the stores |
| the doctor's office | the clothing stores |
| those doctors' offices | the stores in the bazaar |
| the store | the hospital |

2. _____ usee kahãã lee jaaũũ?

| | |
|---|---|
| I | we |
| he | she |
| they | John |

C. Transform the following sentences according to the model given:

kyaa mãĩ jaaũũ?          ..... kyaa woo jaaee?

1. kyaa mãĩ hooTal mẽẽ rukũũ?

2. kyaa mãĩ is paark mẽẽ ghuumũũ?

3. kyaa mãĩ yee phal xariidũũ?

4. kyaa mãĩ DaakTar see milũũ?

5. kyaa mãĩ is dawaaxaanee mẽẽ kaam karũũ?

6. kyaa mãĩ kal raat aap kee ghar aaũũ?

7. kyaa mãĩ isii aspataal see dawaa lũũ?

8. kyaa mãĩ aagree mẽẽ hii wyaapaar karũũ?

9. kyaa mãĩ jaan koo eek patr likhũũ?

10. kyaa mãĩ isiighar mẽẽ rahũũ?

D. Transform the following sentences according to the model given:

yee santaraa acchaa hai. ..... yee santaree acchee hãĩ.

   1. yee baccaa kis kaa hai?

   2. yee dawaaxaanaa bahut acchaa aur mašhuur hai.

   3. yee dukaan kitnii duur hai?

   4. laRkii bazaar jaatii hai.

   5. bas kahãã see chuuTtii hai?

   6. dhoobii kahãã kaam kartaa hai?

   7. yee TikaT pahlee darjee kaa hai.

   8. patnii ghar kaa kaam kartii hai.

   9. yee jaghee bahut mašhuur hai.

  10. gaaRii kitnee bajee aatii hai.

  11. laRkaa paark mẽẽ ghuumtaa hai.

  12. us kaa bhaaii kuch kapRee xariidtaa hai.

  13. khiRkii khulii hai.

  14. us kii bahin biimaar hai.

  15. meeraa moozaa kahãã hai?

  16. dawaa kahãã miltii hai?

  17. yee kamraa bahut acchaa hai.

  18. meeraa bhaaii wyaapaar kartaa hai.

  19. yee dukaan sadar bazaar mẽẽ hai.

  20. laRkaa isii ghar mẽẽ rahtaa hai.

E.  Transform the following simple present imperfect tense sentences into optative sentences according to the model given:

mãĩ bazaar jaataa hũũ ..... kyaa mãĩ bazaar jaaũũ?

   1. mãĩ patr likhtaa hũũ.

   2. ham dawaaxaanee see dawaa leetee hãĩ.

   3. woo paark mẽẽ ghuumtaa hai.

4. mãĩ dhoobii koo kapRee deetaa hũũ.

5. us kaa bhaaii wyaapaar kartaa hai.

6.  woo pleeTfaarm par ruktaa hai.

7. mãĩ usee aagree kaa kiraayaa bataataa hũũ.

8. naukar ghar kaa kaam kartaa hai.

9. mãĩ DaakTar see miltaa hũũ.

10. raam kii bahin us kii baat suntii hai.

11. woo laRkaa isii hooTal mẽẽ rahtaa hai.

12. laRkii kuch kapRaa xariidtii hai.

F.  Translate orally:

1. He will be in the hospital at this time.

2. Will he be in the hospital at this time?

3. Where will he be at this time?

4. Where will the doctor be at this time?

5. John is sick.

6. John has been sick since last night.

7. Is someone sick in your house?

8. Who is sick in your house?

9. My daughter has been sick since last night.

10. My son has had a fever since last night.

11. The store will be open right now.

12. The stores in the bazaar will be open right now.

13. He is a good doctor.

14. He is a very competent doctor.

15. Is he a very competent and famous doctor?

16. Is there a good doctor here in the neighborhood?

17. Dr. Sharma's office is nearby.

18.  Where is Dr. Sharma's office?

19.  Is Dr. Sharma's office very far from here?

20.  Dr. Sharma's office is about a mile from here.

G.  Read the following:

<u>Text of Lesson IV</u>

१ कौन है ?

२ धोबी है, साहब ।

३ अन्दर आ जाओ ।

४ क्या तुम्हीं इस होटल के धोबी हो ?

५ जी हां, मैं ही यहां का काम करता हूं ।

६ अच्छा दो मिनट रुको, अभी कपड़े देता हूं ।

७ लो, ये रहे कपड़े ।

८ अच्छा साहब, लिख लीजिए ।

९ चार पैंट, छह कमीज़, सात बनियाइन, पांच जोड़े मोज़े और नौ रूमाल ।

१० ठीक है, मुफे ये कपड़े जल्दी चाहिए ।

११ बहुत अच्छा, साहब ।

|       |       |
|-------|-------|
| एक    | छह    |
| दो    | सात   |
| तीन   | आठ    |
| चार   | नौ    |
| पांच  | दस    |

<u>Text of Lesson V</u>

१ नमस्ते, कहिए, क्या मैं आप के लिए कुछ कर सकता हूं ।

२ क्या आप के पास कोई कमरा खाली है ?

३ आपको कैसा कमरा चाहिए - सिंगल या डबल ?

४ डबल, मेरे साथ मेरी पत्नी भी हैं ।

५ अच्छा, आइए, कमरा देख लीजिए ।

६ इस कमरे में सभी सुविधाएं हैं ।

७ कहिए, आपको पसन्द है ?

८ ठीक है, मुझे पसन्द है ।

९ इसका किराया कितना है ।

१० आपके लिए केवल दस रुपए रोज़ ।

११ ठीक है, तब मैं इसे ले लूंगा ।

## Text of Lesson VI

१ कहिए, आपको क्या चाहिए ?

२ मैं कुछ कार्ड, लिफ़ाफ़े आदि लेना चाहता हूं ।

३ तब अगली खिड़की पर जाइए ।

४ यहां मनीआर्डर लिए जाते हैं ।

५ मुझे दस पोस्ट कार्ड और बारह लिफ़ाफ़े दे दीजिए ।

६ ये लीजिए, और कुछ चाहिए ?

७ जी हां, पन्द्रह नए पैसे वाले तीस टिकट भी दे दीजिए ।

८ क्या आपके पास अन्तर्देशीय पत्र भी हैं ?

९ जी हां, कितने चाहिए ?

१० सात, साथ ही दस हवाई पत्र भी दे दीजिए ।

११ लीजिए ये रहे आपके टिकट, अन्तर्देशीय पत्र और हवाई पत्र ।

१२ कितने पैसे हुए ?

१३ कुल तेरह रुपए ।

१४ ये लीजिए तेरह रुपए ।

| | |
|---|---|
| ग्यारह | सोलह |
| बारह | सत्रह |
| तेरह | अठारह |
| चौदह | उन्नीस |
| पन्द्रह | बीस |

# LESSON XI

## Conversation -- Extending an Invitation

### RAM NATH

| | |
|---|---|
| namastee | Hello |

### JOHN

| | |
|---|---|
| baiThnaa | to sit down |
| namastee, aaiyee, andar aaiyee. | Hello.  Come in. |
| baiThiyee. kahiyee, kyaa haalcaal hai? | Please take a seat.  How are you? |

### RAM NATH

| | |
|---|---|
| kripaa | kindness, mercy |
| sab aap kii kripaa hai.* | Everything is fine. |
| kašT | trouble, inconvenience |
| mãĩ aap koo eek kašT deenaa caahtaa hũũ.** | I want to ask a favor of you. |
| parsõõ | the day before yesterday, the day after tomorrow |
| tiisraa | third |
| pahar | part of the day |
| tiisraa pahar | late afternoon |
| aašaa | Asha |
| warš | year |

---

\* The style of this lesson is generally more formal than that of any previous lessons.  This particular expression means literally "everything is fine by your kindness."

\*\* Literally "I want to give (cause) you an inconvenience."

139

| waršgããTh | birthday |
|---|---|
| parsõõ tiisree pahar meerii chooTii laRkii aašaa kii waršgããTh hai. | My young daughter Asha is having a birthday cele- bration the day after tomorrow in the afternoon. |
| daawat | dinner |
| aur us kee baad šaam koo eek daawat hai. | And there's a dinner after it. |
| praarthnaa | request |
| meerii praarthnaa hai ki aap us mẽẽ aaẽẽ.* | I would like you to come. |
| laanaa | to bring |
| aur saath hii apnii patnii aur baccõõ koo bhii laaẽẽ. | And bring your wife and children with you too. |

JOHN

| awašy | certainly |
|---|---|
| mãĩ too awašy aa jaaũũgaa. | I will certainly come. |
| par | but |
| kee baaree mẽẽ | about, concerning |
| jaannaa | to know |
| par apnii patnii kee baaree mẽẽ nahĩĩ jaantaa. | But I don't know (for sure) about my wife. |

RAM NATH

| kyõõ | why |
|---|---|
| din | day |
| kyõõ? kyaa wee us din xaalii nahĩĩ hãĩ? | Why? Isn't she free that day? |

JOHN

| jii nahĩĩ. yee baat nahĩĩ hai. | No, that's not the reason. |
|---|---|

---

* Literally "my request is that you should come to it."

| | |
|---|---|
| tabiyat | condition, health |
| aajkal | nowadays |
| xaraab | bad |
| meerii patnii kii tabiyat aajkal xaraab hai. | My wife's health isn't very good these days. |
| isliyee | therefore |
| isliyee mãĩ nahĩĩ kah saktaa ki wee aa sakẽẽgii yaa nahĩĩ. | Therefore, I can't say whether she can come or not. |
| phir bhii | however |
| koošiš | attempt |
| koošiš karnaa | to try |
| phir bhii mãĩ unhẽẽ laanee kii koošiš karũũgaa. | However, I will try to bring her. |

RAM NATH

| | |
|---|---|
| pataa | address |
| kyaa aap meeree ghar kaa pataa jaantee hãĩ? | Do you know my address? |

JOHN

| | |
|---|---|
| jii nahĩĩ. | No. |

RAM NATH

| | |
|---|---|
| nagar | town, city |
| ašook nagar | Ashok Nagar, name of a suburb |
| makaan | house |
| meeraa ghar ašook nagar mẽẽ hai--makaan nambar soolaa. | My house is in Ashok Nagar --house number 16. |
| saRak | road, street |
| kinaaraa | edge, bank |
| yee makaan saRak kee | The house is right on the |

141

kinaaree par hii hai.*        street.

                        JOHN

Thiik hai, mãĩ kitnee      All right, when should I
   bajee aaũũ?                come?

                     RAM NATH

daawat šaam saat bajee     The dinner is at seven p.m.
hai.

aap us samai tak awašy     You should come by that
   aa jaaẽẽ.                  time.

                        JOHN

   pahũcnaa                    to reach

   pahũc jaanaa                to reach

Thiik hai, mãĩ pahũc       O.K., I'll be there.
   jaaũũgaa.

                     RAM NATH

baRii kripaa hoogii.       That will be very kind of
                              you.


               ADDITIONAL  VOCABULARY

   aaj                       today

   kal                       yesterday, tomorrow

   parsõõ                    the day before yesterday,
                                the day after tomorrow

   narsõõ                    two days before yesterday,
                                two days after tomorrow

   na                        not

----

*Literally "the house is right on the edge of the
   street" as opposed to being located off the street
   on some alley or side street.

                        142

GRAMMAR

1. New Nouns

| Masc. I | | Fem. II | |
|---|---|---|---|
| pataa | address | kripaa | kindness |
| kinaaraa | edge, bank | aašaa (no pl.) | Asha |
| Masc. II | | waršgããTh | birthday |
| kašT | trouble, in-convenience | daawat | dinner |
| pahar | part of the day | praarthnaa | request |
| | | tabiyat | condition, health |
| din | day | | |
| nagar | city | koošiš | attempt |
| makaan | house | saRak | street, road |
| warš | year | | |

2. New Verbs

| baiThnaa | to sit | laanaa | to bring |
|---|---|---|---|
| jaannaa | to know | pahũcnaa | to reach |

2.1. New Compound Verbs

Type I

pahũc jaanaa    to reach

Type II

koošiš karnaa    to try

3. New Adjectives in -aa

tiisraa        third

4. New Postpositions

kee baaree mẽẽ        about, concerning

5. Negative

For the present imperfect tense, the present progressive and future tense the negative is expressed

by the negative particle nahĩĩ "not." It is customary in the negative to drop the simple present tense forms of the verb hoonaa, "to be," in the present imperfect and present progressive. The particle nahĩĩ, "not" will occur immediately before the verbal phrase.

| | |
|---|---|
| woo bazaar jaataa hai. | He goes to the bazaar. |
| woo bazaar nohĩĩ jaataa. | He doesn't go to the bazaar. |
| woo bazaar jaa rahaa hai. | He is going to the bazaar. |
| woo bazaar nahĩĩ jaa rahaa. | He isn't going to the bazaar. |
| woo bazaar jaaeegaa. | He'll go to the bazaar. |
| woo bazaar nahĩĩ jaaeegaa. | He won't go to the bazaar. |
| woo phal xariid saktaa hai. | He can buy fruit. |
| woo phal nahĩĩ xariid saktaa. | He can't buy fruit. |
| woo phal xariidnaa caahtaa hai. | He wants to buy fruit. |
| woo phal nahĩĩ xariidnaa caahtaa. | He doesn't want to buy fruit. |
| woo kaam kartaa hai. | He works. |
| woo kaam nahĩĩ kartaa. | He doesn't work. |

With the optative and the imperative the negative particle na is used. The particle na, "not," may also be used with the future tense instead of nahĩĩ, "not."

| | |
|---|---|
| mãĩ bazaar jaaũũgaa. | I'll go to the bazaar. |
| mãĩ bazaar na jaaũũgaa. | } I won't go to the bazaar. |
| mãĩ bazaar nahĩĩ jaaũũgaa. | |
| phal xariidoo. | Buy fruit. |
| phal na xariidoo. | Don't buy fruit. |

| | |
|---|---|
| bazaar jaaiyee | Please go to the bazaar. |
| bazaar na jaaiyee. | Please don't go to the bazaar. |
| kyaa woo bazaar jaaee? | Should he go to the bazaar? |
| kyaa woo bazaar na jaaee? | Shouldn't he go to the bazaar? |
| usee bazaar jaavaa caahiyee. | He should go to the bazaar. |
| usee bazaar na jaanaa caahiyee. | He shouldn't go to the bazaar. |

## 6. Use of Optative

After the form <u>praarthanaa</u>, "request," a subordinate clause may have a verb in the optative or in the polite imperative but not in the present imperfect of the future.

| | |
|---|---|
| meerii praarthnaa hai ki aap us mẽẽ aaẽẽ. | I would like you to come to it. |
| meerii praarthnaa hai ki aap us mẽẽ aaiyee. | |
| meerii praarthnaa hai ki aap meeree saath ghuumnee calẽẽ. | I would like you to take a walk with me. |
| meerii praarthnaa hai ki aap meeree saath ghuumnee caliyee. | |

## 7. The Verb "to try"

If the Hindi verb <u>kooših karnaa</u>, "to try," is used with a dependent infinitive, then the infinitive will be in the oblique form followed by <u>kii</u> since <u>kooših</u> is a feminine noun.

| | |
|---|---|
| mãĩ kooših karũũgaa. | I'll try. |
| mãĩ unhẽẽ laanee kii kooših karũũgaa. | I'll try to bring her. |

145

```
woo aaTh bajee aanee kii          He'll try to come at
    koošiš kareegaa.                  eight o'clock.
```

8. **"Whether ... or not"**

The Hindi equivalent of an English sentence
"whether ... or not" is expressed by <u>ki ... yaa nahĩĩ</u>.
Whereas in English "or not" may be dropped, the <u>yaa
nahĩĩ</u> of Hindi is obligatory.

```
is liyee mãĩ nahĩĩ kah       Therefore I can't say
    saktaa, ki wee aa            whether she can come
    sakẽẽgii yaa nahĩĩ.          (or not).

mãĩ nahĩĩ jaantaa ki         I don't know whether I'm
    mãĩ kal xaalii hũũ           free tomorrow (or not).
    yaa nahĩĩ.
```

9. **Direct Object**

You have learned that the direct object in Hindi
may be in the nominative case but this applies only if
the object is inanimate. If the object is animate,
then the direct object must be in the dative case.
If the direct object is inanimate, it may occasionally
be expressed in the dative case.

```
saath hii woo apnii          He will bring his wife
    patnii koo bhii              with him too.
    laaeegaa.

raam yee phal bazaar see ⎫
    laataa hai.               ⎬ Ram brings this fruit
                              ⎪   from the bazaar.
raam in phalõõ koo bazaar ⎪
    see laataa hai.          ⎭
```

When the direct object is a pronoun, even if it
refers to something inanimate, it is more customary to
use the dative case form.

```
woo usee bhii laaeegaa.      He will bring her too.

raam isee bazaar see         Ram will bring it from the
    laaeegaa.                    bazaar.
```

10. **tiisree pahar**

The period of time from about 3 p.m. to 5 p.m. is
referred to as <u>tiisree pahar</u> in Hindi.

woo kal tiisree pahar         He will come tomorrow
caar bajee aaeegaa.              at four o'clock.

## 11. Writing System

### 11.1. New Consonant Combinations

| pl | प्ल | pleeTfaarm | प्लेटफार्म |
| nh | न्ह | unhẽẽ | उन्हें |
| wy | व्य | wyaapaar | व्यापार |
| cc | च्च | baccaa | बच्चा |
| mm | म्म | ammãã | अम्मां |

### 11.2. Special Consonant Combinations

In some words the consonant combination gy is written by the symbol ज्ञ . Unlike most consonant combinations this symbol has no similarity to either of its parts, g or y.

aagyaa        आज्ञा

### 11.3. Irregular Spellings

| samai | समय |
| jaghee | जगह |
| na | न |

## EXERCISES

Substitute orally in the sentences below the Hindi equivalent of the English given:

1. _____ meerii laRkii kii waršgããTh hai.

tomorrow

the day after tomorrow

this morning

this evening

today

two days after tomorrow

tomorrow night

tomorrow evening

the day after tomorrow at noon

the day after tomorrow in the evening

tomorrow afternoon

tomorrow morning at 10:00.

tomorrow evening at 6:00.

tomorrow night at 8:00.

the day after tomorrow at 7:00 p.m.

the day after tomorrow at 4:00 p.m.

two days after tomorrow at 10:00 a.m.

2.  saath hii _____ bhii laaiyee.

| | |
|---|---|
| your wife | her husband |
| your children | her sister |
| your brother | my brother |
| my friend | your daughters |
| his friend | his friends |
| your daughter | their friends |
| his parents | your sons |
| your parents | your younger son |
| your friends | his servant |
| your children | their servants |
| his sons and daughters | John's brother |
| your brother's children | your servant |

3.  kyaa aap _____ kaa pataa jaantee h\u00e3\u00ee?

| | |
|---|---|
| my house | my friend's house |
| his house | the doctor's office |

148

| | |
|---|---|
| their house | Dr. Sharma's office |
| our house | the hospital |
| the clothing store | the station |
| that clothing store | this park |
| my store | this hotel |
| his store | our store |
| this house | their store |
| that house | my friend's store |

4. mã̃ı _____ laanee kii koošiš karũũgaa.

| | |
|---|---|
| her | my sister |
| him | my sons |
| my wife | their friends |
| my family | Ram's friends |
| John | my daughter |
| his parents | my children |
| his servant | his children |
| his brother | her husband |

5. mã̃ı _____ koošiš karũũgaa.

   to bring her

   to write the letters

   to go to the park

   to give some oranges to Ram

   to buy some fruit

   to meet my friend

   to come tomorrow

   to work

   to give him some money

to live in this house

B. Transform the following sentences into negative sentences according to the model given:

raam patr likhtaa hai ..... raam patr nahĩĩ likhtaa.

1. mãĩ phal xariidtaa hũũ.

2. woo meerii baat suntaa hai.

3. laRkaa neehruu paark mẽẽ ghuumtaa hai.

4. mãĩ dhoobii koo kapRee deetaa hũũ.

5. woo bazaar jaa saktaa hai.

6. tum yee kapRee xariid saktee hoo.

7. meeraa mitr dukaan mẽẽ kaam kartaa hai.

8. woo mujhee apnee baaree mẽẽ bataataa hai.

9. mãĩ raam see milnaa caahtaa hũũ.

10. woo pã̃ac kamiizẽẽ xariidnaa caahtaa hai.

11. woo DaakTar šarmaa kee dawaaxaanee see dawaa
    laataa hai.

12. meeree bhaaii kaanpuur mẽẽ wyaapaar kartee hãĩ.

13. woo meeree saath aagree jaanaa caahtaa hai.

14. meeree maataa-pitaa kal aa rahee hãĩ.

15. usee buxaar hai.

16. DaakTar kaa dawaaxaanaa is samai khulaa rahtaa
    hai.

17. kyaa tum apnee bhaaii koo patr likhnaa caahtee
    hoo.

18. bas yahã̃a see chuuTtii hai.

19. gaaRii pã̃ac nambar kee pleeTfaarm par miltii hai.

20. kyaa aap aaj aagree jaa rahee hãĩ.

21. yee laRkee is ghar mẽẽ rahtee hãĩ.

22. unkii laRkii aath bajee bazaar jaatii hai.

23. gaaRii šaam saat bajee chuuTtii hai.

24. meeree pitaa aajkal ajmeer hooTal mẽẽ rah
    rahee hãĩ.

25. woo apnaa kaam karnee kii koošiš kar rahaa hai.

C. Transform the following sentences according to the
model given:

laRkaa bazaar jaa rahaa hai ... laRkee bazaar jaa
                                          rahee hãĩ.

1. yee nagar bahut mašhuur hai.

2. kyaa aap kii dukaan ašook nagar mẽẽ hai?

3. laRkii kahãã jaa rahii hai.

4. dawaaxaanaa is samai khulaa hoogaa.

5. yee paark bahut prasiddh hai.

6. us kaa makaan bahut duur hai.

7. aap kii baat Thiik hai.

8. us kii bahin kapRee xariid rahii hai.

9. meeraa mitr kapRee kaa wyaapaar kartaa hai.

10. jaan kaa laRkaa likhnee kii koošiš kar rahaa hai.

D. Translate orally:

1. He will be free at that time.

2. Will he be free at that time?

3. Won't she be free at that time?

4. She won't be free tomorrow.

5. She won't be free tomorrow evening.

6. She won't be free tomorrow at 6 p.m.

7. My wife's health isn't very good these days.

8. Is your wife's health good these days?

9. Isn't your wife's health good these days?

10. I can't tell whether he'll come or not.

11. He can't tell whether I'll go to the store or not.

12. I can't tell whether she will go to the store or not.

13. Asha is having a birthday celebration tomorrow.

14. My daughter Asha is having a birthday celebration tomorrow at 4 p.m.

15. My young son Ram is having a birthday celebration the day after tomorrow at 2 p.m.

16. I would like you to come.

17. I would like you and your family to come.

18. I would like you and your wife to come.

19. I would like you, your wife and your children to come.

20. I would like you and your family to come tomorrow at 5 p.m.

E. Read the following:

## Text of Lesson VII

१ सुनिए, क्या आप बता सकते हैं कि आगरे के लिए बस कहां मिलेगी ?

२ जी, यहीं मिलेगी ।

३ कितनी देर में जाएगी ?

४ एक घण्टे में, ठीक आठ बजे छूटेगी ।

५ आप पांच नंबर के प्लेटफार्म पर चले जाइए ।

६ वहां बस तैयार मिलेगी ।

७ क्या आपके पास टिकट है ?

८ अभी नहीं, टिकट कहां मिलते हैं ?

९ आगरे के लिए न ?

१० सामने चार नंबर की खिड़की पर ।

११ आगरे का किराया क्या है ?

१२ किस दर्जे का - पहले या दूसरे ?

152

१३ पहले दर्जे का ।

१४ ज़रा ठहरिए, अभी बताता हूं ।

१५ लगभग तीन रुपए लगेंगे ।

१६ बहुत अच्छा, धन्यवाद ।

## Text of Lesson VIII

१ नमस्ते, कहिए, क्या हालचाल है ?

२ सब ठीक है, आप कैसे हैं ?

३ अच्छा हूं ।

४ आप कहां जा रहे हैं ।

५ घूमने जा रहा हूं ।

६ क्या आप भी घूमने चल रहे हैं ?

७ जी नहीं, मैं इस समय अपने एक मित्र से मिलने जा रहा हूं ।

८ मुझे उनसे कुछ ज़रूरी काम है ।

९ और एक घंटे बाद ही वे बाहर चले जाएंगे ।

१० आप किधर जा रहे हैं ?

११ मैं नेहरू पार्क तक जाऊंगा ।

१२ घूमने के लिए वह जगह बहुत अच्छी है ।

१३ मैं हमेशा वहीं जाता हूं ।

१४ तब ठीक है, मैं थोड़ी दूर तक आपका साथ दूंगा ।

१५ मेरे मित्र का घर उसी ओर है ।

१६ बहुत अच्छा, चलिए तब चलें ।

## Text of Lesson IX

१ नमस्ते, कहिए, कहां जा रहे हैं ?

२ स्टेशन, मेरे बड़े भाई आ रहे हैं ।

३ उन्हें लेने स्टेशन जा रहा हूं ।

४ वे कहां से आ रहे हैं ?

153

५ कानपुर से, वहां वे व्यापार करते हैं ।

६ ऐसा, वे क्या व्यापार करते हैं ?

७ कानपुर में उनकी कपड़े की दुकान है ।

८ वे सूती, ऊनी, रेशमी – सभी तरह के कपड़े का काम करते हैं ।

९ क्या वे अकेले ही आ रहे हैं ?

१० जी नहीं, उनके साथ उनका परिवार भी है – उनकी पत्नी, उनके दो बच्चे और उनका नौकर ।

११ अच्छा, तब तो आपको जल्दी जाना चाहिए ।

१२ गाड़ी का वक्त हो रहा है ।

१३ जी हां, अब मुझे आज्ञा दीजिए ।  नमस्ते ।

| | |
|---|---|
| छोटा | आदमी |
| बहिन | औरत |
| मां-बाप, माता-पिता | लड़का |
| अम्मां, मां, माता | लड़की |
| पिता, बाप | पति |

154

# LESSON XII

## Conversation -- Buying Books

### CLERK

kahiyee, mãĩ aap kee liyee    Hello.   What can I do for
    kyaa kar saktaa hũũ?         you?

### JOHN

    hindii                 Hindi

    kitaab                 book

mãĩ kuch hindii kii           I want to buy some Hindi
    kitaabẽẽ leenaa caahtaa       books.
    hũũ.

hindi kii kitaabẽẽ kidhar     Where are the Hindi books?
    hãĩ?

### CLERK

    idhar                 this direction

aap meeree saath idhar        Come this way with me.
    aaiyee.

yee rahĩĩ hindii kii          Here are the Hindi books.
    kitaabẽẽ.

aap koo kaisii kitaabẽẽ       What kind of books do you
    caahiyee.                    need?

### JOHN

    jin                 which

    aasaanii            ease

    siikhnaa            to learn

mãĩ aisii kitaabẽẽ caahtaa I want to buy books from
    hũũ jin see mãĩ aasaanii    which I can learn Hindi
    see hindii siikh sakũũ.    easily.

### CLERK

aap kitnii hindii jaantee  How much Hindi do you know?
    hãĩ?

155

JOHN

zaadaa, zyaadaa       much, more

mãĩ zaadaa hindi nahĩĩ    I don't know much Hindi.
jaantaa.

bool leenaa        to be able to speak

kuch kuch bool leetaa    I can speak it a little.
hũũ.

CLERK

paRh leenaa        to be able to read

kyaa aap hindii paRh    Can you read Hindi?
leetee hãĩ?

JOHN

jii hãã, mãĩ paRh too   Yes, I can read it easily.
aasaanii see leetaa
hũũ.

samajhnaa         to understand

kaThinaaii         difficulty

leekin, samajhnee mẽẽ kuch But I have some difficulty
kaThinaaii hootii hai.  understanding it.

CLERK

samaacaar         news

samaacaar patr      newspaper

kyaa aap samaacaar patr Can you read the newspapers?
paRh leetee hãĩ?

JOHN

muškil           difficulty, difficult

zaruur           certainly

hãã, paRh leetaa hũũ,   Yes, I can read it but I
samajhnee mẽẽ zaruur   certainly have some diffi-
kuch kuch muškil hootii culty in following it.
hai.

CLERK

| rahnaa | to be |

acchaa, deekhiyee, yee kitaab aap kee liyee kaisii raheegii?
All right, please see how this book will be for you?

JOHN

| kaThin | difficult |

yee too kaThin hai.
This is difficult.

| saral | easy, simple |

is see kuch saral kitaab diijiyee.
Please give me a simpler book than this one.

CLERK

yee deekhiyee, yee kaisii raheegii?
Look at this.  How will this be?

JOHN

hãã, yee Thiik hai.
Yes, this is all right.

CLERK

| darjaa | class, grade |

yee tiisree darjee kii kitaab hai.
This is a third grade book.

JOHN

| cauthaa | fourth |

tab mujhee duusree, tiisree aur cauthee darjee kii kitaabẽẽ dee diijiyee.
Then give me the second, third and fourth grade books.

CLERK

| šabd | word |

| šabd kooš | dictionary |

kyaa aap koo eek šabd kooš bhii caahiyee?
Do you need a dictionary too?

157

JOHN

matlab                          meaning

šabd kooš, šabd kooš        "šabd kooš," what does
  kaa matlab kyaa hai?         "šabd kooš" mean?

CLERK

aŋgreezii                       English

Dikšnarii                       dictionary

aŋgreezii mẽẽ šabd-kooš     "šabd-kooš" means dictionary
  kaa matlab hai--Dikšnarii.   in English.

JOHN

acchaa, jii hãã, caahiyee.  Oh, yes, I want one.

jis                             which

kyaa aap kee paas kooii     Do you have a dictionary
  aisaa šabd-kooš hai,         which has the meanings of
  jis mẽẽ hindii šabdõõ       Hindi words in English?
  kaa matlab aŋgreezii
  mẽẽ hoo.

CLERK

jii hãã, yee liijiyee.      Yes, here it is.

JOHN

huaa                            became

Thiik hai, in sab kaa       All right.  How much are all
  daam kitnaa huaa?            these?

CLERK

caudaa rupaee.              Fourteen rupees.

JOHN

bahut acchaa, yee liijiyee  Very well, here are
  caudaa rupaee.               fourteen rupees.

CLERK

dhanyawaad, namastee        Thanks, goodbye.


158

# GRAMMAR

## 1. New Nouns

| Masc. II | | Fem. I | |
|---|---|---|---|
| samaacaar | news | hindii (no pl.) | Hindi |
| samaacaar patr | newspaper | aasaanii (no pl.) | ease |
| šabd | word | kaThinaaii | difficulty |
| šabdkooš | dictionary | aŋgreezii (no pl.) | English |
| matlab | meaning | Dikšnarii | dictionary |

| Fem. II | |
|---|---|
| kitaab | book |

## 2. New Verbs

| | | | |
|---|---|---|---|
| siikhnaa | to learn | paRhnaa | to read, study |
| boolnaa | to speak | samajhnaa | to understand |

### 2.1. New Compound Verbs

#### Type I

| | |
|---|---|
| bool leenaa | to be able to speak |
| paRh leenaa | to be able to read |

## 3. New Adjectives in -aa

| | |
|---|---|
| cauthaa | fourth |

## 4. Verb rahnaa

The verb rahnaa besides having the meanings "to live, stay, remain," can also be used as an alternative for hoonaa, "to be," in certain contexts.

yee kaisii raheegii?     How will this be?

yee aap kee liyee kaisii How will this be for you?
raheegii?

The form rahaa of this verb with the inflection

159

<u>rahaa</u>, <u>rahee</u>, <u>rahii</u>, <u>rahĩĩ</u> may be used in a pointing
out situation as an equivalent of "here are," "there
are" etc.

| | |
|---|---|
| yee rahee kapRee. | Here are the clothes. |
| yee rahĩĩ hindii kii kitaabẽ̃. | Here are the Hindi books. |
| woo rahaa ajmeerii hooTal. | There's the Ajmer hotel. |

Note the contrast in the following sentences:

| | |
|---|---|
| woo rahaa ajmeerii hooTal. | There's the Ajmer Hotel. |
| ajmeerii hooTal wahãã hai. | The Ajmer Hotel is over there. |

## 5. Emphatic Forms

The emphatic forms of <u>yee</u> "this," <u>woo</u> "that," are
respectively <u>yahii</u> and <u>wahii</u>.

## 6. Relative Pronoun

The relative pronoun <u>joo</u>, "who," "which," "that"
in Hindi has the following forms:

| | Sg. | Pl. |
|---|---|---|
| Nom. | joo | joo |
| Dat. | { jisee | jinhẽ̃ |
| | jis koo | jin koo |
| Obl. | jis | jin |

The relative pronoun in Hindi may be used in the
same way as the English relative pronoun, i.e., referring back to some object already mentioned. It
takes the case form required by the construction in
which it occurs.

| | |
|---|---|
| basẽ̃, joo aagree jaatii hãĩ, pããc nambar kee pleeTfaarm see chuuTtii hãĩ. | The buses, which go to Agra, leave from platform number five. |

160

| | |
|---|---|
| wee kamiizẽẽ, jin kaa daam pããc rupaee hai, yahĩĩ miltii hãĩ. | The shirts which cost five rupees are available here. |
| (woo) kitaab, joo mãĩ paRh rahaa hũũ, bahut acchii hai. | The book I'm reading is very good. |
| yee wahii laRkaa hai, jisee buxaar kii dawaa caahiyee. | This is the boy who needs medicine for a fever. |
| yee wahii aspataal hai, jis mẽẽ DaakTar šarmaa kaam kartee hãĩ. | This is the hospital in which Dr. Sharma works. |
| yee wahii laRkaa hai, jis kaa ghar ašook nagar mẽẽ hai. | This is the boy whose house is in Ashok Nagar. |
| kyaa yee wahii laRkee hãĩ jinhẽẽ hindii paRhnaa caahiyee. | Are these the boys who should study Hindi? |
| mãĩ aisii kitaabẽẽ caahtaa hũũ, jin see hindii siikh sakũũ. | I want books from which I can learn Hindi. |

Note that in the above sentences the Hindi equivalent of "this is the boy who..." is literally "this is that boy who..." using the emphatic form <u>wahii</u> for "that," <u>yee wahii laRkaa hai, joo</u>....

In Hindi, many sentences with the relative pronoun may occur in two different word orders as in the third sentence above. One word order is similar to the English, literally "the book that I'm reading...," <u>kitaab joo mãĩ paRh rahaa hũũ....</u>" The other word order is different from any possible English word order, literally "which book I'm reading, (that) is very good," <u>joo kitaab mãĩ paRh rahaa hũũ, (woo) bahut acchii hai.</u> Compare the following sentences carefully with the preceding ones.

| | |
|---|---|
| joo basẽẽ aagree jaatii hãĩ, wee pããc nambar kee pleeTfaarm see chuuTtii hãĩ. | The buses, which go to Agra, leave from platform No.5. |
| jin kamiizõõ kaa daam pããc rupaee hai, wee yahĩĩ miltii hãĩ. | The shirts, which cost five rupees, are available here. |

| | |
|---|---|
| jis laRkee koo buxaar kii dawaa caahiyee, woo yahii hai. | This is the boy, who needs medicine for a fever. |
| jis aspataal mẽẽ DaakTar šarmaa kaam kartee hãĩ, woo yahii hai. | This is the hospital, in which Dr. Sharma works. |
| jis laRkee kaa ghar ašook nagar mẽẽ hai, woo yahii hai. | This is the boy, whose house is in Ashok Nagar. |
| jin laRkõõ koo hindii paRhnaa caahiyee, wee yahii hãĩ? | Are these the boys, who should study Hindi? |
| jin kitaabõõ see mãĩ hindii siikh sakũũ, wee mãĩ caahtaa hũũ. | I want books from which I can learn Hindi. |

Note that in this type of sentence, where English has "this is the boy who needs medicine," Hindi has literally "which boy needs medicine, this is that one."

## 7. Repetition

Certain items in Hindi may be repeated for emphasis. This will apply to the word kuch, kooii and frequently to adjectives.

| | |
|---|---|
| mãĩ kuch kuch bool leetaa hũũ. | I can speak it a little. |
| kooii kooii santaraa acchaa hootaa hai. | Only some oranges are good. |
| mujhee baRee baRee santaree caahiyee, chooTee chooTee nahĩĩ. | I want some big oranges, not small ones. |

The English equivalent of the above sentences will carry emphatic stress on the words "a little," "some," "big," and "small."

## 8. Postposition see

The postposition see is used with some nouns to form an adverbial expression which then may be the equivalent of an English adverbial expression such as "with difficulty," "with ease" or the equivalent of an English adverb such as "easily."

162

| | |
|---|---|
| kaThinaaii see | with difficulty |
| aasaanii see | with ease, easily |

## 9. Postposition mẽẽ

In this lesson the postposition mẽẽ occurs with an infinitive form of the verb. This is the equivalent of English "in" plus the "-ing" form of the verb.

| | |
|---|---|
| leekin samajhnee mẽẽ kuch kaThinaaii hootii hai. | But there is some difficulty in understanding. |
| mujhee wahãã tak pahũcnee mẽẽ deer hoogii. | I'll take a long time in reaching there (i.e., to reach there). |

## 10. Comparative

With the exception of a very few forms, Hindi does not have any special form for the comparative of an adjective or an adverb. The Hindi equivalent of an English comparative form followed by "than" is usually expressed by the ordinary form of the adjective along with the postposition see equating with the English postposition "than." The Hindi phrase with see will precede the adjective.

| | |
|---|---|
| woo laRkaa acchaa hai. | That boy is good. |
| woo laRkaa mujh see acchaa hai. | That boy is better than I am. |
| raam aašaa see baRaa hai. | Ram is older than Asha. |
| yee bazaar us bazaar see chooTaa hai. | This bazaar is smaller than that bazaar. |
| is see kuch saral kitaab diijiyee. | Please give me a simpler book than this one. |

The word zaadaa can be used as a positive form like bahut, both meaning "much." This usage is common in negative sentences.

| | |
|---|---|
| mãĩ bahut hindii nahĩĩ jaantaa. | I don't know much Hindi. |
| mãĩ zaadaa hindii nahĩĩ jaantaa. | |

The word zaadaa can be used as a comparative,

meaning "more" or "too much." It is frequently used
this way, either by itself or with a following adjective, in situations where the thing that something
is being compared with is not stated.

yee zaadaa hai.                     This is too much.

yee paark zaadaa baRaa          { This park is bigger
  hai.                              (bigger than I thought).

                                    This park is too big
                                      (bigger than it should
                                      be).

## 11. Writing System

## 11.1. Consonant Combinations

| | | | |
|---|---|---|---|
| kT | क्ट | DaakTar | डाक्टर |
| rm | र्म | šarmaa | शर्मा |
| ddh | द्ध | prasiddh | प्रसिद्ध |
| sp | स्प | aspataal | अस्पताल |
| šT | ष्ट | kašT | कष्ट |
| rš | र्ष | waršgããTh | वर्षगांठ |
| pr | प्र | praarthnaa | प्रार्थना |
| rth | र्थ | praarthnaa | प्रार्थना |
| šy | श्य | awašy | अवश्य |
| zy | ज्य | zyaadaa | ज़्यादा |
| šk | श्क | muškil | मुश्किल |
| bd | ब्द | šabd | शब्द |
| gr | ग्र | aŋgreezii | अंग्रेज़ी |
| kš | क्श | Dikšnarii | डिक्शनरी |

## 11.2. Irregular Spellings

zaadaa, zyaadaa          ज़्यादा

## 11.3. New Symbol

In some items Hindi uses the symbol ੑ underneath

164

a consonant symbol to indicate <u>ri</u>.  So far you have
met only the word

     kripaa         कृपा

## EXERCISES

A.  Substitute in the sentences below the Hindi equivalent of the English given:

1.  mãĩ _____ nahĩĩ jaantaa.

| | |
|---|---|
| Hindi | that man |
| English | that woman |
| much Hindi | those women |
| much English | these men |
| him | your son |
| his friend | his parents |
| this man | your friends |
| this woman | your friend, Ram Lal |
| these women | his elder brother |
| those men | his sister |

2.  _____ mujhee kuch muškil hoogii.

    in reading Hindi

    in writing Hindi

    in speaking Hindi

    in understanding Hindi

    in reading a Hindi book

    in understanding a Hindi book

    in reading a Hindi newspaper

    in reading an English book

    in reading an English newspaper

    in writing a letter in English

in writing a letter in Hindi

in understanding a Hindi newspaper

in reading a third grade book

in reading a fourth grade Hindi book

in understanding a fourth grade Hindi book

3. kyaa aap kee paas _____ kitaabɛ̃ɛ̃ bhii hɛ̃ɛ̃?

simpler than these                smaller than this

better than this                  bigger than that

easier than these                 more new than these

more difficult than these

4. kyaa aap _____ paRh leetee hɛ̃ɛ̃.

Hindi                             these books

English                           these Hindi books

Hindi books                       these English books

Hindi newspapers                  these Hindi newspapers

English books                     these English newspapers

English newspapers

5. woo _____ kii koošiš kareegaa.

to learn Hindi                    to bring his wife with
                                    him
to read Hindi
                                  to be (reach) there at
to buy some Hindi books             10 a.m.

to go to a bookstore              to work in the hotel

to bring his wife                 to buy a dictionary

                                  to live in this house.

B. Substitute orally in the sentences below the Hindi
equivalent of the English given, making changes, if
necessary:

1. _____ aap kee liyee kaisaa raheegaa.

166

| this | this hotel |
|---|---|
| this book | these socks |
| this newspaper | these shirts |
| this dictionary | these handkerchiefs |
| this room | these |

C. Change the following sentences into negative sentences using the correct form of the negative.

1. dawaaxaanee see dawaa laaiyee.

2. mujhee zukaam aur buxaar kii dawaa diijiyee.

3. kyaa aap aašaa kii waršgããTh mẽẽ aaẽẽgee.

4. mãĩ is dukaan see kapRee xariidũũgaa.

5. kyaa woo aagree kee liyee eek TikaT lee?

6. aap koo aaj apnee mitr see milnaa caahiyee.

7. meeraa mitr meeree liyee paark mẽẽ Thahreegaa.

8. meeree bhaaii kaanpuur mẽẽ wyaapaar karẽẽgee.

9. aap koo isTeešan jaanaa caahiyee.

10. aap koo hindii kaa samaacaar patr paRhnaa caahiyee.

11. kyaa raam kaa mitr is hooTal mẽẽ Thahree?

12. woo apnee saath apnii patnii koo laaeegaa.

13. kyaa yee aadmii is ghar mẽẽ rahee?

14. kyaa mãĩ neehruu paark mẽẽ ghuumũũ?

15. kyaa gaaRii pããc bajee chuuTeegii?

16. kyaa mãĩ us see milũũ?

17. woo kal aašaa kii waršgããTh mẽẽ aaeegii.

18. usee eek šabd kooš xariidnaa caahiyee.

19. kyaa jaan kee maataa pitaa isTeešan jaaẽẽ?

20. "waršgããTh" šabd kaa matlab šabd kooš mẽẽ deekhoo.

21. aagraa bahut acchaa nagar hoonaa caahiyee.

22. yee aurat is aspataal see dawaa leegii.

23. yee kitaab aap kee liyee acchii raheegii.

24. yahãã baiThiyee.

25. kyaa DaakTar šarmaa is samai aspataal mẽẽ milẽẽgee?

D. Transform the following sentences according to the model given:

yee laRkaa bazaar jaanaa ..yee wahii laRkaa hai joo
   caahtaa hai.                 bazaar jaanaa caahtaa hai.

1. yee laRkaa dawaa leenaa caahtaa hai.

2. yee laRkii hooTal mẽẽ kaam karnaa caahtii hai.

3. yee laRkaa phal xariidnaa caahtaa hai.

4. yee laRkii hindii siikhnaa caahtii hai.

5. yee laRkee hindii kaa samaacaar patr paRhnaa caahtee hãĩ.

6. kyaa yee laRkiyãã paark mẽẽ ghuumnaa caahtii hãĩ?

7. yee laRkaa aašaa kaa baRaa bhaaii hai.

8. yee laRkii ašook nagar mẽẽ rahtii hai.

9. yee laRkiyãã kal kaanpuur jaaẽẽgii.

10. yee laRkee hooTal mẽẽ Thahrẽẽgee.

11. kyaa yee naukar ghar kaa sab kaam kareegaa.

12. yee bas aagree jaaeegii.

13. kyaa yee gaaRii aaTh bajee chuuTtii hai?

14. yee jaghee ghuumnee kee liyee bahut acchii hai.

15. yee kitaab bahut saral hai.

E. Translate orally:

1. What does this word mean?

168

2. What does this word mean in English?

3. What does this Hindi word mean in English?

4. This is a dictionary.

5. This is a Hindi dictionary.

6. This dictionary has the meanings of Hindi words in English.

7. I need a dictionary.

8. Do I need a dictionary?

9. I don't need a dictionary.

10. Give me some Hindi books.

11. Give me some third grade Hindi books.

12. Can I have (take) some third grade Hindi books?

13. I have some difficulty in understanding Hindi.

14. I have some difficulty in writing Hindi.

15. He has some difficulty in understanding Hindi newspapers.

16. These boys have some difficulty in speaking Hindi.

17. Do you read newspapers?

18. Can you read Hindi newspapers?

19. He should read Hindi newspapers.

20. He can read Hindi books and newspapers.

F. Read the following:

## Text of Lesson X

१ क्या यहां पड़ोस में कोई अच्छा डाक्टर है ।

२ हां, लेकिन बात क्या है ?

३ क्या आपके यहां कोई बीमार है ?

४ जी हां, मेरी छोटी लड़की को कल रात से जुकाम हो गया है ।

५ और इसी कारण से उसे कुछ बुखार भी है ।

169

६ अरे, यह तो बड़े अफ़सोस की बात है ।

७ देखिए यहां से कुछ ही दूर पर डाक्टर शर्मा का दवाख़ाना है ।

८ आप उसे वहां ले जाएं ।

९ क्या डाक्टर शर्मा एक अच्छे डाक्टर हैं ?

१० जी हां, बहुत थोग्य, चतुर और प्रसिद्ध ।

११ क्या उनका दवाख़ाना इस समय खुला होगा ?

१२ जी हां, उनका दवाख़ाना सुबह सात बजे से दोपहर बारह बजे
   तक और शाम पांच बजे से रात बारह बजे तक खुला रहता है ।

१३ इस समय वे दवाख़ाने में ही होंगे ।

१४ अच्छा, तब मैं चलूं नहीं तो देर हो जाएगी ।

अस्पताल

## Text of Lesson XI

१ नमस्ते, आइए, अन्दर आइए, बैठिए, कहिए, क्या हालचाल है ?

२ सब आपकी कृपा है ।

३ मैं आपको एक कष्ट देना चाहता हूं ।

४ परसों तीसरे पहर मेरी छोटी लड़की आशा की वर्षगांठ है ।

५ और उसके बाद शाम को एक दावत है ।

६ मेरी प्रार्थना है कि आप उसमें आएं ।

७ और साथ ही अपनी पत्नी और बच्चों के भी लाएं ।

८ मैं तो अवश्य आ जाऊंगा ।

९ पर अपनी पत्नी के बारे में नहीं जानता ।

१० क्यों ?  क्या वे उस दिन खाली नहीं हैं ?

११ जी नहीं, यह बात नहीं है ।

१२ मेरी पत्नी की तबियत आजकल खराब है ।

१३ इसलिए मैं नहीं कह सकता कि वे आ सकेंगी या नहीं ।

१४ फिर भी मैं उन्हें लाने की कोशिश करूंगा ।

१५ क्या आप मेरे घर का पता जानते हैं ?

170

१६ जी नहीं ।

१७ मेरा घर अशोक नगर में है – मकान नंबर सोलह ।

१८ यह मकान सड़क के किनारे पर है ।

१९ ठीक है, मैं कितने बजे आऊं ?

२० दावत शाम सात बजे है ।

२१ आप उस समय तक अवश्य आ जाएं ।

२२ ठीक है, मैं पहुंच जाऊंगा ।

२३ बड़ी कृपा होगी ।

| | |
|---|---|
| आज | कल |
| परसों | नरसों |

## Text of Lesson XII

१ कहिए, मैं आपके लिए क्या कर सकता हूं ?

२ मैं कुछ हिन्दी की किताबें लेना चाहता हूं ।

३ हिन्दी की किताबें किधर हैं ?

४ आप मेरे साथ इधर आइए ।

५ ये रहीं हिन्दी की किताबें ।

६ आपको कैसी किताबें चाहिए ?

७ मैं ऐसी किताबें चाहता हूं जिनसे मैं आसानी से हिन्दी सीख सकूं ।

८ आप कितनी हिन्दी जानते हैं ?

९ मैं ज्यादा हिन्दी नहीं जानता ।

१० कुछ कुछ बोल लेता हूं ।

११ क्या आप हिन्दी पढ़ लेते हैं ?

१२ जी हां, मैं हिन्दी पढ़ तो आसानी से लेता हूं ।

१३ लेकिन समझने में कुछ कठिनाई होती है ।

१४ क्या आप समाचार पत्र पढ़ लेते हैं ?

१५ हां, पढ़ लेता हूं, समझने में जरूर कुछ कुछ मुश्किल होती है ।

१६ अच्छा, देखिए, यह किताब आपके लिए कैसी रहेगी ?

171

१७ यह तो कठिन है ।

१८ यह देखिए, यह कैसी रहेगी ?

१९ हां, यह ठीक है ।

२० यह तीसरे दर्जे की किताब है ।

२१ तब मुझे दूसरे, तीसरे और चौथे दर्जे की किताबें दे दीजिए ।

२२ क्या आपको एक शब्द कोश भी चाहिए ?

२३ शब्द कोश ? शब्द कोश का मतलब क्या है ?

२४ अंग्रेज़ी में शब्द कोश का मतलब है डिक्शनरी ।

२५ अच्छा, जी हां, चाहिए ।

२६ क्या आपके पास कोई ऐसा शब्द कोश है जिसमें हिन्दी शब्दों
का मतलब अंग्रेज़ी में हो ।

२७ जी हां, यह लीजिए ।

२८ ठीक है, इन सबका दाम कितना हुआ ?

२९ चौदह रुपए ।

३० बहुत अच्छा, ये लीजिए चौदह रुपए ।

३१ धन्यवाद, नमस्ते ।

G.  Read the following:

I.      १ कल तीसरे पहर मेरे मित्र राम लाल की छोटी लड़की आशा
        की वर्षगांठ है ।

        २ यह उसकी चौथी वर्षगांठ है ।

        ३ इसलिए कल मैं राम लाल जी के घर जाऊंगा ।

        ४ मेरे साथ मेरी पत्नी और मेरे बच्चे भी जाएंगे ।

        ५ उनके यहां वर्षगांठ के बाद एक दावत भी है ।

        ६ यह दावत शाम सात बजे है ।

        ७ इसलिए हमें वहां शाम सात बजे तक पहुंच जाना चाहिए ।

II.     १ मेरा मित्र जान हिन्दी जानता है ।

        २ वह हिन्दी आसानी से पढ़ लेता है ।

172

३ और उसे हिन्दी की किताबें और समाचार पत्र पढ़ने में
कोई कठिनाई नहीं होती ।

४ वह हिन्दी समझ भी लेता है ।

५ हिन्दी समझने में उसे ज्यादा मुश्किल नहीं होती ।

६ लेकिन उसे हिन्दी लिखने में अभी बहुत कठिनाई होती है ।

७ उसे चाहिए कि वह जल्दी हिन्दी लिखना सीखे ।

## REVIEW III

A.  Substitute orally in the sentences below the Hindi
equivalent of the English given.

1.  kyaa aap _____ aagree lee jaanaa caahtee hãĩ?

this man                    your sons and daughters

this woman                  my servant

your children               your younger brother

my children                 your servant

your wife                   your elder brother's family

your family                 her friends

his servant                 these clothes

your books                  this medicine

your father                 your elder sister

his parents                 his friends

her children                these men

these children              these women

2.  yee dukaan _____ khulii rahtii hai.

from 7 a.m. to 9 p.m.   from 2 p.m. to 10 p.m.

from 9 a.m. to 5 p.m.   from 5 p.m. to 1 a.m.

from 8 a.m. to 6 p.m.   from 3 p.m. to 12 midnight

from 10 a.m. to 7 p.m.  from 4 p.m. to 11 p.m.

173

from 8 a.m. to 8 p.m.

3.  usee _____ koošiš karnaa caahiyee.

        to go to the bazaar

        to bring the medicine

        to read this book

        to speak in English

        to learn Hindi

        to buy a Hindi dictionary

        to meet his parents

        to see a room in the hotel

        to bring the medicine from the hospital

        to bring the medicine from the doctor's office

        to know about this city

        to live in this house

        to be there by 7 p.m.

        to tell about this town

        to work in this store

        to write a book

        to go by bus

        to live in a new house

        to live in this city

        to buy a Hindi newspaper

4.  woo _____ nahĩĩ jaantaa.

| my house | your friend |
|---|---|
| my address | my friend, John |
| my children | this woman |
| your father | my sister |

her parents

this man

this place

this doctor

this boy

these women

Ram's store

Nehru Park

our house

these men

the time of the train

the time of the train for
   Agra

this hotel's address

my brother's store

English

5. aagree kee liyee gaaRii _____ chuuTtii hai.

at 8 a.m.          at 4 p.m.          at 5 p.m.

at 10 p.m.         at 8 p.m.          at 10 a.m.

at 3 p.m.          at 9 a.m.          at 7 p.m.

at 12 noon         at 1 p.m.          at 7 a.m.

6. _____ kii tabiyat kal raat see acchii nahĩĩ
                                                   hai.

my wife

his sister

their son

this woman

this boy

that man

my elder brother

his friend's wife

her husband

his mother

our father

that boy

this girl

that woman

my servant's wife

my friend's son

our father's friend

my younger sister

John's younger brother

this man

7. kyaa jaan koo _____ kuch muškil hoogii?

      in going to Kanpur

      in working in the store

175

in working in the clothing store

in reaching there by 9 a.m.

in buying these medicines

in living in this city

in telling your address

in meeting the doctor

in learning Hindi

in learning to write Hindi

in reading Hindi

in understanding English

in speaking these words

8.  mãĩ nahĩĩ jaantaa _____.

whether he will come

whether she is sick

whether he knows Hindi

whether he likes this city

whether he lives in this house

whether he has a clothing store

whether he has an elder brother

whether this doctor is a good one

whether his house is on the street

whether he wants to buy a dictionary

whether the hospital will be open at this
    time.

whether his wife is coming today

whether he is going to the dinner tomorrow

whether he wants to live in this house

9. kyaa yee kitaabẽẽ ＿＿＿＿＿＿ hãĩ.

      easier than those books

      more difficult than those books

      simpler than those books

      bigger than those books

      smaller than those books

      newer than those books

10. meeree bhaaii ＿＿＿＿＿＿ kaa wyaapaar kartee hãĩ.

| books | clothes |
|---|---|
| medicines | silk cloth |
| cloth | woolen cloth |
| fruit | cotton cloth |

B. Substitute orally in the sentences below the Hindi equivalent of the English given, making changes, if necessary:

1. kyaa ＿＿＿＿＿＿ nayaa hai?

| this hotel | this park |
|---|---|
| this book | this cloth |
| these books | these clothes |
| this dictionary | this bus |
| these dictionaries | these buses |
| these medicines | these streets |
| your house | this news |
| these stores | this newspaper |
| this hospital | these newspapers |

2. raam kii praarthnaa hai ki ＿＿＿＿＿＿ us kee ghar
                                            aaũũ.

    I                she          this man

| | | |
|---|---|---|
| he | they | this woman |
| we | you (polite) | these women |
| you (familiar) | my wife and I | these men |

C. Transform the following sentences according to the model given:

mãĩ kaam kartaa hũũ.  ..... mujhee kaam karnaa
                                                caahiyee.

1. woo laRkaa hindii likhnaa siikhtaa hai.

2. gaaRii doo bajee chuuTtii hai.

3. mãĩ isii hooTal mẽẽ Thahrtii hũũ.

4. woo yahĩĩ baiThtaa hai.

5. mãĩ usee is nagar kee baaree mẽẽ bataataa hũũ.

6. woo aap kii baat samajhtaa hai.

7. meeree pitaa aspataal see dawaa laatee hãĩ.

8. woo yee kitaab paRhnee kii kooših kartaa hai.

9. woo is dukaan kee baaree mẽẽ jaantaa hai.

10. jaan apnee mitr see miltaa hai.

11. woo isii nagar mẽẽ rahtaa hai.

12. laRkii hindii kii kitaabẽẽ paRhtee hai.

D. Transform the following sentences according to the model given:

laRkaa hindii paRhtaa  ..... laRkee hindii paRhtee
  hai.                                                  hãĩ.

1. yee kamraa bahut acchaa nahĩĩ hai.

2. yee kitaab bahut muškil hai.

3. kyaa is samai dawaaxaanaa khulaa hoogaa.

4. makaan saRak kee kinaaree par hai.

5. laRkii hindii mẽẽ likhtii hai.

178

6. meerii bahin aagree mẽẽ rahtii hai.

7. yee khiRkii bahut chooTii hai.

8. yee dawaa buxaar kee liyee acchii hai.

9. kyaa yee laRkii hindii boolnaa jaantii hai.

10. aagree kii gaaRii kab chuuTtii hai?

11. yee šabd kooš aap kee liyee kaisaa raheegaa.

12. yee dukaan bahut baRii hai.

13. meeraa bhaaii ab kaanpuur mẽẽ wyaapaar kareegaa.

14. yee baccaa raam kaa hai.

15. yee santaraa bahut miiThaa hai.

E. Transform the following sentences into negative sentences according to the model given:

mãĩ bazaar jaataa hũũ. ..... mãĩ bazaar nahĩĩ jaataa.

1. aap koo daawat mẽẽ aanaa caahiyee.

2. woo apnee bhaaii see kuch rupaee leetaa hai.

3. is aspataal see dawaa liijiyee.

4. kyaa bas yahãã miltii hai?

5. is mẽẽ pããc rupaee lagẽẽgee.

6. meeraa bhaaii aagree mẽẽ wyaapaar karnaa caahtaa hai.

7. hindii paRhnee kii koošiš kiijiyee.

8. us kaa dawaaxaanaa šaam kee samai khulaa rahtaa hai.

9. kyaa wee pããc bajee aa rahee hãĩ?

10. kal uskii waršgããTh hai.

11. mujhee hindii boolnaa siikhnaa caahiyee.

12. ham wahãã saat bajee tak pahũcẽẽgee.

13. kyaa ham aap kee maataa pitaa see mil saktee hãĩ?

179

14. is samai un koo ghar mẽẽ hoonaa caahiyee.

15. mãĩ hooTal mẽẽ kaam kar saktaa hũũ.

F. Translate orally:

1. We must go now.

2. I want to ask a favor of you.

3. We want to ask a favor of him.

4. That will be very kind of you.

5. That will be very kind of him.

6. I would like you to come to the dinner.

7. We would like you and your family to come to the dinner.

8. He would like us to go to the dinner.

9. Do you know my house?

10. Do you know the address of my house?

11. Do you know where Ashok Nagar is?

12. Do you know where my house is?

13. There is a very good doctor in the neighborhood.

14. There is a very good doctor in Ashok Nagar.

15. Please tell me about the doctor.

16. Please tell me about this town.

17. What time does this hospital open?

18. What time does Dr. Sharma's office open?

19. I don't know when the hospital is open.

20. Tell me whether he wants to come or not.

21. Tell him that I don't want to come.

22. There is a dinner tonight at Ram's house.

23. There will be a dinner tomorrow night at my

friend's house.

24. Will there be a dinner at your house tomorrow night?

25. There should be a dinner after the birthday celebration there.


G. Conversation:

1. A's son is having a birthday celebration. A goes to his friend B's house and invites him formally to come to his place to participate in the celebration and in the dinner to take place thereafter. B. accepts the invitation. Further, A insists that B should bring his family as well with him, and B promises to do so.

2. A's wife is sick and therefore he wants to go to a doctor. He asks his neighbor B about a good doctor. B suggests Dr. Ram Lal and tells that he is a very competent, skillful and well known doctor. A asks when the doctor's office is open and then hurriedly leaves for the doctor's office.

3. A goes to a doctor's office to get some medicine for his wife who has a fever. When he gets there, he finds that he is late and the doctor isn't there. He asks the doctor's assistant B where he can find the doctor now. B tells him that the doctor will be available in the hospital at this time. Then A leaves for the hospital.

4. A meets B on the street. After an exchange of formal greetings, B asks A where he is going. A tells him that he is going to the station to get his parents. B asks about A's parents, where they live, their profession etc. A answers all these questions and tells B that his younger brother and sister are also coming with his parents. Then he takes leave of B and goes to the station.

5. A tells B that he wants to learn Hindi. B asks if he knows Hindi at all. A tells him that he can read Hindi but has some difficulty in understanding and speaking it. B asks A if he can read Hindi newspapers etc. A again tells that he reads them fairly well, but doesn't understand them so well. B suggests that A should buy a dictionary in which he can find the meanings of Hindi words in English and tells him the name of the bookstore where he can get one. A thanks B and leaves.

6. A enters a bookstore and asks for some Hindi books. The clerk shows him some Hindi books which A thinks are difficult for him. Finally, he gets the kind of books he needs and buys them. He further asks for a Hindi-English dictionary and buys that too.

H. Read the following:

I. १ मैं अपने मित्र के लिए कुछ संतरे लेना चाहता हूं ।

२ मेरा मित्र आजकल बीमार है ।

३ उसे जुकाम और बुखार हो गया है ।

४ इस समय वह अस्पताल में है ।

५ संतरे खरीदने के बाद मैं उससे मिलने के लिए अस्पताल जाऊंगा ।

६ यह अस्पताल अशोक नगर में है ।

७ अशोक नगर यहां से बहुत दूर है ।

८ इसलिए मैं बस से जाऊंगा ।

९ अशोक नगर का अस्पताल बहुत अच्छा अस्पताल है ।

१० इसी अस्पताल में डाक्टर राम लाल काम करते हैं ।

११ डाक्टर राम लाल बहुत अच्छे, योग्य और मशहूर डाक्टर हैं ।

१२ वे ही मेरे मित्र को दवा रहे हैं ।

१३ इसलिए मैं समझता हूं कि मेरा मित्र बहुत जल्दी अच्छा हो जाएगा ।

II. १ कल मेरे बड़े भाई कानपुर से आ रहे हैं ।

२ उनके साथ उनकी पत्नी और उनके बच्चे भी आ रहे हैं ।

३ उनके दो लड़कियां और एक लड़का हैं ।

४ वे सभी कल सुबह आठ बजे की गाड़ी से आएंगे ।

५ मैं और मेरी पत्नी उन्हें लेने के लिए स्टेशन जाना चाहते हैं ।

६ मैं कल सुबह स्टेशन ठीक समय से पहुंचना चाहता हूं ।

७ मैं नहीं चाहता कि मुझे देर हो जाय नहीं तो मेरे भाई और उनके परिवार को स्टेशन पर ही रुकना होगा ।

८ इसका कारण यह है कि वे मेरे घर का पता नहीं जानते ।

६ इसलिए मुझे कल आठ बजे तक स्टेशन अवश्य पहुंच जाना चाहिए ।

III. १ मैं रोज़ सुबह घूमने के लिए नेहरू पार्क जाता हूं ।

२ नेहरू पार्क एक बहुत बड़ा और प्रसिद्ध पार्क है ।

३ वहां मेरे बहुत से मित्र घूमने के लिए आते हैं ।

४ घूमने के लिए यह पार्क बहुत अच्छी जगह है ।

५ साथ ही यह पार्क मेरे घर से बहुत दूर भी नहीं है ।

६ यह एक मील से ज्यादा नहीं है ।

७ लेकिन आज मैं घूमने न जा सकूंगा ।

८ आज मुझे अपने एक मित्र से मिलने जाना है ।

९ जिनसे मुझे कुछ ज़रूरी काम है ।

१० इसलिए आज मैं उनसे मिलने जाऊंगा, घूमने नहीं ।

IV. १ मैं कानपुर में अजमेरी होटल में ठहरूंगा ।

२ यह होटल बहुत अच्छा होटल है ।

३ इसमें सिंगिल, डबल सभी तरह के कमरे हैं ।

४ और इन कमरों में सभी तरह की सुविधाएं हैं ।

५ साथ ही इस होटल में कमरों का किराया भी ज्यादा नहीं है ।

६ सिंगिल कमरे का किराया दस रुपए रोज़ और डबल कमरे
   का पन्द्रह रुपए रोज़ ।

७ यह होटल स्टेशन से बहुत दूर भी नहीं है ।

८ लगभग एक मील होगा ।

९ स्टेशन से होटल तक जाने के लिए बस भी मिलती है ।

१० इससे ठहरने के लिए यह होटल सबसे अच्छी जगह है ।

V. १ मैं परसों सुबह आगरे जाना चाहता हूं ।

२ लेकिन मैं नहीं जानता कि आगरे के लिए बस कितने बजे छूटती है ।

३ इसलिए मुझे आज ही बस स्टेशन जाना चाहिए ।

४ और बस छूटने के समय के बारे में जानने की कोशिश करना चाहिए ।

# LESSON XIII

## Conversation -- Visiting Someone

### JOHN

| | |
|---|---|
| श्री | Mr. |
| मोहन लाल | Mohan Lal |
| जी | particle of respect |
| क्या श्री मोहन लाल जी घर पर हैं ? | Is Mr. Mohan Lal in? |

### SERVANT

| | |
|---|---|
| दफ्तर | office |
| नहीं लौटे | has not come back |
| जी नहीं, वे अभी दफ्तर से नहीं लौटे । | He has not come back from the office yet. |

### JOHN

| | |
|---|---|
| लौटना | to return |
| वे कब तक लौटेंगे ? | When will he return? |

### SERVANT

| | |
|---|---|
| मैं नहीं जानता । | I don't know. |
| आम तौर पर | usually, ordinarily |
| साढ़े | plus one half |
| आसपास | vicinity |
| के आसपास | about, approximately |
| वापस | back |
| वापस आना | to come back, return |

184

आम तौर पर वे साढ़े पांच बजे Usually he comes back at
के आसपास वापस आते हैं ।   about 5:30.

क्या आप उनसे मिलना चाहते हैं ? Do you want to see him?

JOHN

हां, मुझे उनसे कुछ ज़रूरी काम   Yes, I have some important
है ।   work with him.

SERVANT

इंतज़ार   waiting

इंतज़ार करना   to wait for, to expect

तब क्या आप उनका इंतज़ार Will you wait for him then?
करेंगे ?

JOHN

जी नहीं, अभी तो चार ही No, it's only four o'clock
बजे हैं । right now.

डेढ़ one and a half

अभी तो उनके वापस आने में There is still an hour and
डेढ़ घंटे की देर है । a half before he comes
  back. (In his coming back
  there is a delay....)

SERVANT

पहले   before

जी हां, लेकिन वे कभी कभी Yes sir, but sometimes he
कुछ पहले भी आ जाते हैं । comes a little earlier
  too.

JOHN

कम   little, less

185

| कम से कम | at least |
|---|---|
| पड़ना | to fall, to have to, must |
| फिर भी मुझे कम से कम एक घंटे रुकना पड़ेगा । | Even then I'll have to wait for an hour at least. |
| इस समय मुझे जल्दी है, इसलिए मैं न रुक सकूंगा । | I'm in a hurry right now, so I won't be able to wait (for him). |

SERVANT

| फिर | again |
|---|---|
| तो क्या आप शाम को फिर उनसे मिलने आएंगे ? | Will you come again in the evening to see him? |

JOHN

| क्या वे शाम को घर पर ही रहेंगे ? | Will he be at home in the evening? |

SERVANT

| कहीं नहीं | nowhere |
|---|---|
| जी हां, वे शाम को कहीं नहीं जाते । | Yes sir, he doesn't go anywhere in the evening. |

JOHN

| तब मैं शाम को उनसे मिलने आऊंगा । | Then I'll come to see him in the evening. |
|---|---|
| बता देना | to tell |
| उन्हें बता देना कि मैं अशोक होटल में रह रहा हूं । | Tell him that I'm staying in the Ashok Hotel. |
| अगर | if |

186

| | |
|---|---|
| टेलीफोन | telephone |
| टेलीफोन करना | to call on the phone |
| अगर वे शाम को खाली न हों, | If he isn't free in the |
| तो मुझे टेलीफोन कर दें । | evening, he should phone me. |

## SERVANT

| | |
|---|---|
| कह देना | to tell |
| बहुत अच्छा, मैं कह दूंगा । | All right, I'll tell him. |

## NUMERALS

| | | |
|---|---|---|
| इक्कीस | (ikkis, ikkiis) | twenty-one |
| बाइस | (baais, baaiis) | twenty-two |
| तेइस | (teeis, teeiis) | twenty-three |
| चौबीस | (caubis, caubiis) | twenty-four |
| पच्चीस | (paccis, pacciis) | twenty-five |
| क्ब्बीस | (chabbis, chabbiis) | twenty-six |
| सत्ताइस | | twenty-seven |
| अट्ठाइस | | twenty-eight |
| उनतीस | (untis, untiis) | twenty-nine |
| तीस | | thirty |

## ADDITIONAL VOCABULARY

| | |
|---|---|
| सवा | plus one quarter |
| पौन | three quarters |
| पौने | less one quarter |
| ढाई | two and a half |
| श्रीमान | Mr. |
| श्रीमती | Mrs. |

187

कुमारी          Miss

GRAMMAR

1. New Nouns

   Masc. II                          Fem.I

   दफ़्तर          office        कुमारी      Miss

   इंतज़ार         waiting       श्रीमती     Mrs., Miss

   आसपास  (no pl.) vicinity

   टेलीफ़ोन        telephone

   श्रीमान्‌        Mr.

2. New Verbs

   लौटना                    to return

   पड़ना                    to fall, to have to, must

2.1. New Compound Verbs

   Type I

   बता देना        to tell

   कह देना         to tell

   Type II

   इंतज़ार करना      to wait

   टेलीफ़ोन करना     to call on the phone

3. New Postpositions

   के आसपास         about, approximately

4. Numerical Fractions

   The word साढ़े "plus one half" is used with numerals
three and above as follows:

         साढ़े तीन            three and a half

188

| साढ़े पांच | five and a half |
| साढ़े दस बजे | at 10:30 |

Note that "one and a half" and "two and a half"
are not expressed by using साढ़े but by special words:

| डेढ़ | one and a half |
| ढाई | two and a half |

The word सवा when used by itself means "one and a
quarter" and, when used with numbers above one, means
"plus one quarter."

| सवा बजे | at 1:15 |
| सवा तीन बजे | at 3:15 |
| सवा दो | two and a quarter |

The word पौन means "three quarters" and also
12:45 when used with बजा or बजे.

| पौन बजा है | It is 12:45 |
| पौन बजे हैं | |
| पौन रुपए | three quarters of a rupee |

The form पौने means "less one quarter" when used
with numbers above one:

| पौने दो | one and three quarters |
| पौने सात | six and three quarters |
| पौने पांच बजे | at 4:45 |

The forms साढ़े, सवा, पौन and पौने always precede the
numeral.

5. Terms of Address

The form श्री can be used with a person's family
name, male or female, married or unmarried, much as in
English one used Mr., Mrs., Miss. In this case the

189

respectful particle जी may also be used or may not be used. If the whole name is used, then जी must precede the last name. The form श्री may also be used with a person's first names, in which case जी must be used.

| | |
|---|---|
| श्री मोहन लाल जी | Mr. Mohan Lal |
| श्री शर्मा | Mr. Sharma |
| श्री शर्मा जी | |
| श्री मोहन लाल शर्मा | Mr. Mohan Lal Sharma |
| श्री मोहन लाल जी शर्मा | |

The forms श्रीमान् "Mr.," श्रीमती "Mrs.," and कुमारी "Miss" may be used as in English:

| | |
|---|---|
| श्रीमान् मोहन लाल जी | Mr. Mohan Lal |
| श्रीमती आशा शर्मा | Mrs. Asha Sharma |
| कुमारी आशा शर्मा | Miss Asha Sharma |

The forms श्रीमान्, श्रीमती and कुमारी may be used along with जी but without any name in which case they are roughly equivalent to "sir," "madam," and "miss":

| | |
|---|---|
| श्रीमान् जी | sir |
| श्रीमती जी | madam |
| कुमारी जी | miss |

Note that the form श्री followed immediately by जी is not used in Hindi.

6. पड़ना

The Hindi verb पड़ना literally "to fall," has the meaning "to have to, must" when used with a dependent infinitive. In this usage, the subject is in the dative case. The infinitive may be used in the masculine singular form in which case the form of the verb पड़ना will always be in third person masculine singular. Alternatively both the infinitive and the verb पड़ना may agree in number and gender with the direct object, if the direct object is in the nominative case.

मुझे बाज़ार जाना पड़ेगा ।    I'll have to go to the bazaar.

मुझे किताबें खरीदना पड़ेगा ।  
मुझे किताबें खरीदनी पड़ेंगी ।    } I'll have to buy books.

मुझे रोज़ बहुत से पत्र लिखना  
   पड़ता है ।  
मुझे रोज़ बहुत से पत्र लिखने  
   पड़ते हैं ।    } I have to write many letters every day.

7. इंतज़ार करना

The expression इंतज़ार करना means "to wait, to wait for, to expect" and the person waited for is expressed by the का form of the noun or pronoun.

मैं उनका इंतज़ार कर रहा हूं ।    I am waiting for him.

वह आज पांच बजे मेरा इंतज़ार    He will wait for (expect)  
करेगा ।    me today at 5 o'clock.

8. Infinitive

The infinitive may be used as an imperative. When used this way, the infinitive is less polite than the imperative in -iyee and more polite than the imperative in -oo. A common situation in which the -naa form would be proper would be the case of an older brother addressing a younger brother who is no longer a child and, therefore, could not properly be addressed by the -oo form and yet to use the -iyee form would be formal to the point of impoliteness. The -naa form is less

191

abrupt than the -oo form. Compare the avoidance of
abruptness in English by saying, "why don't you read
this letter" or "you ought to read this letter"
instead of "read this letter."  English is not strictly comparable to Hindi since these English expressions
might be used where Hindi would use -iyee.

| | |
|---|---|
| उन्हें बता देना । | Why don't you tell him. |
| यह पत्र पढ़ना । | You ought to read this letter. |
| पार्क में न घूमना । | You shouldn't walk in the park. |

## 9.  Conditional Sentence

A conditional sentence referring to an event in
the future, may have the verb of the "if" clause in
either the future or the optative and will have the
verb of the result clause in the future.  This is
comparable to the English construction with the verb
of the "if" clause in the present and the verb of the
result clause in the future.

| | |
|---|---|
| अगर वे आएंगे तो मैं उन्हें किताब दूंगा । | If he comes, I'll give him the book. |
| अगर वे आएं तो मैं उन्हें किताब दूंगा । | |
| अगर वह कमरा देखेगा तो वह उसे ले लेगा । | If he sees the room, he'll take it. |

Note that the sentence in the conversation doesn't
quite follow the pattern discussed above, since it has
an optative form of the verb in both clauses.

| | |
|---|---|
| अगर वे शाम को खाली न हों तो मुझे टेलीफोन कर दें । | If he isn't free in the evening, he might phone me. |

If the optative is used in the result clause, then
the optative must also be used in the "if" clause and
the sentence implies probability like English "may" or
"might."

192

अगर वे आएं तो मैं उन्हें      If he comes, I might give

किताब दूं ।     him a book.

## 10. Writing System

### 10.1. Consonant Combinations

Some symbols that do not lend themselves to the joint writing that has been discussed previously are written separately but with the symbol ، called हल्‌न्त underneath the first consonant indicating that there is no vowel between this consonant and the following one. The items, that you have met, which may be written this way are the following:

daftar   दफ़्तर      aTThaais   अट्ठाइस

### 10.2 New Consonant Combinations

| | | | |
|---|---|---|---|
| šr | श्र | šrii | श्री |
| tt | त्त | sattaais | सत्ताइस |
| kk | क्क | ikkiis | इक्कीस |
| bb | ब्ब | chabbiis | छब्बीस |

### 10.3 Irregular Spellings

šriimaan    श्रीमान्‌

This word is irregular since it is always written with हल्‌न्त at the end.

### 10.4 Postpositions

Postpositions, when used with pronouns, are normally written along with the pronoun as a single word.

इसका कमरा       his room

When used with nouns, the postposition is normally written as a separate word:

राम का कमरा     Ram's room

## EXERCISES

A. Substitute orally in the sentences below the Hindi equivalent of the English given:

1. क्या आप ----- इंतज़ार कर रहे हैं ?

| | |
|---|---|
| for him | for your family |
| for his brother | for their families |
| for my parents | for your mother |
| for your sister | for your friends |
| for my friend | for our children |
| for my friends | for your wife |
| for your elder brother | for Mr. Ram Lal |
| for your children | for Mr. Mohan Lal Sharma |
| for his family | |

2. वह ----- आ जाएगा ।

| | | |
|---|---|---|
| at 5:30 p.m. | at 5:45 p.m. | at 10:45 p.m. |
| at 8:15 p.m. | at 12.30 p.m. | at 10:15 a.m. |
| at 10:45 a.m. | at 8:45 a.m. | at 1:30 p.m. |
| at 7:30 p.m. | at 1:15 p.m. | at 4:30 p.m. |
| at 9:45 a.m. | at 6:15 p.m. | at 2:30 p.m. |
| at 7:30 a.m. | at 12:45 p.m. | at 1:30 a.m. |

3. मैं राम की दुकान से ----- किताबें खरीदना चाहता हूं ।

| | |
|---|---|
| some | twenty-three |

one dozen

twenty-seven

twenty-five

twenty-two

twenty-eight

twenty-six

twenty-one

thirty

twenty-four

at least thirty

twenty-nine

4. मुझे यहां ----- रुकना पड़ेगा ।

    for one hour

    for at least one hour

    for two and a half hours

    for about an hour and a half

    for about an hour and a quarter

    for three and three quarters of an hour

    for at least three and a quarter hours

    for five and a half hours

    for about four and three quarters of an hour

    for four and a quarter hours

    for at least two and a half hours

    for about two and three quarters of an hour

5. अगर वे शाम को ----- तो मुझे टेलीफोन कर दें ।

    is free

    isn't free

    goes out

    doesn't go out

    goes to the bazaar

    doesn't go to the bazaar

```
goes for a walk

doesn't go for a walk

goes to his store

doesn't go to his store

goes to the dinner

doesn't go to the dinner

goes to the dinner at Ram's house

doesn't go to the dinner at Ram's house
```

B.  Substitute orally in the sentences below the Hindi equivalent of the English given, making other changes, if necessary:

1. अगर ----- शाम को बाज़ार जाएं तो उसे टेलीफ़ोन कर दें ।

| | |
|---|---|
| they | Mr. Ram Lal |
| he | Mr. Ram Nath Sharma |
| you (polite) | Asha |
| she | your son |

C.  Transform the following sentences according to the model given:

वह ये किताबें खरीदेगा । ----- उसे ये किताबें खरीदना पड़ेगा ।

1. मैं अस्पताल से दवा लाऊंगा ।

2. तुम राम को दस रुपए दोगे ।

3. मैं कुछ कमीज़ें खरीदूंगा ।

4. वे ये फल अपने घर ले जाएंगे ।

5. वह ये पत्र लिखेगा ।

6. आप कुछ मोज़े खरीदेंगे ।

7. हम आपको सभी बातें बताएंगे ।

8. मैं बाज़ार से कुछ संतरे लाऊंगा ।

9. मैं यह किताब पढ़ूंगा ।

10. वह मुझे इस शहर के बारे में बताएगा ।

11. मैं हिन्दी पढ़ूंगा ।

12. तुम ये शब्द सीखोगे ।

13. मैं अपने मित्र के लिये दवा ले जाऊंगा ।

14. हम यह घर खरीदेंगे ।

15. मैं यह सिंगिल कमरा लूंगा ।

D. Transform the following sentences according to the model given:

क्या मैं बाज़ार जाऊं ? ----- मुझे बाज़ार जाना चाहिए ।

1. क्या वह पार्क में घूमने जाए ?

2. क्या मैं शाम को आपसे मिलने आऊं ?

3. क्या मैं इसी अस्पताल से दवा लूं ?

4. क्या हम उसके यहां काम करें ?

5. क्या मैं उसे ये बातें बता दूं ?

6. क्या मेरी लड़की हिन्दी लिखना सीखे ?

7. मैं ये दवाएं कहां से खरीदूं ?

8. क्या मैं आपके लिये बस स्टाप पर रुकूं ?

9. क्या वह बाज़ार से कुछ संतरे लाए ?

10. मैं कितने बजे आपका इंतज़ार करूं ?

11. क्या मैं यह किताबें पढ़ूं ?

12. क्या मैं आपको इस कमरे का किराया बताऊं ?

13. क्या वह उस नगर में रहे ?

14. क्या वे अपने मित्रों से मिलें ?

15. हम आपके यहां कब पहुंचें ?

E. Transform the following sentences according to the model given:

197

मैं राम की दुकान से दवा ----- दुकान, जिससे मैं दवा लेता हूं,
लेता हूं ।                               राम की है ।

1. वह मेरी दुकान से कपड़ा खरीदता है ।

2. मैं राम के लड़के से कल मिलूंगा ।

3. मेरी पत्नी उसी शहर में रहेगी ।

4. मेरा भाई इसी बाज़ार से फल खरीदता है ।

5. मैं राम के नौकर का इंतज़ार कर रहा हूं ।

6. मैं आजकल यही किताब पढ़ रहा हूं ।

7. राम का परिवार उसी सड़क के किनारे पर है ।

8. उसका मकान इसी सड़क के किनारे पर है ।

9. मैं राम के होटल में ठहरूंगा ।

10. वह उसी गाड़ी से आगरे जाएगी ।

F.  Translate orally:

1.  If I go there, I'll call you on the phone.

2.  If you go there, you should tell me.

3.  If you go there, you should tell me before.

4.  I'll wait for you there.

5.  I'll wait for you there at 5 p.m.

6.  He will wait there for you till 5 p.m.

7.  There is still an hour and a half before he comes back.

8.  There is still an hour and a half before he comes back from the office.

9.  There is still an hour and a quarter before he comes back from the hospital.

10. I'll have to come again.

11. I'll have to come again to see him.

12. I'll have to come again to see him in the evening.

198

13. Should I come again to see him in the evening?

14. I should come again to see him in the evening.

15. Tell him that he is staying in the Ashok Hotel.

16. Tell him that I am staying in the Ashok Hotel.

17. Tell him that I will stay in the Ashok Hotel.

18. Tell him that you will stay in the Ashok Hotel.

19. I'll have to wait for him for about an hour.

20. I'll have to wait for him for one hour at least.

21. He will have to wait for me for at least two hours.

22. Should I wait for him for about an hour?

23. Should I wait for him for one hour at least?

24. You should wait for me for about an hour and a half.

25. You should wait for him for an hour and a half at least.

## Conversation -- Two old friends meet

### SHANKAR DAYAL

| | |
|---|---|
| पहचाना | (you) recognized |
| नमस्ते, कहिए, मुझे पहचाना ? | Hello, did you recognize me? |

### RAM LAL

| | |
|---|---|
| शंकर दयाल | Shankar Dayal |
| अरे हां, तुम तो शंकर दयाल हो । | Oh yes, you are Shankar Dayal. |
| आए | (you) came |
| यहां कब आए ? | When did you come here? |
| से पहले, के पहले | before |
| कभी नहीं | never |
| देखा | (I) saw |
| इससे पहले तो तुम्हें यहां कभी नहीं देखा । | I haven't seen you here before. |

### SHANKAR DAYAL

| | |
|---|---|
| शहर | city |
| आया | (I) came |
| हां, मैं कल ही इस शहर में आया । | I came to this city yesterday. |
| मालूम | knowledge, awareness |
| था | was |
| लेकिन मुझे मालूम न था कि तुम भी इसी शहर में हो । | But I didn't know that you were also in this city. |

## RAM LAL

| | |
|---|---|
| मैं आजकल यहीं हूं । | I am here nowadays. |
| हाल | recent time |
| तबादला | transfer |
| हुआ है | has been |
| हाल ही में यहां मेरा तबादला हुआ है । | I have been transferred here recently. |
| कैसे | what for, how? |
| तुम यहां कैसे आए ? | How did you come here? |

## SHANKAR DAYAL

| | |
|---|---|
| कंपनी | company |
| सेल्स मैनेजर | sales manager |
| दौरा | tour |
| आया हूं | (I) have come |
| मैं आजकल एक कंपनी में सेल्स मैनेजर हूं और यहां दौरे पर आया हूं । | Nowadays, I am a sales manager in a company and I've come here on a tour. |

## RAM LAL

| | |
|---|---|
| इरादा | intention |
| कब तक रुकने का इरादा है ? | How long do you intend to stay? |

## SHANKAR DAYAL

| | |
|---|---|
| और | more, else |
| अभी चार पांच दिन और रहूंगा । | I'll be staying four or five days more. |

## RAM LAL

कहां रह रहे हो ?

Where are you staying?

## SHANKAR DAYAL

मार्ग

road, street

सुभाष मार्ग

Subhas Marg, Subhas Road

सुभाष मार्ग पर कानपुर होटल में ।

In the Kanpur Hotel on Subhas Marg.

## RAM LAL

तब एक दिन शाम हमारे यहां आओ न ?

Then come to our place some evening, won't you?

कल शाम खाली हो ?

Are you free tomorrow evening?

## SHANKAR DAYAL

पार्टी

party

कल शाम तो खाली नहीं हूं, एक पार्टी में जाना है ।

I'm not free tomorrow evening, I have to go to a party.

## RAM LAL

तब परसों ?

Then (how about) the day after tomorrow?

## SHANKAR DAYAL

हां, परसों ठीक रहेगा ।

Yes, the day after tomorrow will be fine.

## RAM LAL

तब परसों हमारे यहां आओ ।

Then come to our place the day after tomorrow.

| | |
|---|---|
| महात्मा गांधी मार्ग | Mahatma Gandhi Marg |
| कोठी | house |
| महात्मा गांधी मार्ग पर १८ नंबर की कोठी पर । | At house number 18 on Mahatma Gandhi Marg. |
| प्रतीक्षा | waiting |
| प्रतीक्षा करना | to wait for, to expect |
| मैं तुम्हारी प्रतीक्षा करूंगा । | I'll be expecting you. |

## SHANKAR DAYAL

| | |
|---|---|
| मैं साढ़े पांच बजे तक आ जाऊंगा । | I'll be there by 5:30. |

## GRAMMAR

1. New Nouns

   **Masc. I**

   | | | | |
   |---|---|---|---|
   | तबादला | transfer | | |
   | दौरा | tour | | |
   | इरादा | intention | | |

   **Fem. I**

   | | |
   |---|---|
   | कम्पनी | company |
   | पार्टी | party |
   | कोठी | house |

   **Masc. II**

   | | |
   |---|---|
   | शहर | city |
   | मालूम | awareness knowledge |
   | हाल | recent time |
   | सेल्स मैनेजर | sales manager |
   | मार्ग | road, street |

   **Fem. II**

   | | |
   |---|---|
   | प्रतीक्षा | waiting |

2. New Verbs

   | | |
   |---|---|
   | पहचानना | to recognize |

2.1  New Compound Verbs

Type II

प्रतीक्षा करना        to wait for, to expect

3.  New Postpositions

के पहले

से पहले        before

4.  Form of the Perfect

The perfect form of a Hindi verb may be formed by
adding the inflection -aa, -ee, -ii, -íí to the stem
of the verb.  The inflection is already known and rep-
resents masculine singular, masculine plural, feminine singular, and feminine plural respectively.

| Infinitive | देखना | ख़रीदना | सुनना |
|---|---|---|---|
| Verb Stem | देख | ख़रीद | सुन |
| Perfect -- Masc. Sg. | देखा | ख़रीदा | सुना |
| Masc. Pl. | देखे | ख़रीदे | सुने |
| Fem. Sg. | देखी | ख़रीदी | सुनी |
| Fem. Pl. | देखीं | ख़रीदीं | सुनीं |

If the stem of a verb is composed of two or more
syllables and ends in vowel -a- followed by a consonant, then this vowel is dropped in pronunciation
when the perfect endings are added.  This, however,
will not be indicated in the writing.

| Infinitive | समझना | samajhnaa |
|---|---|---|
| Verb Stem | समझ | samajh |
| Perfect -- Masc. Sg. | समझा | samjhaa |
| Masc. Pl. | समझे | samjhee |
| Fem. Sg. | समझी | samjhii |
| Fem. Pl. | समझीं | samjhíí |

If the stem ends in a vowel, then the masculine

singular ending is -yaa, always written या, the mascu-

204

line plural ending is -ee written ए or ये , the feminine singular and plural endings are -ii and -īī respectively, usually written ईं, ई but occasionally यी and यीं as well.

| | | |
|---|---|---|
| Infinitive | बताना | आना |
| Verb stem | बता | आ |
| Perfect -- Masc. Sg. | बताया | आया |
| Masc. Pl. | बताए (बताये) | आए (आये) |
| Fem. Sg. | बताई (बतायी) | आई (आयी) |
| Fem. Pl. | बताईं (बतायीं) | आईं (आयीं) |

Some verbs have an irregular stem used in the formation of the perfect form. The ones you have met so far are the following:

| | | | | | |
|---|---|---|---|---|---|
| Infinitive | लेना | देना | करना | होना | जाना |
| Perfect -- Masc. Sg. | लिया | दिया | किया | हुआ | गया |
| Masc. Pl. | लिए | दिए | किए | हुए | गए |
| Fem. Sg. | ली | दी | की | हुई | गई |
| Fem. Pl. | लीं | दीं | कीं | हुईं | गईं |

## 5. Perfect Tense

The perfect form of the verb is used by itself as a perfect tense. This tense usually equates with the English simple past tense. The negative is expressed by नहीं .

| | |
|---|---|
| वह बाज़ार गया । | He went to the bazaar. |
| वह यहां कब आया ? | When did he come here? |
| मैं होटल में रुकी । | I stayed in the hotel. |
| बस यहां से छूटी । | The bus left from here. |

205

वह बाज़ार नहीं गया ।　　He did not go to the bazaar.

6. Present Perfect Tense

The present perfect tense is formed by using the perfect form followed by the simple present of the verb होना "to be." This usually equates with the English present perfect ("has gone" etc.).

वह बाज़ार गया है ।　　He has gone to the bazaar.

मैं यहां दौरे पर आया हूं ।　I have come here on a tour.

वह ये किताबें लाई है ।　　She has brought these books.

The negative is expressed by नहीं and like the present imperfect, usually drops the simple present of the verb होना "to be." This means that the negative of the perfect tense and the negative of the present perfect tense have the same form.

वह बाज़ार नहीं गया ।　　$\begin{cases} \text{He didn't go to the bazaar.} \\ \text{He hasn't gone to the bazaar.} \end{cases}$

वह यहां नहीं आया ।　　$\begin{cases} \text{He didn't come here} \\ \text{He hasn't come here.} \end{cases}$

7. Simple Past of the Verb होना "to be "

The simple past of the verb होना "to be" has the following forms:

| | |
|---|---|
| Masc. Sg. | था |
| Masc. Pl. | थे |
| Fem. Sg. | थी |
| Fem. Pl. | थीं |

206

Just as the verb होना is the only verb in Hindi which has a simple present, so it is the only verb which has a simple past. The simple past of होना is used as a main verb usually equating with the English "was," "were."

| | |
|---|---|
| मुझे मालूम न था । | I didn't know (wasn't aware). |
| मैं उस समय बाज़ार में थी । | At that time, I was in the bazaar. |
| उसके भाई कल आगरे में थे । | His brothers were in Agra yesterday. |
| ये लड़कियां कल कहां थीं ? | Where were these girls yesterday? |

## 8. "To be to," "to be supposed to"

The Hindi equivalent of the English verb "to be supposed to," "to be to" is the infinitive of the verb dependent upon "to be to," "to be supposed to" along with the verb होना. The subject of the verb is in the dative and as with the verb पड़ना "must," "have to," the infinitive may be used in the masculine singular form under all conditions or it may alternatively agree with the direct object, if the direct object is in the nominative case.

The difference in meaning between the Hindi infinitive plus होना "to be supposed to" construction and the Hindi infinitive plus पड़ना "to have to," "must" construction is very close to that indicated by the translations. The infinitive plus होना construction implies that somebody expects you to do something which

207

you either might or might not do but normally would do.
The infinitive plus पड़ना construction implies greater
urgency or necessity involving pressure by some external
force, human or otherwise.

मुझे एक पार्टी में जाना है । I am (am supposed) to go to
a party.

मुझे यह किताब पढ़ना है । | I'm supposed to read this
मुझे यह किताब पढ़नी है । | book.

राम को कुछ पत्र लिखना है । | Ram is to write some
राम को कुछ पत्र लिखने हैं । | letters.

उसे पांच कमीज़ें ख़रीदना है । |
उसे पांच कमीज़ें ख़रीदनी हैं । | He is to buy five shirts.

Note that the चाहिए construction, when used with a
dependent infinitive equates with an English "should,"
"ought to." The infinitive plus चाहिए construction, the
infinitive plus होना construction and the infinitive
plus पड़ना construction are similar to each other in
that the subject of all the three constructions is in
the dative case and the infinitive may either be in
the masculine singular form or it may agree with the
direct object, if the direct object is in the nominative case.

मुझे यह किताब पढ़ना चाहिए । |
मुझे यह किताब पढ़नी चाहिए । | I should read this book.
मुझे यह किताब पढ़ना है । | I'm supposed to read this
मुझे यह किताब पढ़नी है । | book.

208

मुझे यह किताब पढ़ना पड़ेगा । ⎱ I'll have to read this
मुझे यह किताब पढ़नी पड़ेगी । ⎰ book.

9. मालूम

The word मालूम "knowledge," "awareness" may be used tith the subject in the dative case and with the verb होना "to be" as an alternative of the verb जानना "to know."

मुझे मालूम है कि कल उनके ⎫
यहां दावत है ।            ⎪ I know that there is a
मैं जानता हूं कि कल उनके ⎬    dinner at his place
यहां दावत है ।            ⎭    tomorrow.

10. इरादा

The form इरादा "intention" is used in a con-struction that is similar to the English "it is my intention to go..." with the "to go" expressed by the oblique form of the infinitive plus का . Note the word order of those sentences which state the person involved and those which don't state the person.

मेरा इरादा यह किताब      It is my intention to read
पढ़ने का है ।              this book (I intend to
                        read this book).

कब तक रुकने का इरादा है ? ⎫
आपका इरादा कब तक रुकने ⎬ How long do you intend
का है ?                  ⎭ to stay?

11.  "Four or five"

The Hindi equivalent of the English numeral expression of the type "one or two," "two or three" etc. doesn't use any word equivalent to the English "or."

चार पांच दिन          four or five days

दो तीन घंटे          two or three hours

12. और

The form और besides having the meaning "and" also means "more," "else."

अभी चार पांच दिन और      I'll stay for four or five
रुकूंगा ।              days more.

कुछ और चाहिए ?
और कुछ चाहिए ?    }   Do you need something else?

मुझे एक और चाहिए ।     I need one more.

13. प्रतीक्षा करना

The form प्रतीक्षा "waiting" is an equivalent of इंतज़ार and will occur in the same constructions as इंतज़ार करना:

मैं तुम्हारी प्रतीक्षा करूंगा ।
मैं तुम्हारा इंतज़ार करूंगा ।   } I'll wait for (expect) you.

वह राम की प्रतीक्षा कर
रहा है ।
वह राम का इंतज़ार कर
रहा है ।            He is waiting for Ram.

आज शाम छह बजे मेरी
प्रतीक्षा कीजिए ।
आज शाम छह बजे मेरा
इंतज़ार कीजिए ।       Please wait for (expect)
me today at 6 p.m.

## 14. Writing System

### 14.1 Consonant Combinations

New consonant combinations in this lesson are:

| ls | ल्स | seels | सेल्स |
| rg | र्ग | maarg | मार्ग |
| rT | र्ट | paarTii | पार्टी |
| tm | त्म | mahaatmaa | महात्मा |

Combinations of the above type, whose components are obvious, will not be noted in future lessons.

### 14.2 Irregular Spellings

The symbol क्ष "kš" is irregular, since the components are not similar either to "k" क or "š" ष or "š" श .

pratiikšaa    प्रतीक्षा

The following spelling is also irregular:

maalum    मालूम

### EXERCISES

A. Substitute orally in the sentences below the Hindi equivalent of the English given:

1. मैं कल शाम ----- प्रतीक्षा कहूँगा ।

| | |
|---|---|
| for you (familiar) | for her children |
| for your father | for Mr. Ram Nath |
| for your mother | for Mr. Ram Nath Sharma |
| for his friend | for Mr. Sharma's family |
| for his parents | for my friends |
| for her sister | for my friend and his wife |
| for her elder brother | for my friend and his family |

2. मुझे ----- एक पार्टी में जाना है ।

       tomorrow

       the day after tomorrow

       two days after tomorrow

       tomorrow in the evening

       tomorrow at 5 p.m.

       tomorrow at 5 o'clock in the evening

       tomorrow at 8:45 p.m.

       tomorrow at 5:30 p.m.

       the day after tomorrow at 6:30 p.m.

       the day after tomorrow at 7:15 p.m.

       the day after tomorrow at 8:30 p.m.

       the day after tomorrow at 6:45 p.m.

3. _____ यह बात मालूम न थी ।

| I | my wife |
| he | Ram Nath |
| we | Ram Nath's sister |
| they | Asha |
| she | Asha's husband |
| his parents | this man |

4. अभी ----- और रहने का इरादा है ?

| how many days | seven or eight days |
| a few days | five or six days |
| some time | two or three hours |
| two days | four or five hours |
| four days | seven or eight hours |

four or five days          three or four hours

three or four days         five or six hours

two or three days

5. तो आपका इरादा कब तक ----- का है ?

to stay here               to go there

to stay in this city       to go to the doctor's office

to live in this house      to stop at the station

to return from Agra        to work

to come here               to work in this store


6. यह वही आदमी है ----- ।

who lives in Agra

who should go to the bazaar

who will buy some Hindi newspapers

who reads English books

who studies Hindi

who brought medicine for me

who has come from Ajmer

who works in the fruit store

who will tell you about that hotel

who was at the bus stop this morning

who should learn to read Hindi

whose daughter learns Hindi

whose son learns Hindi in this school

whose house is near the hospital

whose house is in my neighborhood

whom I will see tomorrow morning

whom you should give these books

213

whom he will tell about you

B. Substitute orally in the sentences below the Hindi equivalent of the English given, making other changes, if necessary:

1. _____ आज ही इस शहर में आया हूं ।

| | |
|---|---|
| I (masc.) | they (masc.) |
| she | I (fem.) |
| you (masc., familiar) | you (masc., polite) |
| we (fem.) | they (fem.) |
| he | we (masc.) |
| you (fem., polite) | you (fem., familiar) |

2. _____ आज ही यहां पहुंचा ।

| | |
|---|---|
| I (masc.) | they (masc.) |
| she | I (fem.) |
| you (masc., polite) | you (masc., familiar) |
| we (fem.) | they (fem.) |
| he | we (masc.) |
| you (fem., familiar) | you (fem., polite) |

C. Transform the following simple present tense sentences to simple past tense sentences according to the model given:

वह अपने घर में है । ----- वह अपने घर में था ।

1. क्या डाक्टर दवाखाने में हैं ?
2. मेरी पत्नी घर में है ।
3. मुझे यह बात मालूम है ।
4. क्या तुम घर पर हो ?
5. उसे कुछ जुकाम है ।
6. यह दवा अच्छी नहीं है ।

7. यह कमीज़ अच्छी नहीं है ।

8. इसका दाम पांच रुपए है ।

9. क्या वे दौरे पर हैं ?

10. आपकी लड़की कहां है ?


D. Transform the following present imperfect tense sentences to perfect tense sentences according to the model given:

वह बाज़ार जाता है । ----- वह बाज़ार गया ।

1. वे दफ़्तर से कब लौटते हैं ?

2. राम बाज़ार से दवा लाता है ।

3. गाड़ी वहां पांच बजे पहुंचती है ।

4. वह अपने घर कब आता है ?

5. इसे खरीदने में पांच रुपए लगते हैं ।

6. ये किताबें कहां मिलती हैं ?

7. बस बस स्टाप पर रुकती है ।

8. क्या आप इस पार्क में घूमते हैं ?

9. वह फल खरीदने बाज़ार जाता है ।

10. यह बस कहां से छूटती है ?


E. Transform the following present imperfect tense sentences to present perfect tense sentences according to the model given:

वह बाज़ार जाता है । ----- वह बाज़ार गया है ।

1. यह गाड़ी वहां से पांच बजे छूटती है ।

2. ये किताबें उसी दुकान पर मिलती है ।

3. आप यह सब कहां से लाते हैं ?

4. वह यहां से फल ले जाती है ।

5. क्या आप कभी इस पार्क में भी घूमते हैं ?

6. क्या बस यहां केवल पांच मिनट रुकती है ?

7. इसमें दस रुपए लगते हैं ।

8. वह अशोक होटल में ठहरती है ।

9. राम यह दवा अस्पताल से लाता है ।

10. मेरे भाई बाज़ार जाते हैं ।


F.  Transform the following sentences according to the model given:

वह स्टेशन जाता है । ----- उसे स्टेशन जाना है ।

1. वह हिन्दी की किताबें पढ़ता है ।

2. मैं यह बात समझता हूं ।

3. क्या आप उसी होटल में ठहरते हैं ?

4. मैं इसी कम्पनी में काम करता हूं ।

5. क्या तुम बाज़ार से समाचार पत्र खरीदते हो ?

6. वह अंग्रेज़ी के इन शब्दों का मतलब जानता है ।

7. मैं हिन्दी बोलना सीखता हूं ।

8. वह पत्र लिखता है ।

9. क्या वह बस-स्टाप पर रुकता है ।

10. वह कितने बजे दफ़्तर जाता है ?


G.  Translate orally:

1.  I know that he is in this city.

2.  I don't know where he lives in this city.

3.  He is a sales manager nowadays.

4.  Nowadays, he is a sales manager in a company.

5.  Nowadays, I am a doctor in the Ashok Nagar
      Hospital.

6.  I have been transferred to this place.

7.  I have been transferred to this place recently.

8.  Then come to our place some evening, won't you?

9. You won't go to the hospital tomorrow morning, will you?

10. He is going on a tour, isn't he?

11. He should come to this city tomorrow.

12. Should he come to this city tomorrow?

13. If he comes to this city, he will certainly see me.

14. If they come to this city, they will buy some Hindi books.

15. If I come here on a tour, I'll bring you some books.

16. If we come here, we will stay with you.

17. If she buys some books, she'll buy them from your store.

18. If my parents come here, I'll tell you.

19. If you go there, please tell me.

20. If you are sick, go to Dr. Sharma's office.

## Conversation -- Entering School

### PRINCIPAL

कहिए, मैं आपके लिए क्या कर
सकती हूं ?

Hello, what can I do for
you?

### KELKAR

भर्ती

admission

मैं अपनी छोटी लड़की की भर्ती
के बारे में आपके पास आया
हूं ।

I have come to see you about
the admission of my
younger daughter.

### PRINCIPAL

कराना

to have done, to get
done

भर्ती कराना

to have admitted, to
get admitted

आप उसे किस दर्जे में भर्ती
कराना चाहते हैं ?

Which grade do you want to
get her admitted to?

### KELKAR

आठवां

eighth

आठवें दर्जे में ।

In eighth grade.

### PRINCIPAL

पढ़ती थी

used to study

अभी तक वह कहां पढ़ती थी ?

Where has she been studying
up to now?

### KELKAR

पूना

Poona

पूने में ।

In Poona.

पिछला

last, previous

साल

year

पिछले साल तक मैं पूने में था
और मेरी लड़की वहीं पढ़ती
थी ।

I was in Poona till last
year and my daughter was
studying there.

अभी हाल में ही मेरा तबादला
यहां हुआ है ।

I have just recently been
transferred here.

स्कूल

school

यहां आने पर मुझे मालूम हुआ
कि यह स्कूल इस नगर का
सबसे अच्छा स्कूल है ।

After coming here, I have
learned that this is the
best school in the city.

रखना

to put

और इसलिए मैं उसे इसी स्कूल
में रखना चाहता हूं ।

And therefore, I want to
put her in this school.

## PRINCIPAL

भाषा

language

मातृभाषा

native language, mother
tongue

आपकी लड़की की मातृभाषा
क्या है ?

What is your daughter's
native language?

## KELKAR

मराठी

Marathi

मराठी ।

Marathi.

## PRINCIPAL

पता

awareness, knowledge

219

| पता होना | to be aware, to know |
|---|---|
| प्रदेश | state, province |
| पढ़ाई | instruction, study |
| आपको तो पता ही होगा कि इस प्रदेश के सभी स्कूलों में हिन्दी में पढ़ाई होती है । | You must be aware that in all the schools of this province instruction is given in Hindi. |
| विषय | subject |
| हमारे स्कूल में भी सभी विषयों की पढ़ाई हिन्दी में होती है । | In our school too instruction in all the subjects is given in Hindi. |

KELKAR

| जानकारी | knowledge, information |
|---|---|
| जी हां, मुझे इस बात की जानकारी है । | Yes, I know about that. |
| मेरी लड़की वहां स्कूल में हिन्दी भी पढ़ती थी । | My daughter studied Hindi too in school. |
| विचार | thought, idea |
| मेरा विचार है कि उसे हिन्दी में कोई कठिनाई न होगी । | I don't think she will have any difficulty in Hindi |

PRINCIPAL

| तब तो ठीक है । | Then it's all right. |
|---|---|
| सातवां | seventh |
| पास | pass |
| पास करना | to pass |
| सर्टिफिकेट | certificate |

आपके पास उसके सातवां दर्जा | You must certainly have her
पास करने का सर्टिफिकेट तो | seventh grade certificate.
होगा ही ।

## KELKAR

जी हां, है । | Yes, I have.

## PRINCIPAL

मेज देना | to send

तब आप उसे कल सुबह यहां भेज | Then please send her here
दीजिए । | tomorrow morning.

लोग | people

नाम | name

लिख लेना | to write

नाम लिख लेना | to enroll

हम लोग इस स्कूल में उसका नाम | We will enroll her in this
लिख लेंगे । | school.

## KELKAR

बहुत अच्छा, मैं भेज दूंगा । | O.K., I'll send her.

नमस्ते । | Good-bye.

## GRAMMAR

1. New Nouns

| Masc. I | | Fem. I | |
|---------|---|--------|---|
| पूना | Poona | भर्ती | admission |
| पता | knowledge, awareness | पढ़ाई | study, instruction |
| | | मराठी | Marathi |
| | | जानकारी | knowledge, information |

221

| Masc. II | | Fem. II | |
|---|---|---|---|
| साल | year | भाषा | language |
| स्कूल | school | मातृभाषा | native language |
| प्रदेश | state, province | | |
| विषय | subject | | |
| विचार | thought, idea | | |
| पास | pass | | |
| सर्टिफिकेट | certificate | | |
| लोग | people | | |
| नाम | name | | |

## 2. New Verbs

| | | | |
|---|---|---|---|
| कराना | to get done, to have done | भेजना | to send |
| रखना | to put | | |

## 2.1 New Compound Verbs

### Type I

| | | | |
|---|---|---|---|
| भेज देना | to send | लिख लेना | to write |

### Type II

| | |
|---|---|
| भर्ती कराना | to get admitted, to have |
| पता होना | to be aware of, to know |
| नाम लिखना | to enroll |

## 3. New Adjectives in -aa

| | | | |
|---|---|---|---|
| आठवां | eighth | पिछला | last, previous |
| सातवां | seventh | | |

## 4. Past Imperfect Tense

The past imperfect form of the verb is composed of

222

the imperfect form of the verb plus the simple past of the verb होना "to be." Note that although both forms show inflection for gender and number, it is only the simple past of the verb होना "to be" that will show the feminine plural inflection -<u>ĩĩ</u>.

| | | | |
|---|---|---|---|
| Masc. Sg. | देखता था | पढ़ता था | जाता था |
| Masc. Pl. | देखते थे | पढ़ते थे | जाते थे |
| Fem. Sg. | देखती थी | पढ़ती थी | जाती थी |
| Fem. Pl. | देखती थीं | पढ़ती थीं | जाती थीं |

This form of the verb will frequently equate with the English "used to" form of the verb.

| | |
|---|---|
| मैं रोज़ सुबह बाज़ार जाता था । | I used to go to the bazaar every morning. |
| वह इसी स्कूल में पढ़ती थी । | She used to study in this school. |
| वह कभी कभी मुझे पत्र लिखता था । | Sometimes, he used to write me letters. |

This form of the verb may also be used to refer to events in the past, which continued over a period of time where English is likely to use a form like "was studying," "has been studying":

| | |
|---|---|
| वह अभी तक कहां पढ़ती थी ? | Where has she been studying up to now? |

5. <u>Causative Verbs</u>

Many verbs in Hindi, besides having a form which will be called here the basic form, will have another form, which will be called the first causative. Thus

223

the verb करना "to do" is classified as a basic form
of the verb, and the verb कराना "to get done," "to
have done" is the first causative.  The first causative
will have a complete inflection paralleling that of
the basic verb:

| | | |
|---|---|---|
| Infinitive | करना | कराना |
| Imperfect (masc. sg.) | करता | कराता |
| Present Imperfect (3rd, masc.sg.) | करता है | कराता है |
| Past Imperfect (3rd, masc.sg.) | करता था | कराता था |
| Perfect (masc.sg.) | किया | कराया |
| Present Perfect (3rd, masc.sg.) | किया है | कराया है |
| Present Progressive (3rd, masc.sg. | कर रहा है | करा रहा है |
| Optative (3rd, sg.) | करे | कराए |
| Future (3rd, masc.sg.) | करेगा | कराएगा |
| Imperative (familiar) | करो | कराओ |
| Imperative (polite) | कीजिए | कराइए |

For the verb करना "to do" (and for most verbs that
are transitive) the basic verb will imply that the
subject performs the action, whereas the first causative will imply that the subject gets somebody else,
i.e., causes somebody else, to perform the action.
This will apply to the verb करना by itself and also
to verb phrases with करना such as काम करना "to work,"
टेलीफोन करना "to call on the phone" etc.

| | |
|---|---|
| वह क्या कर रहा है ? | What is he doing? |
| वह क्या करा रहा है ? | What is he getting done? |
| मैं यह काम कर रहा हूं । | I'm doing this work |

| | |
|---|---|
| मैं यह काम करा रहा हूं । | I'm getting this work done. |
| वह मुझे टेलीफोन करेगा । | He will call me on the phone. |
| वह मुझे टेलीफोन कराएगा । | He will have me called up (i.e., he will get his secretary to do it). |
| वे उसे स्कूल में भर्ती करेंगे । | He will admit him to the school. |
| वे उसे स्कूल में भर्ती कराएंगे । | He will get him admitted to the school. |
| वह यह नहीं कर सकता । | He can't do it. |
| वह यह नहीं करा सकता । | He can't get it done. |
| वह यह काम नहीं करना चाहता। | He doesn't want to do it. |
| वह यह काम नहीं कराना चाहता । | He doesn't want to get it done. |

The person that one gets to do something is expressed in Hindi by means of the postposition से .

| | |
|---|---|
| वह मुझे अपने नौकर से टेलीफोन कराएगा । | He will get his servant to call me up. |

## 6. Ordinal Numerals

The ordinal numerals first, second, third, and fourth are irregular in formation in Hindi.  The inflection is that of a regular adjective in -aa.

| | | | |
|---|---|---|---|
| पहला | first | तीसरा | third |
| दूसरा | second | चौथा | fourth |

The ordinal number "sixth" has the following variants:

| | |
|---|---|
| छटवां | chaTwãã |

225

| | |
|---|---|
| छठवां | chaThwãã |
| छठा | chaThaa |

Other ordinal numerals are formed by adding वां to the cardinal numerals.

| | | |
|---|---|---|
| पांचवां | pããcwãã | fifth |
| सातवां | saatwãã | seventh |
| बारहवां | baarhwãã | twelfth |
| पन्द्रहवां | pandrhwãã | fifteenth |
| बीसवां | biiswãã | twentieth |
| पच्चीसवां | pacciiswãã | twenty-fifth |

All the ordinals ending in वां have the following inflections:

| | |
|---|---|
| Masc. Sg. | पांचवां |
| Masc. Pl. | पांचवें |
| Fem. | पांचवीं |

## 7. विचार

The form विचार "thought," "idea" is frequently used where English uses the verb "think." For English "I think" the Hindi expression is literally "my thought is," मेरा विचार है ।   Where English has the negative of the verb "to think," i.e., "I don't think he is coming," Hindi uses the negative in the subordinate clause, literally "my thought is that he isn't coming": मेरा विचार है कि वह नहीं आ रहा ।

मेरा विचार है कि वह बाज़ार जायगा ।   I think he is going to the bazaar.

मेरा विचार है कि वह बाज़ार     I don't think he is going
नहीं जायगा ।                 to the bazaar.

## 8. जानकारी

The form जानकारी  "knowledge," "information" may
be used in situations where English uses the verb "to
know about."  The person who knows is in the dative
case, and the thing known about is expressed by the का
form of the noun or pronoun.

मुझे इस बात की जानकारी     I know about that.
है ।

क्या उन्हें मेरे आने की       Does he know about my
जानकारी है ?            coming?

## 9. "Must"

Where English uses "must be" meaning that something
is almost sure to be true rather than in the meaning of
obligation, Hindi uses the future of the verb होना.
Where in English a sentence of this kind frequently
has in it "certainly" or "surely," Hindi frequently
has ज़रूर, अवश्य, तो -- ही ।

आपके पास उसका सर्टिफिकेट     You must certainly have her
तो होगा ही ।              certificate.

## 10. Agreement

The का forms, मेरा, उसका  etc., are sometimes
separated from the noun they modify.  Thus in the
sentence:

आपके पास उसके सातवां दर्जा     You must have her

पास करने का सर्टिफिकेट तो     seventh grade certifi-

होगा ही ।             cate.

the उसके modifies the infinitive करने and is in the
oblique because करने is oblique. This is like the
English "her passing seventh grade."

उनकी कपड़े की दुकान       his clothing store

In the above phrase उनकी modifies दुकान and is in
the feminine form.

## 11. Superlative Construction

Where English uses the superlative form of the
adjective, Hindi uses the positive form of the adjective preceded by सबसे. This type of expression is
identical with the comparative type, discussed in
Lesson XII, in that both use a से construction.

यह स्कूल इस नगर का सबसे     This is the best school in

अच्छा स्कूल है ।          the city.

## 12. लोग

The word लोग may be used in the meaning "people"
and may also be used after a noun or pronoun merely to
indicate that the preceding noun or pronoun is plural.
This use of लोग with pronoun is quite common and
acceptable in Hindi, but the use of लोग with noun is
generally not considered good Hindi and should therefore be avoided.

लोग इसके बारे में क्या     What do people say about

कहते हैं ?            it?

हम लोग उसका नाम लिख लेंगे । We will enroll her.

इस नगर में डाक्टर लोग       The doctors in this city

अच्छे हैं ।                  are good.

## 13. Writing System

### 13.1 Irregular Spellings

The following words have an irregular spelling:

| wišai | विषय |
| bhaašaa | भाषा |
| maatribhaašaa | मातृभाषा |

There are many items in Hindi written as if they should be pronounced -ay at the end, but these are all pronounced -ai. In the future, these forms will not be given in the list of irregular spellings.

## EXERCISES

A. Substitute orally in the sentences below the Hindi equivalent of the English given:

1. _____ इस बात की जानकारी न थी ।

| I | Ram Lal's sister |
| he | Mr. Ram Lal |
| we | that girl |
| they | that boy |
| she | my friend |
| his brother | this woman |

2. मुझे _____ किताब दे दीजिए ।

| fourth | twenty-eighth |
| eighth | seventeenth |

|            |                |
|------------|----------------|
| tenth      | twenty-fifth   |
| twelfth    | thirtieth      |
| thirteenth | twenty-second  |
| nineteenth | twenty-fourth  |
| twenty-first | twenty-sixth |

3. अगर वह आएगा ----- ।

 then I'll see him

 then I'll go with him

 then he will go with me to the bazaar

 then I'll give him these Hindi books

 then he will certainly see me

 then he will be able to study Hindi

 then he will give me a call before he comes

 then I'll give him the medicine

 then he will bring his daughter's certificate

4. मुझे _____ पता न था ।

| of this thing | of his being here |
|---------------|-------------------|
| of this book  | of his going to Agra |
| of this place | of his coming here |
| of his return | of his coming here today |

5. _____ में पूने में था ।

 till last year

 till yesterday

 till the day before yesterday

 till two days before yesterday

 till last night

till 8 o'clock last night

till 3 p.m. yesterday

till 10 a.m. yesterday

6. मेरे पास ----- किताब नहीं थी ।

| | |
|---|---|
| his | his brother's |
| their | your son's |
| your | your daughter's |
| Ram Lal's | her younger sister's |
| John's | her elder brother's |
| his friends' | that woman's |

7. मैं कल उस लड़के से मिला ----- ।

who lives in Agra

who works in the hospital

who is your friend

who is your friend's son

who studies Hindi

who studies Hindi in your class

whose name is Ram Lal

whose parents live in Kanpur

whose parents will go to Agra tomorrow

from whom you got this book

B. Substitute orally in the sentences given below the Hindi equivalent of the English given, making other changes. if necessary:

1. _____ कभी कभी हिन्दी की किताबें खरीदता था ।

| | |
|---|---|
| I (masc.) | we (masc.) |
| she | I (fem.) |

you (masc., polite)    you (masc., familiar)

we (fem.)              they (fem.)

they (masc.)           he

you (fem., familiar)   you (fem., polite)

2. आपके पास ----- तो होगा ही ।

her certificate       a Hindi dictionary

that book             envelopes

a ticket              postcards

some oranges          some five-new-pice stamps

medicines             some handkerchiefs

my address            some undershirts

C.  Transform the following present imperfect tense
sentences to past imperfect tense sentences according
to the model given:

राम बाज़ार जाता है । ----- राम बाज़ार जाता था ।

1. मैं यहीं पढ़ती हूं ।

2. वह कभी कभी मुझे पत्र लिखता है ।

3. हम अंग्रेज़ी सीखना चाहती हैं ।

4. क्या आप इसी दुकान से कपड़े खरीदते हैं ?

5. वे लड़कियां अशोक नगर में रहती हैं ।

6. आप उस स्कूल में हिन्दी सीख सकते हैं ।

7. मैं कुछ कुछ हिन्दी बोल लेता हूं ।

8. वे औरतें दुकान में काम करती हैं ।

9. क्या तुम आज बाज़ार जाना चाहते हो ?

10. मैं यहीं से हिन्दी की किताबें खरीदती हूं ।

D.  Transform the following present imperfect sentences
to perfect tense sentences according to the model
given:

वह बाज़ार जाता है । ----- वह बाज़ार गया ।

1. आप दफ़्तर से कब लौटते हैं ?

2. मेरा भाई इसी बस-स्टाप पर रुकता है ।

3. क्या वह पांच बजे घर आता है ?

4. आगरे के लिए गाड़ी सात बजे छूटती है ।

5. हिन्दी की किताबें कहां मिलती हैं ?

6. शब्द कोश खरीदने में दस रुपए लगते हैं ।

7. डाक्टर कितने बजे दवाखाने आते हैं ?

8. मैं अस्पताल से दवा लाता हूं ।

9. मेरे पिता स्कूल जाते हैं ।

10. हम पांच बजे दफ़्तर से वापस आते हैं ।

E. Transform the following sentences according to the model given:

वह स्टेशन जाता है । ----- उसे स्टेशन जाना पड़ा ।

1. वह हिन्दी पढ़ता है ।

2. मैं अशोक होटल में ठहरता हूं ।

3. मेरा भाई दौरे पर जाता है ।

4. वह राम लाल को टेलीफोन करती है ।

5. मेरा नौकर घर का सब काम करता है ।

6. मैं उसे होटल का पता बताता हूं ।

7. वह हिन्दी की किताबें खरीदता है ।

8. मेरे मातापिता उसी घर में रहते हैं ।

9. मैं मराठी लिखना सीखता हूं ।

10. हम इसी स्टेशन पर रुकते हैं ।

F. Transform the following sentences according to the model given:

किताब कहां मिलती है ? ----- किताबें कहां मिलती थीं ?

233

1. यह धोबी कहां काम करता है ?

2. लड़का यह बात जानता है ।

3. बस यहीं से छूटती है ।

4. औरतें राम को कुछ कपड़ा देती हैं ।

5. आगरे का टिकट कहां मिलता है ?

6. क्या नौकर घर का सब काम करता है ?

7. लड़की इसी स्कूल में पढ़ती है ।

8. मैं अस्पताल से दवा लाता हूं ।

9. गाड़ी इसी प्लेटफ़ार्म से छूटती है ।

10. मेरा भाई उसी शहर में व्यापार करता है ।

G.  Translate orally:

1.  You certainly must have her certificate.

2.  He certainly must have my address.

3.  You certainly must have his books.

4.  You certainly must have her seventh grade certificate.

5.  They certainly must have this hotel's address.

6.  I'll get you admitted to the school.

7.  I'll get his son admitted to the school.

8.  I'll get my friend admitted to the school tomorrow.

9.  Can you get my brother admitted to the school tomorrow?

10. Should I get my daughter admitted to this school?

11. He used to study Hindi here.

12. What subjects do you study in this school?

13. What languages do you study in the school?

14. What languages will he study in the school?

234

15. What languages can I study in this school?

16. This is the best school in the city.

17. This is the best bookstore in this bazaar.

18. I think this is the best book of this year.

19. I think Ram Lal is the best boy in the school.

20. I don't think she used to work here.

21. I don't think she knows how to write Hindi.

22. I don't think his native language is Marathi.

23. I don't think you should see him tomorrow.

24. I don't think he has been transferred here recently.

25. I don't think the instruction is given in Hindi here.

# LESSON XVI

## Conversation -- An Accident

### RAM NATH

| यात्रा | trip, journey |
|---|---|
| कहिए, कल आपकी यात्रा कैसी रही ? | Hello, how was your trip yesterday? |

### BILL

| जब | when |
|---|---|
| लौट रहा था | was coming back |
| मुसीबत | trouble |
| पड़ जाना | to get (in), be involved (in) |
| यात्रा तो अच्छी रही, पर जब मैं लौट रहा था, उस समय बड़ी मुसीबत में पड़ गया । | The trip was fine but when I was coming back, I got in trouble. |

### RAM NATH

| क्यों, क्या हुआ ? | Why, what happened? |
|---|---|

### BILL

| मोटर | car |
|---|---|
| दुर्घटना | accident |
| मोटर-दुर्घटना | car accident |
| मोटर-दुर्घटना हो गई । | There was a car accident. |

### RAM NATH

| अरे, कैसे ? | Oh, how? |
|---|---|

236

| लौटते | returning |
|---|---|
| हो गई थी | had happened |
| कल लौटते समय मुझे शाम हो गई थी । | It got dusk when I was coming back yesterday (lit.: at the time of my returning, the evening had happened). |
| पानी | water, rain |
| बरस रहा था | was raining |
| उस समय पानी बरस रहा था । | It was raining at that time. |
| काफ़ी | quite, rather, enough |
| अंधेरा | darkness |
| हो गया था | had happened |
| और काफ़ी अंधेरा हो गया था । | And it had gotten quite dark. |

RAM NATH

| मौसम | weather |
|---|---|
| ख़राब | bad |
| तब तो मौसम काफ़ी ख़राब हो गया था । | Then the weather had gotten quite bad. |

BILL

| सावधानी | caution |
|---|---|
| चलाना | to drive |
| चला रहा था | was driving |
| मैं तो बहुत सावधानी से अपनी | I was driving my car very |

237

| | |
|---|---|
| मोटर चला रहा था । | cautiously. |
| पर | but |
| तभी | just then |
| सामने से | from in front |
| आने वाला | coming |
| टकरा जाना | to run into |
| पर तभी सामने से आने वाली एक मोटर मेरी मोटर से टकरा गई । | But just then a car coming from the opposite direction (in front of me) ran into my car. |

RAM NATH

| | |
|---|---|
| तेज़ी | speed |
| आ रही थी | was coming |
| क्या वह मोटर बहुत तेज़ी से आ रही थी ? | Was that car coming very fast? |

BILL

| | |
|---|---|
| जी हां, वह मोटर बहुत तेज़ी से आ रही थी । | Yes, it was coming very fast. |
| लगना | to seem |
| ब्रेक | brake |
| और लगता है, उसके ब्रेक भी अच्छे न थे । | And, it seems its brakes weren't good (either). |
| मोटरवाला | the driver |
| कोहरा | fog |
| वजह | reason, cause |
| पाना | to get, to find, to be possible to |

238

मोटरवाला कोहरे की वजह से देख नहीं पाया और टकरा गया ।

The driver couldn't see on account of the fog and ran into me.

RAM NATH

चोट

injury

आपको चोट तो नहीं आई ?

You didn't get hurt, did you?

BILL

बचना

to be saved

बच जाना

to be saved

जी नहीं, मैं तो बच गया पर उसे कुछ चोट आई ।

No, I was safe, but he got somewhat hurt.

RAM NATH

सचमुच

really, in reality

पड़ गए थे

were involved

तब तो आप सचमुच मुसीबत में पड़ गए थे ।

Then you really were involved in trouble.

BILL

जी हां, इस वजह से कल रात मैं काफ़ी देर तक घर न लौट सका ।

Yes, because of this I couldn't come home till quite late last night.

239

GRAMMAR

1.  <u>New Nouns</u>

<u>Masc. I</u>                    <u>Fem. I</u>

अंधेरा (no pl.) darkness  सावधानी (no pl.) caution

कोहरा (no pl.) fog       तेज़ी    (no pl.) speed

<u>Masc. II</u>                   <u>Fem. II</u>

पानी (no pl.) water, rain यात्रा    trip, journey

मौसम          weather    मुसीबत    trouble

ब्रेक           brake      मोटर      car

                         दुर्घटना   accident

                         वजह       reason, cause

                         चोट       injury

2.  <u>New Verbs</u>

बरसना              to rain

चलाना              to drive

टकराना             to collide, to run into

लगना               to seem

पाना               to get, to find, to be
                      possible to

बचना               to be saved

Note that in this lesson you have met a new
causative verb that pairs off with a basic form like
the basic form करना, causative form कराना,discussed in
Lesson XV:

<u>Basic form</u>              <u>Causative form</u>

चलना      to go         चलाना   to drive, to cause
                                   to go

240

## 2.1 New Compound Verbs

### Type I

पढ़ जाना     to get into, to be involved in

टकरा जाना    to collide, to run into

बच जाना      to be saved

### Type II

यात्रा करना    to travel, to take a trip

## 3. Past Perfect Tense

The past perfect of a verb is formed by using the simple past form of the verb होना along with the perfect form of the verb. If the verb agreement is feminine plural, only the auxiliary will show the inflection for plural, -_īī_; the main verb will show only the feminine inflection -_ii_.

| | | |
|---|---|---|
| Masc. Sg. | देखा था | गया था |
| Masc. Pl. | देखे थे | गए थे |
| Fem. Sg. | देखी थी | गई थी |
| Fem. Pl. | देखी थीं | गई थीं |

The past perfect is used in Hindi where English uses the past perfect forms like "had gone," "had written" etc.

वह उस समय तक नहीं लौटा था ।    He hadn't come back by that time.

कल लौटते समय मुझे शाम हो गई थी ।    While I was returning yesterday, evening fell.

The past perfect tense is also used in Hindi where

241

English will use just the past tense. In stating a
series of events in the past, the first is likely to
be in the past perfect and the others in the perfect.
Many uses of the past perfect derive from this
situation in that they will imply that something more
is going to be stated.

| | |
|---|---|
| मैं कल आगरे गया था, वहां मैं एक मित्र से मिला... | Yesterday I went to Agra, I met a friend there... |
| क्या आप कल आगरे गए थे ? | Did you go to Agra yester-day? |
| वह कल मुझसे मिला था । | He met me yesterday. |

## 4. Past Progressive Tense

The present progressive is formed by using the
present perfect of the verb रहना along with the stem
of the main verb, e.g., जा रहा है. The past progressive
is formed similarly by using the past perfect of the
verb रहना along with the stem of the main verb, e.g.,
जा रहा था. This usually equates with the English past
progressive "was reading," "was going" etc.

| | |
|---|---|
| पानी बरस रहा था । | It was raining. |
| क्या वह मोटर बहुत तेज़ी से आ रही थी ? | Was that car coming very fast? |

## 5. Verb Review

The forms of the imperfect, present imperfect and
past imperfect are parallel to those of the perfect,
present perfect and past perfect.

मिलता         मिला

मिलता है      मिला है

मिलता था     मिला था

## 6. "When" Clause

Where English uses a "when" clause to express the
time at which something was taking place, Hindi may
use the word समय preceded by the imperfect form of the
verb in the oblique case. Thus where English has "when
I was returning," Hindi may have literally "at the time
of returning" लौटते समय . The person involved in the
action may be expressed in Hindi by the का form, thus
उसके लौटते समय, मेरे लौटते समय, राम के लौटते समय although the
person is likely to be omitted if the context is clear
without it.

| | |
|---|---|
| कल लौटते समय मुफे शाम हो गई थी । | It got dusk when I was coming back yesterday. |
| पानी बरसते समय मैं बाहर नहीं जा सकता । | I can't go out when it's raining. |

The time of the action is simultaneous with that of
the main verb, i.e., लौटते समय will mean "when I was
returning" if the main verb is past but will mean
"when I am returning" if the main verb is present.

| | |
|---|---|
| (मेरे) बाज़ार जाते समय मोटर दुर्घटना हो गई । | There was a car accident when I was going to the bazaar. |
| पार्क में उसके घूमते समय मैं | I'll see him when he is |

243

उससे मिल लूंगा ।                    taking a walk in the park.

7. वाला

The form वाला is used in two constructions:

1. वाला may be added to the oblique form of the
infinitive of a verb.  Such a form may be used as a
verbal adjective modifying a noun or it may be used
as an agentive noun.  When used as an adjective, it
has the regular inflection, i.e., वाला , वाले and वाली
and frequently equates with an English clause introduced by "who," "which," e.g.,

बाज़ार से आनेवाला लड़का
The boy coming from the
bazaar.
The boy who is coming from
the bazaar.

सामने से आनेवाली एक मोटर
मेरी मोटर से टकरा गई ।
A car coming from the opposite direction ran into
my car.

हिन्दी बोलने वाला लड़का
इसी कमरे में है ।
The boy, who speaks Hindi,
is in this room.

रेशमी कपड़े खरीदनेवाली
लड़की इसी शहर में रहती
है ।
The girl, who is buying the
silk clothes, lives in
this city.

When used as a noun, the masculine form ends in
वाला and has the inflection of a masculine class I
noun, and the feminine form ends in वाली and has the
inflection of a feminine class I noun.  An agentive

244

noun means a person who performs the action of the infinitive. Thus बोलने वाला "the person speaking" or "the speaker."

| | |
|---|---|
| बहुत यात्रा करने वाले मुझे पसन्द नहीं हैं । | I don't like those, who travel a lot. |
| दवा देने वाला इस समय अस्पताल में नहीं है । | The dispenser is not in the hospital right now. |

2. वाला may be added to a noun or adjective. This form usually makes a noun but in some cases may also be used as an adjective. The inflection will be that mentioned in the preceding section. When used as a noun, it means a person connected in some way with the meaning of the noun to which it is added. Thus मोटर-वाला "a person connected with a car" or "a driver." Some other useful nouns of this sort are:

| | |
|---|---|
| दुकानवाला | the storekeeper |
| फलवाला | the fruit vender |
| बसवाला | the bus conductor |
| पानीवाला | the water carrier |

Nouns of this pattern are made fairly freely in Hindi but not referring to people of higher social status. When used as an adjective, the construction with वाला simply makes an adjective out of the preceding noun. Thus:

| | |
|---|---|
| तीन पांच नए पैसे वाले लिफ़ाफ़े पांच नए पैसे वाले तीन लिफ़ाफ़े | Three five-new-pice envelopes |

|  |  |
|---|---|
| पांच बजे वाली बस । <br> पांच बजे की बस । | The five o'clock bus |
| मुझे अच्छी वाली कमीज़ दे दीजिए । | Give me the good shirt. |
| आगरे वाले डाक्टर कानपुर वाले डाक्टरों से अच्छे हैं । | The Agra doctors are better than the Kanpur doctors. |

8. पाना

The verb पाना "to get," "to find" may be used along with the stem form of another verb in the meaning "to be possible to," "to get a chance to." This construction with पाना may frequently be translated by English "can," "be able to," but it differs from the सकना construction in that it implies the accomplishment of the act, whereas सकना doesn't imply whether an act is accomplished or not.

|  |  |
|---|---|
| मोटरवाला कोहरे की वजह से देख नहीं पाया । | The driver couldn't see (didn't get a chance to see) on account of the fog. |
| मैं दफ़्तर में ही काम कर पाता हूं, घर में नहीं । | I can (get to) work in the office but not at home. |
| मैं बाज़ार जाना चाहता था लेकिन नहीं जा पाया । | I wanted to go to the bazaar but didn't get to go. |
| मैं कल यह किताब पढ़ सकता हूं । | I can read this book tomorrow (with no implication of getting it done). |

246

9. "To rain"

The expression "to rain" in Hindi is पानी बरसना.
It is not customary to omit पानी unless the context is
clear.

10. से

One more adverbial expression like आसानी से is
तेज़ी से "fast, quickly."

11. Irregular Spellings

Words in Hindi, which are written as if they end
in -ah are usually pronounced -ai.

वजह                 wajai

EXERCISES

A. Substitute orally in the sentences below the Hindi
equivalent of the English given:

1. क्या आप ----- जानते हैं ?      (Use a वाला construction)

that boy who lives in Ashok Nagar

the boy who works in the Kanpur Hotel

the girl who studies Hindi

the girl who is buying fruit

my friend who is going to Agra tomorrow

Ram's brother who is coming from Kanpur
  tomorrow

my son who is learning Hindi in school

the doctor who works in that hospital

the boy who studies in the seventh grade

the woman who works in the clothing store

the man who takes a walk in the park

247

2. मोटर दुर्घटना में ----- कुछ चोट आई ।

| | |
|---|---|
| he | my parents |
| I | their friends |
| we | that boy |
| they | that girl |
| my wife | the driver |
| his daughter | that driver |

3. मुझे ----- दे दीजिए ।

three five-new-pice stamps

twenty one-new-pice stamps

ten fifteen-new-pice envelopes

twelve five-new-pice postcards

twenty-five ten-new-pice inland letters

thirty two-new-pice stamps

one dozen five-new-pice postcards

one ten-new-pice inland letter

sixteen fifteen-new-pice envelopes

four five-rupee shirts

one dozen good shirts

one two-rupee undershirt

one dozen one-rupee handkerchiefs

4. ----- इस समय यहां नहीं है ।

the dispenser

the fruit vender

the bus conductor

the store keeper

248

the water carrier

the driver

5. कल ----- बहुत देर हो गई थी ।

    when I was coming back

    when I was coming back from the station

    when I was coming back from the hospital

    when I was buying clothes from the store

    when I was coming back from the party

    when I was going to Ram's house

    when I was going to see Ram's parents

    when I was calling him up on the phone

    when I was coming to your house

    when I was coming back from their friend's
      house

    when I was taking a walk in the park

    when I was going to the doctor's office

6. मैं बहुत सावधानी से ----- चला रहा था ।

| | |
|---|---|
| my car | my friend's car |
| his car | my parents' car |
| their car | his friend's car |
| the new car | her parents' car |
| my new car | my wife's parents' car |

7. तभी ----- मेरी मोटर से टकरा गई ।

    a car

    a new car

    his car

249

that man's car

a car coming from the opposite direction

a car coming from the left

a car coming from the right

John's car coming from the left

Ram's car coming from the opposite direction

a new car coming from the right

B.  Substitute orally in the sentences below the Hindi
equivalent of the English given, making other changes,
if necessary:

1.  ----- उस समय तक घर नहीं पहुंचा था ।

| | |
|---|---|
| I (masc.) | he |
| she | we (fem.) |
| they (masc.) | you (masc., familiar) |
| you (fem., familiar) | Mr. Ram Lal |
| we (masc.) | you (masc., familiar) |
| they (fem.) | you (fem., polite) |
| you (masc., polite) | Asha |
| I (fem.) | that woman |

2.  ----- उस समय कपड़े खरीद रहा था ।

| | |
|---|---|
| I (masc.) | I (fem.) |
| she | you (masc., familiar) |
| you (masc., polite) | we (fem.) |
| they (fem.) | Mr. Mohan Lal |
| we (masc.) | you (fem., polite) |
| you (fem., familiar) | he |
| they (masc.) | that man |

250

C. Transform the following present imperfect tense
sentences to past progressive tense sentences:

वह बाज़ार जाता है । ----- वह बाज़ार जा रहा था ।

1. वह इसी होटल में रहता है ।

2. हम इसी दुकान से कपड़े ख़रीदते हैं ।

3. उसकी बहिन हिन्दी पढ़ती है ।

4. क्या तुम उस समय दफ़्तर से आते हो ?

5. क्या आप इसी पार्क में घूमते हैं ?

6. लड़का अस्पताल से दवा लाता है ।

7. क्या आप इसी दुकान से किताबें लेते हैं ?

8. मैं उसे सिंगिल कमरे का किराया बताता हूं ।

9. क्या तुम मेरी बात नहीं सुनते ?

10. नौकर ये कपड़े धोबी के यहां ले जाता है ।

11. मैं इसी होटल में काम करता हूं ।

12. हम लोग हिन्दी सीखते हैं ।

13. उन दिनों यहां पानी बरसता है ।

14. हम लोग उनके दर्जे में हिन्दी में बोलते हैं ।

15. मैं धोबी को कपड़े देता हूं ।

D. Transform the following present imperfect tense
sentences to past perfect tense sentences:

वह बाज़ार जाता है । ----- वह बाज़ार गया था ।

1. राम इसी दुकान से दवा लाता है ।

2. यह बस कितने बजे छूटती है ?

3. वह कुछ फल ख़रीदने बाज़ार जाता है ।

4. बस इसी बस-स्टाप पर रुकती है ।

5. ये किताबें इसी दुकान पर मिलती हैं ।

6. इसे ख़रीदने में बीस रुपए लगते हैं ।

7. आप दफ़्तर से कब लौटते हैं ?

251

8. गाड़ी पांच नम्बर के प्लेटफ़ार्म पर ठहरती है ।

9. मेरे पिता पांच बजे स्कूल से वापस आते हैं ।

10. आप यह सब कहां से लाते हैं ?

11. आप वहां कितनी देर रुकते हैं ?

12. क्या इसे लेने में पांच रुपए ही लगते हैं ?

13. क्या वह पांच बजे घर लौटता है ?

14. क्या हिन्दी की किताबें यहां नहीं मिलतीं ?

15. क्या नौकर आपके कपड़े धोबी के यहां ले जाता है ?

E.  Transform the following sentences according to the model given:

वह बाज़ार गया । ----- वह बाज़ार नहीं जा पाया ।

1. लड़के यहां सात बजे पहुंचे ।

2. उसके भाई कानपुर में दस दिन ठहरे ।

3. लड़की अपने साथ अपना सर्टिफ़िकेट लाई ।

4. मैं कल अपने मित्र के घर गया ।

5. आशा पांच दिन से ज्यादा इस नगर में रही ।

6. वह आदमी पांच बजे दफ़्तर से वापस आया ।

7. हम राम को अपने साथ पार्टी में ले गए ।

8. वह औरत आगरे से परसों लौटी ।

9. मैं कल राम के माता पिता से मिला ।

10. वे अपने साथ अपने परिवार को लाए ।

F.  Translate orally:

1.  He drives his car very cautiously.

2.  I was driving my car very cautiously.

3.  He is driving his car very cautiously.

4.  Ram will drive his car very cautiously.

5.  You should drive your car very cautiously.

6. Was John driving his car very cautiously?

7. Wasn't he driving his car very cautiously?

8. The weather isn't very good today.

9. The weather was very bad here yesterday.

10. The weather had gotten quite bad this morning.

11. The weather was very bad, when I was coming back.

12. It seems the weather had gotten quite bad when you were coming back.

13. He got hurt in the accident.

14. Did the boy get hurt in the accident?

15. He didn't get hurt in the accident, did he?

16. He couldn't see on account of the fog.

17. He couldn't see the car coming from the opposite direction on account of the fog.

18. My car ran into a car coming from the opposite direction.

19. Did his car run into the car coming from the opposite direction?

20. Just then, a car coming from the left ran into my car.

21. My friend got into trouble last night.

22. My brother got into trouble last night on account of the car accident.

23. Did you get into trouble yesterday?

24. How did you get into trouble yesterday?

25. What trouble did you get into yesterday?

REVIEW IV

A.  Substitute orally in the sentences below the Hindi
equivalent of the English given:

1. वह आदमी ----- प्रतीक्षा कर रहा है ।

       for his wife

       for his wife to come

       for the car

       for good weather

       for the office to open

       for the rain to stop

       for a telephone call

       for the bus

       for his son

       for me to leave the party

       for his friend's telephone call

       for the servant to bring the newspapers

       for his daughter's admission

       for his brother's return from the trip

       for the bus to stop

       for the bus to leave

2. क्या राम को ----- मालूम है ।

| | |
|---|---|
| about the accident | about these books |
| about the dinner | about my telephone call |
| about my trip | about this school |
| about your trip | about yesterday's accident |
| about your transfer | about his birthday |

254

3. क्या ----- इसकी जानकारी है ?

| | |
|---|---|
| he | his friend |
| they | his family |
| you (polite) | their daughter |
| you (familiar) | these children |
| your servant | the boys |

4. वह इस समय ----- से मिलने गया है ।

| | |
|---|---|
| the doctor | Mrs. Asha |
| Mr. Ram Lal | Mrs. Asha Sharma |
| Mr. Mohan Lal Sharma | Mrs. Ram Pal |
| Miss Asha | Mrs. Ram Pal Sharma |
| Miss Asha Sharma | |

5. ----- कि वह लड़का आज सुबह भी आया था ।

| | |
|---|---|
| I think | her husband thinks |
| he thinks | my brother thinks |
| Mr. Sharma thinks | my sister thinks |
| my wife thinks | my parents think |

6. राम का इरादा ----- का है ।

to go to his office

to wait for his wife

to buy a new car

to learn to drive a car

to drive this new car

to go on a tour

to study in this school

to make a trip

to wait till it's dark

255

to visit his friend

to wait for his phone call

to celebrate his daughter's birthday

to study Hindi here

7. क्या ----- इस दावत के बारे में मालूम है ?

| | |
|---|---|
| Ram | that woman |
| he | this girl |
| they | that boy |
| you | your father |
| your sister | your wife |
| your younger brother | her husband |
| that man | your elder brother |

8. मुझे ----- जानकारी न थी ।

about it

about this school

about these books

about that car accident

about his going

about his returning

9. क्या आप ----- आदमी से मिले हैं ?　(use a वाला construction)

who drives this car

who drives this new car

who is learning to drive a car

who lives in that big house

who is going to Agra

who likes sweet fruit

who studies Hindi

who knows how to read Hindi

who enrolls the students in this school

who comes back from Agra tomorrow

who works in the office opposite me

who studies languages

10. क्या आप उस आदमी को जानते हैं, ----- ?

who got hurt in the accident

who speaks Marathi

whose native language is Hindi

who intends to go on tour with you

who knows about the accident

who was driving the car in that bad weather

whose daughter is in the seventh grade in your
school

whom we are going to visit tomorrow

who sat near me in the doctor's office

who was driving that car

whose office is near the school

for whom you brought all those books

who has been transferred to Agra recently

who has been waiting for you here for quite
some time

who sat opposite you at the party

who has some difficulty in understanding my
Hindi

11. ----- इरादा इस शहर से बाहर जाने का है ।

my

his

our

their

that man's

this boy's

this doctor's

my daughter's

his wife's

her husband's

her husband's brother

her husband's younger brother

her husband's elder sister

their parents

12. कल ----- पानी बरस रहा था ।     (use जाते समय construction)

when I was driving the car

when the boys were coming back from the dinner

when I was returning from my trip

when he was going to the store

when he was buying those books

when he was waiting

when I was working in the office

when Ram was walking in the park

when the bus was leaving

13. वह ----- आपकी प्रतीक्षा करेगा ।

at 5:15 p.m.        at 12:45 p.m.

at 2:30 p.m.        at 1:30 p.m.

at 6:45 p.m.          at 5:15 p.m.

at 9:15 a.m.          at 11:30 a.m.

at 1:15 p.m.          at 2:45 p.m.

at 3:30 p.m.          at 7:15 a.m.

at 8:45 a.m.          at 10:15 p.m.

at 2:15 p.m.          at 9:45 p.m.

14. इन फलों का दाम ----- है ।

three and a half rupees a dozen

a rupee and a quarter a dozen

a rupee and a half a dozen

two rupees and a quarter a dozen

two rupees and a half a dozen

six rupees and a quarter a dozen

six rupees and a half a dozen

six rupees and three quarters a dozen

eight rupees and a half a dozen

eight rupees and a quarter a dozen

eight rupees and three quarters a dozen

15. यहां से ----- घर किसका है ?

tenth               eighth

sixth               fourth

third               second

seventh             twentieth

fifth               twenty-fifth

ninth               twelfth

first               eleventh

259

B. Substitute orally in the sentences below the Hindi equivalent of the English given, making other changes if necessary:

1. ----- शहर से कल सुबह वापस आया है ।

| the boy | you (masc., polite) |
| I (masc.) | you (fem., familiar) |
| the woman | you (masc., familiar) |
| they (fem.) | you (fem., polite) |
| they (masc.) | we (masc.) |
| I (fem.) | we (fem.) |

2. ----- उस समय दफ़्तर जा रहा था ।

| I (masc.) | you (fem., polite) |
| they (fem.) | you (masc., polite) |
| the boy | we (fem.) |
| I (fem.) | you (masc., polite) |
| that girl | you (fem., polite) |
| they (masc.) | we (masc.) |

3. ----- पिछले साल इसी स्कूल में पढ़ता था ।

| that boy | I (masc.) |
| I (fem.) | we (fem.) |
| we (masc.) | you (polite, masc.) |
| that girl | you (polite, fem.) |
| these boys | you (familiar, masc.) |
| those girls | you (familiar, fem.) |

4. मुझे ----- देखना है ।

| the school | this new car | this state |
| his house | these books | this town |

260

his office       *your store*

C.   Transform the following present imperfect tense sentences to past perfect tense sentences:

वह शाम को लौटता है । ----- वह शाम को लौटा था ।

1. बस यहां पांच मिनट ठहरती है ।

2. क्या आप इसी दुकान से किताबें ख़रीदती हैं ?

3. तुम कितने बजे स्कूल जाते हो ?

4. मेरा मित्र पांच बजे वापस आता है ।

5. आप यहां कितने समय रुकते हैं ?

6. वह लड़का किताबें कहां ले जाता है ?

7. वह आदमी इसी कमरे में बैठता है ।

8. बस इसी सड़क पर मिलती है ।

9. गाड़ी सुबह आठ बजे छूटती है ।

10. इसे ख़रीदने में पन्द्रह रुपए लगते हैं ।

11. ये दवाएं यहीं मिलती हैं ।

12. मैं सुबह इसी पार्क में घूमता हूं ।


D.   Transform the following present imperfect tense sentences to past progressive tense sentences:

वह दवा ख़रीदता है । ----- वह दवा ख़रीद रहा था ।

1. लड़के हिन्दी सीखते हैं ।

2. वह औरत मोटर चलाती है ।

3. मैं उस समय दफ़्तर से वापस आता है ।

4. वह लड़कों को स्कूल के बारे में बताता है ।

5. उन दिनों यहां पानी बरसता है ।

6. मैं भाषाएं सीखती हूं ।

7. हम इसी मकान में रहते हैं ।

8. बच्चे हिन्दी की किताबें पढ़ते हैं ।

9. क्या आप उनकी बात नहीं सुनते ?

10. मेरी बहिन अस्पताल से दवा लाती है ।

E. Transform the following present imperfect tense sentences to present perfect tense sentences:

वह दफ़्तर जाता है । ----- वह दफ़्तर गया है ।

1. ये दवाएं किस दुकान में मिलती हैं ?

2. गाड़ी क्या यहीं रुकती है ?

3. राम लाल जी इसी दफ़्तर में बैठते हैं ।

4. बस पांच बजे से पहले नहीं छूटती ।

5. क्या आपके पिता कभी इस पार्क में घूमते हैं ?

6. क्या तुम यह किताबें स्कूल से लाते हो ?

7. क्या आप कभी इस होटल में भी ठहरते हैं ?

8. मोटर चलाना सीखने में कितने रुपए लगते हैं ?

9. हम पड़ोस के अस्पताल से ही दवा लाते हैं ।

10. वे लड़कियां पांच बजे तक इसी मकान में रहती हैं ।

F. Transform the following sentences according to the model given:

वह बाज़ार जाता है । ----- वह बाज़ार नहीं जा पाया ।

1. लड़के अंग्रेज़ी पढ़ते हैं ।

2. मैं मोटर चलाना सीखता हूं ।

3. नौकर सब काम करता है ।

4. वह कपड़े ख़रीदता है ।

5. लड़कियां दवाएं लाती हैं ।

6. क्या आप उनकी भाषा समझते हैं ?

7. वह पत्र लिखती है ।

8. मैं मोटर देखता हूं ।

G. Transform the following sentences according to the

model given:

लड़का बाज़ार जाता है । ----- लड़के को बाज़ार जाना पड़ेगा ।

1. लड़कियां मोटर चलाना सीखती हैं ।

2. नौकर घर का सब काम करता है ।

3. वह बच्चे को इसी स्कूल में भर्ती कराता है ।

4. मेरा छोटा भाई इसी मकान में रहता है ।

5. औरतें कपड़ा ख़रीदती हैं ।

6. मैं इसी कमरे में बैठता हूं ।

7. हम सातवें दर्जे में उसका नाम लिखते हैं ।

8. तुम मेरी बात सुनते हो ?

9. तुम मेरी बात नहीं सुनते ।

10. वह लड़का अपने पिता के आने की प्रतीक्षा करता है ।


H.   Conversation:

1.   A gets a telephone call from the hospital informing
     him that his wife has had an accident and is in the
     hospital.  A finds out the details and leaves his
     office hurriedly informing his secretary about it
     and asking him to take messages for him during his
     absence.

2.   A has recently been transferred to Agra and is new
     to the town.  He looks up his old friend who is in
     Agra now and asks for his help in finding a place
     to live, telling him what kind of place he wants.

3.   A is asked some advice by B, a new arrival in town,
     about getting his children admitted into school.
     A asks for the details, suggests which schools to
     go to and offers to accompany B personally to the
     school for getting the children admitted.

4.   A has an appointment to see B.  B is late for the
     appointment.  He explains that due to bad weather
     it took him much longer to drive down than he ex-
     pected and apologizes for the delay.

5.   B runs into A, an old friend of his, at a party he
     is attending.  B asks A about his family, parents
     etc.  B invites him out to his place later during
     the week to meet his family.  A asks for the

263

address of B's house and how to get there, before
he leaves the party.

6. A calls on B, who isn't at home. A talks to B's
servant who tells him when B will be in and asks
A to wait. However, A leaves a message giving his
name, the place he is staying, and other details
asking B to call him back when he returns.

7. A is an English speaker. The principal of the
school, to which A wants his son to be admitted,
explains that the medium of instruction is only
Hindi and that his son may have some difficulty.
A assures the principal that his son knows Hindi
because he has studied it for a few years in
college in the United States.

8. A hears that B had an accident the previous day.
A calls up to find out about the accident, asking
B's wife if he can do anything for them.

# LESSON XVII

## Conversation -- Invitation to a Village

### JOHN

छुट्टी

अगली छुट्टियों में आप क्या
करेंगे ?

vacation

What are you going to do
during the coming
vacation?

### RAM LAL

गांव

जानेवाला हूं

मैं अपने माता पिता से मिलने
गांव जानेवाला हूं ।

मैं बहुत दिनों से उनसे नहीं
मिला हूं ।

आप छुट्टियों में क्या करेंगे ?

village

am about to go

I am about to go to the
village to see my parents.

I haven't seen them for a
long time.

What are you going to do
during the vacation?

### JOHN

निश्चय

अभी निश्चय नहीं है, कहीं
घूमने जाने का इरादा है ।

certainty

It is not certain as yet,
I intend to take a trip
somewhere.

### RAM LAL

देश

क्या आपने कभी हमारे देश के
गांव देखे हैं ?

country

Have you ever seen the
villages of our country?

## JOHN

भारतीय             Indian

जी नहीं, मैंने भारतीय गांवों
के बारे में पढ़ा है,

No, I have read about Indian
villages,

इच्छा           desire

और तभी से मेरी इच्छा
भारतीय गांव देखने की है ।

and since then I have
wanted to visit an
Indian village,

लेकिन         but

लेकिन अभी तक में जा नहीं
पाया ।

but I haven't been able to
go as yet.

## RAM LAL

क्यों          why

तब आप मेरा साथ मेरे गांव
क्यों नहीं चलते ?

Then why don't you come with
me to my village?

देख लेना        to be able to see

बीत जाना        to pass, to be spent

आप गांव भी देख लेंगे और
आपकी छुट्टियां भी अच्छी
बीत जाएंगी ।

You will be able to see a
village and will enjoy the
vacation too (-- and your
vacation will be spent
nicely too).

## JOHN

हां, यह है तो अच्छा विचार ।     Yes, that's a fine idea.

आपका गांव कितनी दूर है ?     How far is your village?

## RAM LAL

यही कोई           about

266

अस्सी                              eighty

यही कोई अस्सी मील ।               About eighty miles.

रेलगाड़ी                            train

क्या आपके गांव तक रेलगाड़ी          Does the train go to your
जाती है ?                            village?

RAM LAL

जी हां, लगभग तीन घण्टे             Yes, it's about a three
की यात्रा है ।                      hours' trip.

JOHN

तब आप कब चलेंगे ?                 When will you leave then?

RAM LAL

शनिवार                            Saturday
बन्द होना                          to be closed
शनिवार को दफ़्तर बन्द               The office will be closed
होगा ।                            on Saturday.
चल देना                           to go, to start off
उसी दिन शाम को चल देंगे ।          We will leave that evening.

JOHN

तब ठीक है, मैं आपके साथ            Then it's O.K., I'll go
चलूंगा ।                          with you.
असुविधा                          inconvenience
आपको कोई असुविधा तो               Then it won't be incon-
नहीं होगी ?                         venient for you?

RAM LAL

खुशी                              pleasure, happiness

267

जी नहीं, मुझे बड़ी खुशी होगी । No, I'll be very glad.

अच्छा, अब मैं चलूं । नमस्ते ।   All right, I should leave

now.  Goodbye.

नमस्ते ।

Goodbye.

## DAYS

| | |
|---|---|
| इतवार | Sunday |
| सोमवार | Monday |
| मंगलवार, मंगल | Tuesday |
| बुधवार, बुध | Wednesday |
| बृहस्पतिवार, गुरुवार | Thursday |
| शुक्रवार, शुक्र | Friday |
| शनिवार, शनीचर | Saturday |
| हफ़्ता, सप्ताह | week |

## NUMERALS

| | | |
|---|---|---|
| इकतीस | (iktis, iktiis) | thirty-one |
| बत्तीस | (battis, battiis) | thirty-two |
| तैंतीस | (tãĩtis. tãĩtiis) | thirty-three |
| चौंतीस | (cãũtis, cãũtiis) | thirty-four |
| पैंतीस | (pãĩtis, pãĩtiis) | thirty-five |
| छत्तीस | (chattis, chattiis) | thirty-six |
| सैंतीस | (sãĩtis, sãĩtiis) | thirty-seven |
| अड़तीस | (aRtis, aRtiis) | thirty-eight |
| उनतालीस | (untaalis, untaaliis) | thirty-nine |

चालीस    (caalis, caaliis)    forty

GRAMMAR

1.  <u>New Nouns</u>

<u>Masc. II</u>                           <u>Fem. I</u>

गांव        village        छुट्टी       vacation

निश्चय       certainty      रेलगाड़ी      train

देश         country        खुशी        happiness, pleasure

<u>Fem. II</u>

इच्छा       desire, wish

असुविधा     inconvenience

2.  <u>New Verbs</u>

बीतना               to pass, to be spent

2.1  <u>New Compound Verbs</u>

<u>Type I</u>

देख लेना             to be able to see

बीत जाना            to pass, to be spent

चल देना             to go, to leave

<u>Type II</u>

बन्द होना            to be closed

3. ने <u>Construction</u>

Certain verbs used in any form involving the perfect will express the subject of the verb by using the
postposition ने with the subject.

A noun used with the postposition ने is in the
oblique case form. Pronouns used with the postposition

269

ने are irregular, some using the nominative, some using
the oblique and some using a special form.

|  | Sg. | | Pl. | |
|---|---|---|---|---|
|  | Nom. | ने Form | Nom. | ने Form |
| 1st Per. | मैं | मैंने | हम | हमने |
| 2nd Per. |  |  | तुम | तुमने |
|  |  |  | आप | आपने |
| 3rd Per. | वह | उसने | वे | उन्होंने |
|  | यह | इसने | ये | इन्होंने |
| Rel. Pr. | जो | जिसने | जो | जिन्होंने |
| Interr. Pr. | कौन,क्या | किसने | कौन | किन्होंने |
| Indef. Pr. | कोई | किसीने |  | किन्होंने |
|  | कुछ | कुछने |  |  |

The verbs which appear in this construction are
all those verbs that are transitive, i.e., take a
direct object, with three exceptions:

1. A small number of transitive verbs do not appear
in this construction. So far लाना is the only transitive verb of this type you have met.

| मैं ये फल लाया । | I brought this fruit. |
|---|---|
| वह ये किताबें लाया है । | He has brought these books. |
| क्या आप ही ये कपड़े लाए | Did you bring these |
| थे? | clothes? |

2. Some verbs that may occur with or without an
object, are used in the ने construction, when there is
an object expressed, and are used without ने when there

270

is no object expressed. The only verb that you have

met so far of this type is समझना ।

मैं समझा ।                          I understood.

मैंने आपकी बात समझी ।                I understood you (i.e.,

                                    what you said).

3. Verbs which take a direct object expressed by the
postposition से will normally express the subject by the
ने form, when the perfect form of the verb is used. This
is true for example of the verb कहना "to say," "to tell"
which takes a direct personal object expressed by से .

राम उससे कहता है ।                  Ram tells him.

राम ने उससे कहा ।                   Ram told him.

However, the verb मिलना "to meet," which also has a
direct personal object expressed by the postposition से,
does not use the ने construction when the verb is in
the perfect form.

मैं उससे दो बजे मिलूंगा ।           I'll see him at two o'clock.

मैं उससे दो बजे मिला ।              I saw him at two o'clock.

लड़की उससे दो बजे मिली ।            The girl saw him at two

                                    o'clock.

The agreement of the verb is as follows:

1. If the direct object is in the nominative case,
the verb will agree with the direct object in number
and gender.  The direct object may appear in the nominative case only if it is inanimate.

मैंने वे किताबें पढ़ीं ।            I read those books.

271

मैंने पांच लिफ़ाफ़े खरीदे ।     I bought five envelopes.

उसने अपना काम किया ।     He did his work.

2. If the direct object is in the को form, then the verb does not agree with either the subject or the object but is arbitrarily used in the masculine singular form. The direct object is always in the को form if the object is animate and is sometimes in the को form if the direct object is inanimate.

उसने लड़के को देखा ।
{ He saw the boy.
{ She saw the boy.

क्या आपने मेरे मित्रों को     Didn't you recognize my
नहीं पहचाना था?     friends?

क्या राम ने उन किताबों     Has Ram read those books?
को पढ़ा है ?

4. वाला

A new use of वाला with the oblique form of the infinitive is to express an action which is about to take place.

मैं जानेवाला हूं ।     I am about to go.

राम कुछ किताबें खरीदनेवाला     Ram is about to buy some
है ।     books.

गाड़ी छूटने वाली है ।     The train is about to leave.

5. इच्छा

The word इच्छा "desire," "wish" is used with the verb होना where English would use the verb "want to." Where English uses the infinitive with "want," Hindi uses the infinitive with का construction, i.e., the

272

form की agreeing with इच्छा (feminine).  In the following sentences note the word order, when a possessive
adjective is used with इच्छा.

हिन्दी पढ़ने की इच्छा          the desire to study Hindi

मेरी इच्छा हिन्दी बोलने        I want to speak Hindi.

की है ।

## EXERCISES

A.  Substitute orally in the sentences below the Hindi
equivalent of the English given:

1. मेरी इच्छा ----- है ।

> to go to a village
>
> to go to an Indian village
>
> to visit my parents
>
> to take a trip
>
> to take a trip somewhere
>
> to take a trip during the vacation
>
> to learn Hindi
>
> to learn to speak Hindi
>
> to buy some clothes
>
> to buy some envelopes

2. उसका गांव ----- है ।

| | |
|---|---|
| how far | thirty-seven miles |
| thirty miles | thirty-three miles |
| thirty-eight miles | thirty-six miles |
| thirty-two miles | thirty-one miles |
| thirty-nine miles | thirty-five miles |
| thirty-four miles | forty miles |

3. क्या आपके दफ़्तर में ----- छुट्टी है ?

| | |
|---|---|
| on Monday | on Thursday |
| on Saturday | on Friday |
| on Wednesday | tomorrow |
| on Tuesday | the day after tomorrow |
| on Sunday | two days after tomorrow |

4. ----- भी अच्छी बीत जायगी ।

| | |
|---|---|
| his vacation | the night |
| your holiday | the evening |
| the morning | |

5. ----- कोई असुविधा तो नहीं होगी ।

| | |
|---|---|
| you (familiar) | your father |
| he | his family |
| they | her husband |
| you (polite) | his sister |
| your brother | your elder brother |

6. ----- यह किताब नहीं पढ़ी ।

| | |
|---|---|
| I | the boy |
| he | the girl |
| we | my friend |
| they | his sister |
| she | this man |
| this woman | that woman |

7. मैं ----- उनसे नहीं मिला हूं ।

| | |
|---|---|
| for a long time | since last Wednesday |
| for the last two weeks | since last Monday |

274

for the last three years

for the last so many days

since last Saturday

since last Friday

8. तब मैं आपसे ----- मिलूंगा ।

at 2:30 p.m. on Friday

at 11:30 a.m. on Wednesday

at 7:30 p.m. on Monday

at 5:45 p.m. on Thursday

at 6:15 p.m. on Tuesday

at 8:30 a.m. on Sunday

at 3:45 p.m. on Saturday

at 4:00 p.m. tomorrow

at 3:30 p.m. on Thursday next

9. ----- बड़ी खुशी होगी ।

| | |
|---|---|
| I | my wife |
| we | my family |
| they | our friends |
| he | my elder brother |
| my parents | this man |

B. Substitute orally in the sentences below the Hindi equivalent of the English given making changes, if necessary:

1. ----- अगली छुट्टियों में गांव जानेवाला हूं ।

| | |
|---|---|
| I (masc.) | I (fem.) |
| she | we (masc.) |
| you (masc., familiar) | you (fem., familiar) |

we (fem.)                    you (masc., polite)

they (masc.)                 they (fem.)

you (fem., polite)           John and his wife

he                           this man


C.  Transform the following future tense sentences to
perfect tense sentences according to the model given:

मैं कल हिन्दी पढ़ूंगा । ----- मैंने कल हिन्दी पढ़ी ।

1. हम उसे यह बात बताएंगे ।

2. क्या आप परसों कपड़े खरीदेंगे ।

3. वह लड़की कल दर्जे में हिन्दी बोलेगी ।

4. मैं कल आपका काम करूंगा ।

5. मेरा मित्र कल अंग्रेज़ी समाचार पत्र पढ़ेगा ।

6. उसकी बहिन कल राम को कुछ रुपए देगी ।

7. क्या तुम परसों कुछ किताबें खरीदोगे ?

8. मैं आपकी बात सुनूंगा ।

9. हम कल एक मकान देखेंगे ।

10. मेरा भाई कल शाम पांच बजे मेरी प्रतीक्षा करेगा ।

11. मैं आपकी किताबें भेज दूंगा ।

12. लड़के कल इसी दुकान से दवाएं लेंगे ।

13. मैं कल राम को टेलीफ़ोन करूंगा ।

14. हम उसी होटल में दो कमरे लेंगे ।

15. क्या उसकी लड़की इस साल हिन्दी सीखेगी ?


D.  Transform the following present progressive tense
sentences to perfect tense sentences according to the
model given:

वह हिन्दी पढ़ रही है । ----- उसने हिन्दी पढ़ी ।

1. मैं कपड़े खरीद रहा हूं ।

2. क्या आप उसकी बात सुन रहे हैं ?

276

3. मैं इस साल हिन्दी सीख रहा हूं ।

4. उसका भाई कुछ लिफ़ाफ़े खरीद रहा है ।

5. राम धोबी को कपड़े दे रहा है ।

6. क्या तुम मेरी बात सुन रहे हो ?

7. लड़का अस्पताल से दवा ले रहा है ।

8. मैं राम के आने की प्रतीक्षा कर रहा हूं ।

9. **हम डाक्टर शर्मा के दवाखाने से दवा ले रहे हैं ।**

10. मैं उसे कुछ किताबें भी भेज रही हूं ।

E.  Transform the following future tense sentences to past perfect tense sentences:

मैं अगले साल हिन्दी पढ़ूंगा । ----- मैंने पिछले साल हिन्दी पढ़ी थी ।

1. क्या तुम अगले साल कुछ किताबें भेज दूंगी ?

2. उसकी बहिन अगले साल कुछ सूती कपड़े खरीदेगी ।

3. लड़का धोबी को कपड़े देगा ।

4. मैं परसों आपकी किताबें भेज दूंगी ।

5. क्या आप इसी दुकान से दवा लेंगे ?

6. हम इसे ये बातें बता देंगे ।

7. **लड़की अगले साल हिन्दी सीखेगी ।**

8. राम शाम पांच बजे मेरी प्रतीक्षा करेगा ।

9. हम इसी दुकान से संतरे लेंगे ।

10. क्या आप मेरी बात सुनेंगे ?

11. लड़का हिन्दी लिखेगा ।

12. मैं उसे अगले साल कुछ डिक्शनरियां दूंगी ।

13. हम अगले हफ़्ते नेहरू पार्क देखेंगे ।

14. क्या आप कल शाम छ: बजे मेरा इंतज़ार करेंगे ?

15. क्या आपका नौकर मेरा काम कर देगा ?

F.  Translate orally:

1. I intend taking a trip this year.

2. Do you intend to take a trip somewhere during the vacation?

3. Have you seen an Indian village?

4. He wants to visit an Indian village.

5. Does John want to go to see an Indian village?

6. Since then I have wanted to go to India.

7. I have studied about Indian villages.

8. I have studied about Indian people.

9. He must have studied about Indian villages.

10. You must have seen Indian books.

11. You will enjoy your vacation.

12. Did you enjoy your vacation?

13. Why don't you come with me to my village?

14. Why didn't he go to the city with you?

15. Why don't you come to my house with me?

16. Does the train go to your village?

17. Does the bus go to his village?

18. I don't think the bus goes to his village.

19. Do you think the bus goes to Ram's village?

20. The office will be closed on Saturday.

21. The store will be closed at 9 p.m.

22. The office is closed today.

23. The doctor's office was closed when I went there.

24. The clothing store was closed yesterday at 7 p.m.

25. The fruit store was not closed on Friday at 2:30 p.m.

# LESSON XVIII

## Conversation -- A Hindi Film

### RAM PAL

क्या कल शाम आप खाली हैं ?       Are you free tomorrow
                                  evening?

ख़ास                              important, special

### BILL

कल शाम मुझे कोई ख़ास काम          I don't have anything
नहीं है ।                         special to do tomorrow
                                  evening.

क्यों ? क्या बात है ?             Why? What's the matter?

### RAM PAL

फ़िल्म                            film

मैं कल शाम एक हिन्दी फ़िल्म       I'm going to see a Hindi
देखने जा रहा हूं ।               film tomorrow evening.

पसन्द करना                       to like

क्या आप मेरे साथ चलना            Would you like to go with
पसन्द करेंगे ?                   me?

### BILL

ज़रूर ।                           Certainly.

आए                               coming

मुझे भारत आए इतने दिन हो          It has been a long time
गए लेकिन अभी तक मैंने एक          since I came to India but
भी हिन्दी फ़िल्म नहीं             I haven't seen a Hindi
देखी ।                           film yet.

279

सिनेमा              movie

मैं बड़ी खुशी से आपके साथ     I will be glad to go to the
सिनेमा देखने चलूंगा ।         movie with you.

शुरू होना             to begin

फ़िल्म कितने बजे शुरू होती है ?    When does the movie begin?

RAM PAL

साढ़े छह बजे ।           At half past six.

BILL

तब तो फ़िल्म नौ साढ़े नौ     Then the movie will last
बजे तक चलेगी ।         until nine or nine thirty.

लम्बा              long

मैंने सुना है कि हिन्दी फ़िल्में    I have heard that Hindi
काफ़ी लम्बी होती हैं ।      films are quite long.

RAM PAL

आम तौर पर           generally, ordinarily

जी हां, आम तौर पर हिन्दी     Yes, Hindi films are
फ़िल्में अंग्रेज़ी फ़िल्मों से      usually longer than
ज्यादा लम्बी होती हैं ।       English films.

एक फ़िल्म लगभग ढाई घण्टे    A film runs for about two
चलती है ।            and a half hours

BILL

सच                true

नाचना              to dance

नाच               dance, dancing

गाना              song, singing, to sing

भरपूर              filled with

280

| | |
|---|---|
| भरपूर होना | to be filled with |
| क्या यह सच है कि हिन्दी फ़िल्में नाच-गानों से भरपूर होती हैं ? | Is it true that Hindi films are full of dancing and singing? |

RAM PAL

| | |
|---|---|
| अक्सर | often, usually |
| कई | many |
| जी हां, अक्सर हिन्दी फ़िल्मों में आठ-दस गाने और कई नाच होते हैं । | Yes, there are usually eight to ten songs and many dances in a Hindi film. |
| दिलचस्पी | interest |
| आपको तो नाच-गाने में बहुत दिलचस्पी है । | You are very much interested in dancing and singing. |
| सोचना | to think |
| शायद | perhaps |
| इसीलिए मैंने सोचा कि शायद आप हिन्दी फ़िल्म देखना पसन्द करें । | Therefore, I thought you might like to see a Hindi film. |

BILL

| | |
|---|---|
| जी हां, ज़रूर । | Yes, certainly. |
| मैं आपके साथ ज़रूर चलूंगा । | I'll certainly go with you. |

MONTHS

| | |
|---|---|
| जनवरी | January |
| फ़रवरी | February |
| मार्च | March |
| अप्रैल | April |

281

| | |
|---|---|
| मई | May |
| जून | June |
| जुलाई | July |
| अगस्त | August |
| सितम्बर | September |
| अक्टूबर | October |
| नवम्बर | November |
| दिसम्बर | December |
| महीना, मास | month |

## NUMERALS

| | | |
|---|---|---|
| इकतालीस | (iktaalis, iktaaliis) | forty-one |
| बयालीस | (bayaalis, bayaaliis) | forty-two |
| तितालीस | (titaalis, titaaliis) | forty-three |
| चवालीस | (cawaalis, cawaaliis) | forty-four |
| पैंतालीस | (pãĩtaalis, pãĩtaaliis) | forty-five |
| कयालीस | (chayaalis, chayaaliis) | forty-six |
| सैंतालीस | (sãĩtaalis, sãĩtaaliis) | forty-seven |
| अड़तालीस | (aRtaalis, aRtaaliis) | forty-eight |
| उनचास | | forty-nine |
| पचास | | fifty |

## GRAMMAR

1. <u>New Nouns</u>

<u>Masc. I</u>          <u>Fem. I</u>

सिनेमा cinema          दिलचस्पी (no pl.) interest

गाना song, singing

महीना month

| Masc. II | | Fem. II | |
|---|---|---|---|
| नाच | dance, dancing | फ़िल्म | film |
| मास | month | | |

## 2. New Verbs

| | |
|---|---|
| सोचना | to think |
| नाचना | to dance |
| गाना | to sing |

## 2.1 New Compound Verbs

### Type II

| | |
|---|---|
| पसन्द करना | to like |
| शुरू करना | to begin |

## 3. New Adjectives in -aa

| | |
|---|---|
| लम्बा | long |

## 4. Compound Verbs

Many compound verbs formed with करना as the second element of the compound will also form a compound with होना instead of करना as the second element. Some of these compounds with करना will have the same meaning as the compounds with होना but will be used in a different syntactic construction.

Compounds of this type that you have met so far are:

| | | |
|---|---|---|
| पसन्द करना | पसन्द होना | to like |
| इंतज़ार करना | इंतज़ार होना | to wait for |
| प्रतीक्षा करना | प्रतीक्षा होना | to wait for |

283

| | | |
|---|---|---|
| इरादा करना | इरादा होना | to intend to |
| इच्छा करना | इच्छा होना | to want to |
| विचार करना | विचार होना | to think of |

All of these compounds with करना express the subject by the nominative case. Some of these (पसन्द, इंतज़ार, प्रतीक्षा, इच्छा) when compounded with होना express the subject by the dative case, but others (इरादा, इच्छा, विचार) express the subject by the pronominal adjective form.

मैं यह किताब पसन्द करता हूं ।
मुझे यह किताब पसन्द है ।
> I like this book.

मैं उनका इंतज़ार करता हूं ।
मुझे उनका इंतज़ार है ।
> I wait for him.

मैं उनकी प्रतीक्षा करता हूं ।
मुझे उनकी प्रतीक्षा है ।
> I wait for him.

मैं बाज़ार जाने की इच्छा करता हूं ।
मेरी इच्छा बाज़ार जाने की है ।
मुझे बाज़ार जाने की इच्छा है ।
> I want to go to the bazaar.

मैं बाज़ार जाने का इरादा करता हूं ।
मेरा इरादा बाज़ार जाने का है ।
> I intend to go to the bazaar.

मैं बाज़ार जाने का विचार करता हूं ।
मेरा विचार बाज़ार जाने
> I am thinking of going to the bazaar.

का है ।

Whether the करना construction is present imperfect or present progressive, the equivalent होना construction will be in the simple present. Also whether the करना construction is past imperfect, past progressive or perfect, the equivalent होना construction will be in the simple past.

मैं उनका इंतज़ार करता हूं ।
मैं उनका इंतज़ार कर रहा हूं ।
} मुझे उनका इंतज़ार है ।

मैं उनकी प्रतीक्षा करता था ।
मैं उनकी प्रतीक्षा कर रहा था ।
मैंने उनकी प्रतीक्षा की ।
} मुझे उनकी प्रतीक्षा थी ।

Of these alternative forms, the constructions with होना occur more frequently than those with करना .

5. शायद

Sentences in which शायद "perhaps," "probably," "maybe" occurs, will have the main verbal form in the optative.

शायद आप हिन्दी फ़िल्म
देखना पसन्द करें ।

Perhaps you might like to see a Hindi film.

शायद कल मैं आपको टेलीफ़ोन
करूं ।

Perhaps I will call you on the phone tomorrow.

शायद वह आज आपसे मिले ।

Perhaps he will see you today.

शायद आज शाम को मैं
बाज़ार जाऊं ।

Maybe I'll go to the bazaar this evening.

285

6. "Since"

In time statements of the sort "It is a certain time since somebody did something," the clause "since somebody did something" is expressed by using the perfect form of the verb and expressing the subject in the dative case. The verb form does not agree with anything but must necessarily have the ending -ee.

मुझे भारत आए इतने दिन        So many days have passed
हो गए ।                          since I came to India.

मुझे यह किताब पढ़े कई साल     It has been many years
हो गए हैं ।                      since I read this book.

मुझे उससे मिले कई दिन हो      Many days have passed since
गए ।                            I saw him.

Note the word order of the subject and the object in the clause with the perfect form of the verb:

मुझे उसे देखे तीन दिन हो       It is three days since I
गए ।                            saw him.

उसे मुझे देखे तीन दिन हो       It is three days since he
गए ।                            saw me.

## EXERCISES

A. Substitute orally in the following sentences the Hindi equivalent of the English given:

1. शायद आप ----- पसन्द करें ।

      to see a Hindi film

      to buy some books

      to buy some Hindi books

      to visit a village

      to visit an Indian village

      to go to a movie

      to go to an Indian movie

286

to go to an Indian movie with me

to study Hindi

to learn Hindi

to talk in Hindi

to see him

to see him tomorrow

to stay in this hotel

to take a walk in this park

to buy some sweet oranges

2. क्या ----- हिन्दी फ़िल्म देखना पसन्द है ?

| | |
|---|---|
| you (polite) | his brother |
| he | your friends |
| they | your younger daughter |
| you (familiar) | his elder sister |
| this girl | Asha's husband |
| Ram's wife | this boy |

3. मुझे पांच नए पैसे वाले ----- टिकट दे दीजिए ।

| | |
|---|---|
| forty-six | forty-eight |
| forty-five | forty-one |
| forty-two | forty-nine |
| forty-seven | forty-four |
| forty-three | fifty |

4. ---------- बहुत दिन हो गए । (using the perfect form of the verb)

since he came to India

since he came back to India

since I came back from India

since I saw him

since he saw me

since I saw a film

since I saw a good film

since I saw a good Hindi film

since I bought these clothes

since he went to India

since I read Hindi

since I read Hindi books and newspapers

5. मैं यहां ----- आया था ।

| last year | in December | on Monday |
| last month | in February | on Friday |
| last week | in June | on Wednesday |
| in May | in September | on Saturday |
| in November | in April | on Tuesday |
| in January | in October | on Sunday |
| in August | in July | on Thursday |
| in March | | |

6. क्या उसे ----- बहुत दिलचस्पी है ?

in dancing

in singing

in dancing and singing

in seeing Hindi movies

in seeing English movies

in seeing Indian movies

in going to India

in visiting an Indian village

288

B. Substitute orally in the sentences given below the Hindi equivalent of the English given, making changes if necessary:

1. लड़के ने ----- खरीदे ।

some fruit                      some woolen cloth

one dozen sweet oranges         some silk clothes

some medicines                  one dozen cotton shirts

ten inland letters              a pair of socks

a Hindi newspaper               a bus ticket

some books                      fifty books

C. Transform the following sentences with a करना construction to sentences with a होना construction, according to the model given.

मैं यह फ़िल्म पसन्द करता हूं । ----- मुझे यह फ़िल्म पसन्द है ।

1. मैं यह किताब पसन्द करता हूं ।

2. वह अपने मित्र के आने की प्रतीज्ञा कर रहा है ।

3. क्या आपके भाई इस पार्क में घूमना पसन्द करते हैं ?

4. मैं गाड़ी का इंतज़ार कर रहा हूं ।

5. लड़की स्कूल खुलने की प्रतीक्षा कर रही है ।

6. मेरा मित्र भारतीय फ़िल्में देखना पसन्द करता है ।

7. क्या आप डाक्टर के आने की प्रतीक्षा कर रहे हैं ?

8. मैं गाड़ी छूटने का इंतज़ार कर रहा हूं ।

9. वह लड़की हिन्दी पढ़ना पसन्द करती है ।

10. क्या आप अपने भाई के लौटने की प्रतीक्षा कर रहे हैं ?

D. Transform the following sentences with a करना construction to sentences with a होना construction, according to the model given.

289

वह फल खरीदने की इच्छा ----- उसकी इच्छा फल खरीदने की
करता है ।                              है ।

1. क्या आप आज शाम उस पार्टी में जाने का विचार कर रहे हैं ?

2. जान आगरा देखने का इरादा करता है ।

3. वह भारतीय नाच-गाना सीखने की इच्छा करती है ।

4. मैं आज शाम हिन्दी फ़िल्म देखने का विचार कर रहा हूं ।

5. वह भारत जाने की इच्छा करता है ।

6. मेरी लड़की अगले साल हिन्दी सीखने का विचार कर रही है ।

7. क्या आप इन छुट्टियों में गांव जाने का इरादा कर रहे हैं ?

8. मेरे मित्र एक हिन्दी फ़िल्म देखने का इच्छा करते हैं ।

9. क्या आप अपने बीमार भाई को डा0 शर्मा के यहां ले जाने का
   विचार कर रहे हैं ?

10. मैं हाल में ही बाहर जाने का इरादा कर रहा हूं ।

E.  Transform the following present imperfect tense
sentences to perfect tense sentences, according to the
model given:

वह हिन्दी लिखती है । ----- उसने हिन्दी लिखी ।

1. राम धोबी को कपड़े देता है ।

2. मेरी पत्नी इसी दुकान से फल खरीदती है ।

3. वे लड़कियां इसी स्कूल में पढ़ती हैं ।

4. क्या नौकर आपका सब काम करता है ?

5. वह मुझे अपने दफ़्तर के बारे में बताता है ।

6. आप दवाएं कहां से लेते हैं ?

7. लड़के यहां हिन्दी बोलना सीखते हैं ।

8. वह अपने मित्र को पत्र लिखता है ।

9. मेरे भाई मुझे पांच रुपए देते हैं ।

10. वह अपने मित्र को पत्र भेजता है ।

F. Transform the following sentences according to the model given:

वह बाज़ार जा रहा है । ----- वह बाज़ार जाने वाला है ।

1. मेरी पत्नी अपने लिए कुछ सूती कपड़े खरीद रही है ।

2. वह अपने मित्र को कुछ किताबें भेज रहा है ।

3. मैं राम का नया घर देखने जा रहा हूं ।

4. क्या तुम धोबी को कपड़े दे रहे हो ?

5. वह आज भारत से वापस आ रहा है ।

6. गाड़ी छूट रही है ।

7. लड़के हिन्दी पढ़ रहे हैं ।

8. उसका भाई कुछ संतरे ले रहा है ।

9. क्या पानी बरस रहा है ?

10. वह डाक्टर के यहां से आपके लिए दवा ला रहा है ।

G. Translate orally:

1. The movie lasts until nine o'clock.

2. Will the movie last until nine o'clock?

3. Does the movie last until nine o'clock?

4. The movie doesn't last until nine o'clock.

5. I think the movie lasts until nine o'clock.

6. I don't think the movie lasts until nine o'clock.

7. I have heard that Hindi movies are usually very long.

8. Is it true that Hindi movies are usually very long?

9. Is it true that Hindi films are full of dancing and singing?

10. You are very much interested in dancing and singing, aren't you?

11. Is he very much interested in singing and danc-

291

ing?

12. Are you interested in learning Hindi?

13. My friend is interested in going to India.

14. He should be interested in learning to read and write Hindi.

15. Should he be interested in learning to speak Hindi?

16. When does the movie begin?

17. The school begins at 8 a.m., doesn't it?

18. Hindi films are longer than English films.

19. Hindi films were longer than English films.

20. Hindi films should be longer than English films.

21. English films are better than Hindi films.

22. Hindi films were better than English films.

23. Don't you think that Hindi films were worse than English films?

24. It's true that English films were shorter than Hindi films.

25. I thought that English films were not worse than Hindi films.

## Conversation -- Building a House

### RAM LAL

| | |
|---|---|
| ख़तम | completion, end |
| ख़तम होना | to be finished |
| कहो, आज काम कहां तक ख़तम हुआ ? | Tell me, how far has the work gone today? |

### MOHAN

| | |
|---|---|
| नींव | foundation |
| पूरा | full, complete |
| **पूरा होना** | to be completed |
| नींव पूरी हो गई है । | The foundation has been completed. |
| दीवाल | wall |
| बनाना | to build, to make |
| शुरू हो जाना | to begin |
| कल सुबह से दीवाल बनाना शुरू हो जाएगा । | By tomorrow, the building of the walls will begin. |

### RAM LAL

| | |
|---|---|
| **सामान** | materials |
| क्या तुम्हारे पास सभी सामान है ? | Have you all the materials? |

### MOHAN

| | |
|---|---|
| ईंट | brick |
| चूना | lime |

293

गारा

जी हां, ईंटें, चूना, गारा
आदि सभी है ।

ज़रूरत

लेकिन बहुत जल्दी ईंटों की
ज़रूरत पड़ेगी ।

RAM LAL

बच रहना

कितनी बच रही हैं ?

MOHAN

हज़ार

मेरा विचार है कि दस हज़ार
से ज्यादा न होंगी ।

और वे चार पांच दिन में ख़तम
हो जाएंगी ।

RAM LAL

ख़बर

भेज देना

अच्छा, तब मैं आज ही दुकान
पर ख़बर भेज दूंगा, जिससे
ईंटें समय से आ जाएं ।

मज़दूर

मज़दूरों का क्या हाल है ?

mortar

Yes, we have everything,
bricks, lime, mortar etc.

need

But very soon bricks will
be needed.

to be left

How many are left?

thousand

I don't think there are
more than ten thousand
(left).

And they will be used up in
four to five days.

information, news

to send

O.K., I'll send a request
to the store today, so
that the bricks will
come on time.

laborer, workman

What is the situation re-
garding the workmen?

294

MOHAN

ठीक है, लेकिन अब से हमें
कुछ और मज़दूरों की
ज़रूरत पड़ेगी ।

It is all right, but from
now on we will need some
more laborers.

RAM LAL

कितने ?

How many?

MOHAN

कम से कम

at least

कम से कम एक दर्जन ।

At least a dozen.

RAM LAL

इंतज़ाम

arrangement

इंतज़ाम करना

to arrange

ठीक है, मैं उसका इंतज़ाम कर
दूंगा ।

O.K., I'll make arrange-
ments.

चीज़

thing

और कोई चीज़ चाहिए ?

Do you need anything else?

MOHAN

छत

roof

इस समय तो नहीं, पर अगले
हफ़्ते छत बनाने के सामान
की ज़रूरत पड़ेगी ।

Not right now, but materials
for building the roof will
be needed next week.

RAM LAL

लोहा

steel, iron

लकड़ी

wood

सीमेंट

cement

लोहा, लकड़ी और सीमेंट तो

I have enough steel, wood

295

मेरे पास काफ़ी है ।
इसलिए, कोई कठिनाई नहीं
होगी ।

and cement,

Therefore, there shouldn't

be any difficulty.

MOHAN

तब ठीक है ।

एक बात और है ।

Then it's all right.

There's one more thing.

RAM LAL

क्या ?

What?

MOHAN

पैसा

मुझे कुछ पैसा चाहिए ।

money

I need some money.

RAM LAL

मज़दूरी

क्यों ? क्या तुम्हें मज़दूरी
नहीं मिली ?

wages

Why?  Didn't you get your

wages?

MOHAN

नहीं, मज़दूरी तो मिल गई है ।

एडवांस

पर मुझे कुछ एडवांस चाहिए ।

मेरे बच्चे की तबियत ख़राब

हो गई है और इसलिए मुझे

पैसे की बड़ी ज़रूरत है ।

Yes, I did.

advance

But I need an advance.

My son is not well and

therefore I need money

badly.

RAM LAL

अच्छा, कितना पैसा चाहिए ?

O.K.  How much do you want?

MOHAN

इस समय बीस रुपए काफ़ी

Twenty rupees will be

296

| | |
|---|---|
| होंगे । | enough right now. |

**RAM LAL**

| | |
|---|---|
| अच्छा, ये लो बीस रुपए । | O.K., here are twenty rupees. |

**MOHAN**

| | |
|---|---|
| मेहरबानी | kindness |
| ठीक है, आपकी बहुत मेहरबानी । | O.K., thank you very much. |

**NUMERALS**

| | |
|---|---|
| इक्यावन | fifty-one |
| बावन | fifty-two |
| तिरपन (tirpan, treepan) | fifty-three |
| चउवन, चौवन | fifty-four |
| पचपन | fifty-five |
| छप्पन | fifty-six |
| सत्तावन | fifty-seven |
| अट्ठावन | fifty-eight |
| उनसठ | fifty-nine |
| साठ | sixty |

**GRAMMAR**

1. <u>New Nouns</u>

<u>Masc. I.</u>                                  <u>Fem. I</u>

| | | | | |
|---|---|---|---|---|
| चूना | (no plural) | lime | लकड़ी | wood |
| गारा | (no plural) | mortar | मज़दूरी | wages |
| लोहा | (no plural) | steel, iron | मेहरबानी | kindness |

297

|          | Masc. II          |          | Fem. II              |
|----------|-------------------|----------|----------------------|
| सामान    | materials         | नींव     | foundation           |
| हज़ार     | thousand          | दीवाल    | wall                 |
| मज़दूर     | workman, laborer  | ईंट      | brick                |
| इंतज़ाम    | arrangement       | ज़रूरत    | need                 |
| एडवांस    | advance           | ख़बर      | information, news    |
|          |                   | चीज़      | thing                |
|          |                   | छत       | roof                 |
|          |                   | सीमेंट    | cement               |

## 2. New Verbs

बनाना            to build, make

## 2.1 New Compound Verbs

### Type I

बच रहना          to be left

भेज देना          to send

### Type II

ख़तम होना         to get finished

इंतज़ाम करना       to arrange, to make arrangements

## 3. New Adjectives in -aa

पूरा             full

## 4. Compound Verbs

Some of the compound verbs that are made with होना and करना as the second element, have a different meaning depending upon whether the compound is with होना or with करना. The compound with होना is likely to

298

have a passive meaning (something is being done or something gets done), and the compound with करना is likely to have a transitive meaning (somebody does something). The compounds of this type that you have met so far are

| | | | |
|---|---|---|---|
| बन्द होना | to get closed, to be closed | बन्द करना | to close |
| ख़तम होना | to get finished, to be finished | ख़तम करना | to finish |
| पूरा होना | to get completed, to be completed | पूरा करना | to complete |

Sometimes the meaning of the compound with होना is intransitive whereas the compound with करना is transitive. So far you have met the following forms:

| | | | |
|---|---|---|---|
| शुरू होना | to begin (intransitive) | शुरू करना | to begin (transitive) |

Examples of the use of these forms are:

| | |
|---|---|
| दरवाज़ा बन्द होता है । | The door gets closed. |
| मैं दरवाज़ा बन्द करता हूँ । | I close the door |
| काम ख़तम होता है । | The work gets completed. |
| मैं काम ख़तम करता हूँ । | I complete the work. |
| नींव पूरी होती है । | The foundation gets completed. |
| मैं नींव पूरी करता हूँ । | I complete the foundation. |
| काम शुरू होता है । | The work begins. |
| मैं काम शुरू करता हूँ । | I begin the work. |

299

The form बन्द may be used as an ordinary adjective along with the simple present or simple past of होना whereas the forms शुरू, ख़तम, and पूरा may not be used in this way.

दरवाज़ा बन्द है ।　　　　The door is closed
दरवाज़ा बन्द था ।　　　　The door was closed.

The forms पूरा and बन्द may be used as adjectives with a following noun:

मैंने पूरे दिन काम किया ।　　I worked the whole day.
यह बन्द दुकान किसकी है ?　Whose is this closed store?

Another similar verbal pair is इंतज़ाम होना and इंतज़ाम करना. This pair is similar to the preceding in that the meaning of the form with होना is passive, "arrangements get made" or "are made," and the meaning of the compound with करना is transitive "to make arrangements." This pair is unlike the preceding group in that the thing arranged is expressed by a का construction.

मेरे आगरे जाने का इंतज़ाम　　Arrangements have been made
हो गया है ।　　　　　　　　for my going to Agra.
मैं आगरे जाने का इंतज़ाम　　I am making arrangements
कर रहा हूं ।　　　　　　　　to go to Agra.

5. Time Expressions

Some time expressions are expressed in the oblique case with no postpositions. This is customary with the words दिन, हफ़्ता, महीना, मास, साल, पहर particularly when used with पिछला "last," यह "this," अगला "next."

300

| | |
|---|---|
| मैं पिछले साल भारत गया था । | I went to India last year. |
| मैं इस महीने भारत जाऊंगा । | I will go to India this month. |
| वह अगले हफ्ते भारत जाएगा । | He will go to India next week. |
| उसने पिछले हफ्ते यह किताब पढ़ी । | He read this book last week. |
| मैं तीसरे पहर उनसे मिलूंगा । | I will see him in the after-noon. |

With the days of the week the postposition को is used.

| | |
|---|---|
| वह सोमवार को मुझसे मिला था । | He saw me on Monday. |

With the names of the months the postposition में is used.

| | |
|---|---|
| क्या आप नवम्बर में आगरे गए थे ? | Did you go to Agra in November? |

Note that the expression "on time" may be समय से, समय पर, वक्त से, वक्त पर.

| | |
|---|---|
| गाड़ी समय से छूटेगी । | The train will leave on time. |
| सिनेमा समय से शुरू होगा । | The movie will begin on time. |

6. "Necessity"

Note the following parallel pairs.

| | | |
|---|---|---|
| ज़रूर | अवश्य | certainly |
| ज़रूरी | आवश्यक | necessary |

301

| ज़रूरत | आवश्यकता | necessity, need |
|---|---|---|

आपको बाज़ार ज़रूर (अवश्य)  You should certainly go to
जाना चाहिए ।  the bazaar.

इस समय अस्पताल जाना बहुत  It is very necessary to go
ज़रूरी (आवश्यक) है ।  to the hospital now.

हमें ईंटों की ज़रूरत  We need bricks.
(आवश्यकता) है ।

7. "Thing"

Both the word चीज़ and the word बात are likely to
be translated as "thing" in English.  Usually चीज़
will refer to some material object, and usually बात
will refer to something somebody says or thinks.  Besides this, बात may refer to an incident and be translated by English "affair."

क्या आपको कोई और चीज़  Do you need anything else
चाहिए ?  (any material object)?

क्या उसने कोई और बात  Did he say anything else?
कही थी ?

इस बाज़ार में सभी चीज़ें  All kinds of things are
मिल जाती हैं ।  available in this bazaar.

EXERCISES

A.  Substitute orally in the sentences below the Hindi
equivalent of the English given:

1. अगले हफ़्ते मुझे ----- की ज़रूरत पड़ेगी ।

      materials to build a house

      materials to build a road

materials to build a roof

materials to build the walls

materials to build the walls of this house

some money to buy books

some money to buy clothes

some money to buy books for my daughter

some more workmen to build the foundation

some wood to build this house

some iron to build this house

ten thousand bricks to build this house

2. क्या मेरा सामान ----- आ जाएगा ?

by tomorrow                    by next Thursday

by the day after tomorrow  by next Tuesday

by next Sunday              by next Friday

by next Saturday            by next month

by next Wednesday           by next year

by next Monday              on time

3. मैं ----- आगरे गया ।

last year                   in August

in January                  in November

on Wednesday                on Friday

last week                   on Tuesday

on Thursday                 on Saturday

in April                    last month

4. मैं ----- इंतज़ार कर दूँगा ।

for this                    for these things

for this thing              for iron

for bricks

for mortars

for lime

for wood

for money

for some workmen

for some more workmen

for your wages

for an advance for you

5. मुझे कल से ----- मज़दूर और चाहिए ।

| | |
|---|---|
| sixty | fifty-nine |
| fifty-five | forty-nine |
| fifty-eight | fifty-seven |
| fifty-two | forty-four |
| fifty-four | fifty-one |
| forty-six | fifty-six |
| forty-three | forty-eight |
| fifty-three | fifty |

6. ----- इंतज़ाम कर दीजिए ।

for me to stay

for me to stay in that town

for him to stay here

for him to stay here for a week

for me to go to Kanpur

for him to come here tomorrow

to get medicine from the hospital

for her birthday celebration

304

for her to get admitted to the school

for him to go to see a Hindi movie

7. वह आदमी, -----, यही रहता है । (use a relative clause)

who completed the foundation of this building

who will make arrangements for the building of this house

who gives the wages to the workman

who built this new house

who knows how to sing Hindi songs

who likes Indian movies very much

who told me about your accident

whom my father met the other day in the store

who likes to dance Indian dances

who has been sick for the last few days

who has a clothing store in Agra

whom I have wanted to see for the last one month

B. Substitute orally in the sentences below the Hindi equivalent of the English given, making other changes if necessary.

1. ----- कहां रहता है ? (use a वाला construction)

the man, who works in this store

the girl, who studies Hindi in this school

the man, who sings Indian songs

the workmen, who are building this house

the doctor, who works in this hospital

the boy, who is going to the village tomorrow

your brother, who speaks Hindi

the servant, who works for Ram

2. मैंने ----- ।

read the book

wrote a letter

shut the door

saw your brother

finished your work

began the book

built a house

gave him some money

sent him some books

bought a house

drove a car

got her admitted to the school

C.  Transform the following sentences according to the model given:

क्या आप यह किताब पढ़ ----- जी नहीं, मैंने यह किताब पिछले
रहे हैं ?                                    हफ़ुते पढ़ी थी ।

1. क्या आप पत्र लिख रहे हैं ?

2. क्या आप यह मकान बना रहे हैं ?

3. क्या तुम हिन्दी फ़िल्म देख रहे हो ?

4. क्या आप राम को इस शहर के बारे में बता रहे हैं ?

5. क्या तुम राम की मोटर चला रहे हो ?

6. क्या तुम स्कूल का काम कर रही हो ?

7. क्या आप अपने भाई को कपड़े दे रहे हैं ?

8. क्या आप यह दवाएं ख़रीद रहे हैं ?

9. क्या आप यह सामान बाहर भेज रहे हैं ?

306

10. क्या तुम इस दुकान से फल ले रही हो ?

D.  Transform the following sentences according to the model given:

क्या वह बाज़ार जा रहा है ? ----- कल शायद वह बाज़ार जाए ।

1. क्या वह दुकान बन्द कर रहा है ?

2. क्या वह टिकट ले रहा है ?

3. क्या वह पार्क में घूम रहा है ?

4. क्या वह डाक्टर को टेलीफ़ोन कर रहा है ?

5. क्या वे सिनमा देखने जा रहे हैं ?

6. क्या लड़के स्कूल का काम पूरा कर रहे हैं ?

7. क्या वे पूना से वापस आ रहे हैं ?

8. क्या लड़कियां पार्टी का इंतज़ाम कर रही हैं ?

9. क्या पानी बरस रहा है ?

10. क्या वे कुछ कपड़े ख़रीद रहे हैं ?

E.  Translate orally:

1.  I am going to the bazaar.

2.  My brother is going to the bazaar.

3.  My brother is going to Agra.

4.  My brother went to Agra.

5.  My brother came to Agra.

6.  My brother came from Agra.

7.  My brother returned from Agra.

8.  My brother returned from India.

9.  My brother returned yesterday.

10.  My brother was working yesterday.

11.  They were working yesterday.

12. They were reading yesterday.

13. They were reading this book.

14. They read this book.

15. They wrote this book.

16. They wrote some books.

17. They bought some books.

18. They bought some Hindi books.

19. They often buy Hindi books.

20. The boys often buy Hindi books.

21. The boys never buy Hindi books.

22. The boys never read Hindi books.

23. The boys never read Hindi.

24. The boys never speak Hindi.

25. We never speak Hindi.

F.   Translate orally:

1. He is building a house.

2. He is building a new house.

3. He is beginning to build a new house.

4. He wants to build a new house.

5. They want to build a new house.

6. They are making arrangements to build a new house.

7. They have to build a new house.

8. They have to buy a new house.

9. We have to buy a new house.

10. We have to see a new house.

11. We are waiting to see a new house.

12. We are waiting to see a new film.

13. We saw a new film.

14. He saw a new film.

15. He saw a new car.

16. He drove the new car.

17. He drove to India.

18. He drove to India last year.

19. He returned to India last year.

20. He returned last year.

21. He wanted to return last year.

22. He wanted to work last year.

23. He couldn't work last year.

24. He couldn't work last year because he was sick.

# LESSON XX

## Conversation -- Seasons

### JOHN

|  |  |
|---|---|
| गर्मी | heat, hot season |
| पड़ना | to be, remain |
| आजकल यहां बड़ी गर्मी पड़ रही है । | It is very hot here nowadays. |
| ऐसी गर्मी यहां कब तक पड़ती है ? | How long will it remain so hot here? |

### RAM LAL

|  |  |
|---|---|
| अभी एक डेढ़ महीने और काफ़ी गर्मी रहेगी । | It will be quite hot for a month or a month and a half more. |
| आख़िर | end |
| बरसात | rainy season |
| लेकिन जून के आख़िर तक बरसात शुरू हो जायगी । | But the rainy season will begin by the end of June. |
| ऋतु | season |
| जाड़ा | cold weather |
| आप तो जानते ही हैं कि भारत में तीन ऋतुएं होती हैं --- गर्मी, बरसात और जाड़ा । | You know that there are three seasons in India -- the hot season, the rainy season, and the cold season. |

### JOHN

|  |  |
|---|---|
| कब से कब तक | from when to when |

310

गर्मी कब से कब तक रहती है ?   How long does the hot season last?

RAM LAL

आम तौर पर मार्च से जून तक गर्मी की ऋतु रहती है ।

The hot season usually lasts from March to June.

तेज़   strong, sharp, fast

धूप   sunshine

लू   hot wind

इस दिनों में बड़ी तेज़ धूप होती है, गर्मी पड़ती है और अक्सर लू भी चलती है ।

At that time the sun is very strong, it gets very hot and there is often a hot wind.

जून के आख़िर से बरसात शुरू हो जाती है ।

The rainy season begins by the end of June.

बरसना   to rain

और सितम्बर तक पानी बरसता रहता है ।

And it keeps on raining until September.

आसमान   sky

बादल   cloud

बराबर   continuously

छाया   gathered

तूफ़ानी   stormy

हवा   wind, air

बरसात में आसमान पर बादल बराबर छाए रहते हैं, काफ़ी पानी बरसता है और कभी कभी तूफ़ानी हवाएं भी चलती हैं ।

In the rainy season, the clouds are generally gathered in the sky, it rains a lot, and stormy

311

|                                                  |                                                      |
| ------------------------------------------------ | ---------------------------------------------------- |
|                                                  | winds also blow sometimes.                           |
| ठण्डक                                             | cold, cold season                                    |
| अक्टूबर से फ़रवरी तक ठण्डक पड़ती है ।             | The cold season lasts from October to February.      |

JOHN

|                                        |                               |
| -------------------------------------- | ----------------------------- |
| ठण्ड                                    | cold, cold season             |
| क्या यहां बहुत ठण्ड पड़ती है ?          | Does it get very cold here?   |

RAM LAL

|                                                                        |                                                                         |
| ---------------------------------------------------------------------- | ----------------------------------------------------------------------- |
| वैसा --- जैसा                                                            | as...as                                                                 |
| उत्तरी                                                                   | northern                                                                |
| भाग                                                                     | part                                                                    |
| जी नहीं, यहां वैसी ठण्ड नहीं पड़ती जैसी आपके देश के उत्तरी भागों में ।   | No. It does not get as cold here as in the north-ern part of your country. |
| बर्फ़, बरफ़                                                               | snow, ice                                                               |
| साथ ही यहां बर्फ़ भी नहीं गिरती ।                                        | It does not snow here either.                                           |
| काश्मीर                                                                  | Kashmir                                                                 |
| केवल काश्मीर में तथा कुछ उत्तरी भागों में जाड़े में बर्फ़ गिरती है ।     | It snows only in Kashmir and some northern regions during the cold season. |

JOHN

|                                                                  |                                                                           |
| ---------------------------------------------------------------- | ------------------------------------------------------------------------- |
| दक्षिणी                                                           | southern                                                                  |
| क्या उत्तरी और दक्षिणी भारत में गर्मी का समय एक ही होता है ?     | Is the time of the hot season the same in the north as in the south?      |

# RAM LAL

| | |
|---|---|
| अन्तर | difference |
| जी नहीं, उत्तरी और दक्षिणी भारत में ऋतुओं के समय में अन्तर है । | No, there is a difference in the time of the seasons between North India and South India. |
| के अलावा | besides |
| उत्तर | north |
| दक्षिण | south |
| इसके अलावा एक अन्तर यह भी है कि उत्तर में गर्मियों में ज्यादा गर्मी पड़ती है दक्षिण में उससे कम । | Besides this, there is the difference that in the north, it is hotter in the hot season than it is in the south. |
| मौसम | season, weather |
| मैं आपको उत्तरी भारत के मौसमों के बारे में ही बता रहा था । | I was telling you only about the seasons in North India. |

## DIRECTIONS

| | |
|---|---|
| उत्तर | north |
| दक्षिण | south |
| पूर्व, पूरब | east |
| पश्चिम | west |
| उत्तरी | northern |
| दक्षिणी | southern |
| पूर्वी | eastern |
| पश्चिमी | western |

313

# NUMERALS

| | | |
|---|---|---|
| इकसठ | | sixty-one |
| बासठ | | sixty-two |
| तिरसठ | (tirsaTh, treesaTh) | sixty-three |
| चौंसठ | | sixty-four |
| पैंसठ | | sixty-five |
| छ्याछठ | (chããchaTh) | sixty-six |
| सड़सठ | (sarsaTh, saRsaTh) | sixty-seven |
| अड़सठ | (arsaTh, aRsaTh) | sixty-eight |
| उनहत्तर | | sixty-nine |
| सत्तर | | seventy |

# GRAMMAR

1.  ## New Nouns

### Masc. I

जाड़ा    cold, cold season

### Masc. II

| | |
|---|---|
| आख़िर | end |
| आसमान | sky |
| बादल | cloud |
| भाग | part |
| अन्तर | difference |
| मौसम | season, weather |
| उत्तर | north |
| दक्षिण | south |
| पूर्व, पूरब | east |
| पश्चिम | west |

### Fem. I

गर्मी    heat, hot season

### Fem. II

| | |
|---|---|
| बरसात | rains, rainy season |
| ऋतु | season |
| धूप | sunshine |
| लू | hot wind |
| ठण्ड | cold, cold season |
| ठण्डक | cold, cold season |
| बर्फ़, बरफ़ | snow, ice |

314

2. New Verbs

गिरना     to fall

3. New Adjectives in -aa

कड़ाया     gathered

वैसा     as

जैसा     as

4. Compound Postpositions

के अलावा     besides

5. Seasons

The year is normally divided into three seasons in Hindi, गर्मी the hot season from March to June, बरसात the rainy season, from the end of June to September, and जाड़ा, ठण्ड or ठण्डक the cold season, from October to February. The word for season is either ऋतु or मौसम . With the words गर्मी, जाड़ा, ठण्ड and ठण्डक the verb पड़ना may be used where English will use the verb "to be," but with the word बरसात the verb होना is used.

गर्मी यहां कब तक पड़ती है ?     How long is the hot season here?

बरसात यहां कब तक होती है ?     How long is the rainy season here?

The word बर्फ़ or बरफ़ can mean either "snow" or "ice" and is treated by some people as a masculine noun and by others as a feminine noun. The word बर्फ़ or बरफ़ "snow" is used with the verb गिरना or पड़ना to make a verb "to snow."

315

| कल बर्फ़ गिरी थी । | It snowed yesterday. |
| क्या इस दुकान पर बर्फ़<br>मिलता है ? | Is ice available in this<br>store? |

6. "To keep on"

Where English uses "to keep on" followed by a verb
ending in "ing" as in "to keep on working," Hindi uses
the verb रहना for the English "to keep on" plus the
imperfect form of a verb. As in English the verb "to
keep on" may appear in various tenses, so in Hindi the
verb रहना may appear in various tenses, but the subordinate verb is always in the imperfect form. The
verb forms agree with the subject except when रहना is
in the infinitive form in which case the verb in the
imperfect form is always in the -ee form.

| वह जाता रहता है । | He keeps on going. |
| वह जाती रहती है । | She keeps on going. |
| वे जाते रहते थे । | They kept on going. |
| वह जाता रहा । | He kept on going. |
| वह जाता रहेगा । | He will keep on going. |
| सितम्बर तक पानी बरसता<br>रहता है । | It keeps on raining until<br>September. |
| वह कल पूरे दिन काम करती<br>रही । | She kept on working all day<br>yesterday. |
| राम अगले हफ़्ते भी यह<br>किताब पढ़ता रहेगा । | Ram will keep on reading<br>this book next week too. |
| राम पिछले सितम्बर तक<br>यहां पढ़ता रहा है । | Ram (has) studied here until<br>last September. |

316

| | |
|---|---|
| मुझे यह किताब पढ़ते रहना चाहिए । | I ought to keep on reading this book. |
| हिन्दी पढ़ते रहो । | Keep on studying Hindi. |

7. "As...as"

The Hindi equivalent of English "as...as" is either वैसा ----- जैसा or उतना -----जितना . The construction वैसा ---- जैसा is likely to imply "kinds of" and may be translated variously into English as "as...as," "such...as," "the same way, kind, sort, as."

| | |
|---|---|
| यहां वैसी ठण्ड नहीं पड़ती जैसी उत्तर में । | It does not get as cold here as in the North. |
| यह पार्क वैसा नहीं है, जैसा आपने बताया था । | This park is not the same as you said (such as you said, or the kind that you said). |
| यह दुर्घटना वैसी नहीं थी जैसी मैंने सुनी थी । | This accident was not the same as I had heard. |

The उतना ---- जितना construction implies quantity or degree and is likely to be translated into English by "as...as," "as...much as," "as...many as."

| | |
|---|---|
| वह उतना लम्बा है जितना उसका भाई । | He is as tall as his brother. |
| मुझे हिन्दी पढ़ने की उतनी ही इच्छा है जितनी राम को । | I want to study Hindi as much as Ram does. |

Compare the following sentences.

| | |
|---|---|
| मेरे पास वैसी किताबें नहीं | I don't have the same kind |

हैं, जैसी राम के पास । | of books as Ram does.

मेरे पास उतनी किताबें नहीं हैं, जितनी राम के पास । | I don't have as many books as Ram does.

यह शहर उतना बड़ा नहीं है, जितना कानपुर । | This city is not as big as Kanpur is.

यह शहर वैसा नहीं है, जैसा कानपुर । | This city is not the same as Kanpur (i.e. not like Kanpur).

यहां उतनी गर्मी नहीं पड़ती जितनी उत्तर में । | It is not as hot here as in the north.

यहां वैसी गर्मी नहीं पड़ती जैसी उत्तर में । | They don't have the same kind of heat here as in the north.

## 8. Time Expressions

In English the expression "at that time" or "at this time" may refer to a point in time or duration of time over a period. In Hindi the expression referring to point of time is इस समय, उस समय or इस वक्त, उस वक्त, and the expression referring to duration of time is इन दिनों में, उन दिनों में or इन दिनों, उन दिनों ।

इन दिनों (में) बड़ी तेज़ धूप होती है । | At this time the sun is very strong (over a period of time).

उन दिनों (में) मैं भारत में था । | At that time I was in India (over a period of time).

इस समय वह हिन्दी पढ़ रहा है । | Right now he is studying Hindi (not over a period

318

of time).

Compare the following sentences:

उस समय वह घर में न था ।    At that time he wasn't at
                             home (at that particular

                             point of time).

उन दिनों (में) वह घर में न    He wasn't home at that time
था ।    (during that period of

                             time).

## EXERCISES

A. Substitute orally in the sentences below the Hindi
equivalent of the English given:

1. वह ----- ।

      keeps on going

      keeps on working

      keeps on reading

      keeps on writing

      keeps on speaking

      keeps on driving

      kept on driving

      kept on working

      kept on writing

      kept on reading this book

      will keep on reading this book

      will keep on studying here

      should keep on studying here

      will keep on studying Hindi

has kept on studying Hindi

should keep on studying Hindi

should keep on working

2. ----- बहुत गर्मी पड़ती है ।

here

there

in the North

in the North of India

in the South

in the West

in the West of this country

in the East of this country

in this part of the country

in South India

in North India

3. इसका दाम ----- रुपए है ।

| | |
|---|---|
| sixty-five | sixty-four |
| sixty-nine | forty-four |
| sixty-three | seventy |
| sixty-six | thirty-three |
| sixty-eight | fifty-three |
| sixty-two | twenty-seven |
| sixty-seven | forty-nine |
| sixty-one | twenty-eight |
| fifty-one | fifty |
| fifty-nine | twenty-five |

4. ----- यहां बड़ी गर्मी होगी ।

    for a month and a half

    for two months

    for two months more

    for two and a half weeks

    for a week more

    for how long

    tomorrow morning

    until tomorrow morning

    until next week

    until July

    until Thursday

    until the rainy season

    until the cold season

    in the hot season

5. मेरे भाई ----- आगरे में रहेंगे ।

    from March to June

    from August to December

    from May to November

    from Monday to Wednesday

    from Tuesday to Sunday

    from Friday to Thursday

    from the end of February until September

    from the beginning of April to the end of May

    from the beginning of July to the end of
      October

6. ----- काफ़ी अन्तर है ।

between North India and South India

between my brother and his brother

between India and America

between Hindi and English

between the hot season and the rainy season

between the hot season in India and the hot season
  in America

between the North and the South

between the houses here and in the South

between a village and a city

B. Complete the following sentences by giving the
Hindi equivalent of the English in parentheses:

1. यहां वैसी ठण्ड नहीं पड़ती ----- । (as in the North)

2. मेरे पास वैसी किताबें नहीं हैं ----- । (as Ram does)

3. यह गांव वैसा नहीं है ----- । (as you said)

4. यह स्कूल वैसा नहीं है ----- । (as I thought)

5. ये फल वैसे नहीं हैं ----- । (as I wanted)

6. यह लड़का उतना लम्बा नहीं है ----- । (as my brother)

7. ये कमरे उतने छोटे नहीं हैं ----- । (as I thought)

8. उसके पास उतनी किताबें नहीं हैं ----- । (as I do)

9. यह फ़िल्म उतनी अच्छी नहीं है ----- ।(as yesterday's
                                                                India)
10. यहां उतनी तेज़ धूप नहीं पड़ती ----- । (as in India)

C. Transform the following sentences according to the
model given:

बर्फ़ गिरती है । ----- बर्फ़ गिरती रहती है ।

1. धूप पड़ती है ।

2. पानी बरसता है ।

3. लू चलती है ।

322

4. लड़के गाते हैं ।

5. मज़दूर काम करते हैं ।

6. हम हिन्दी बोलते हैं ।

7. मैं इसे रुपए देती हूं ।

8. वह भारत के बारे में बताता है ।

D.  Transform the following sentences according to the model given:

वह पढ़ रहा था । ----- वह पढ़ता रहा ।

1. आशा नाच रही थी ।

2. लड़के गा रहे थे ।

3. पानी बरस रहा था ।

4. वे सिनेमा देख रहे थे ।

5. मज़दूर मकान बना रहे थे ।

6. बर्फ़ गिर रही थी ।

7. वह कपड़े का व्यापार कर रहा था ।

8. मेरा भाई दवा ले रहा था ।

9. वह हिन्दी सीख रही थी ।

10. औरतें कपड़े भेज रही थीं ।

E.  Transform the following sentences according to the model given:

वह हिन्दी पढ़ता है । ----- उसे हिन्दी पढ़ते रहना चाहिए ।

1. वह लड़कों का नाम लिखता है ।

2. लड़की गाना गाती है ।

3. मैं कपड़े भेजता हूं ।

4. वे आदमी नया मकान बनाते हैं ।

5. मज़दूर नींव पूरी करते हैं ।

6. वे औरतें धोबी को कपड़े देती हैं ।

7. उसका मित्र भारत के बारे में बताता है ।

8. वह एक नई भाषा सीखते हैं ।

F.  Transform the following sentences according to the model given:

वह सिनेमा देखेगा । ----- उसने सिनेमा देखा ।

1. मज़दूर दीवाल बनाएंगे ।

2. लड़की गाना गाएगी ।

3. वह दुर्घटना के बारे में बताएगी ।

4. मैं कल सभी चीज़ें भेजूंगा ।

5. हम समाचार पत्र पढ़ेंगे ।

6. वे औरतें भारतीय नाच नाचेंगी ।

7. क्या आप उसके मित्र को पहचान लेंगे ?

8. मैं उसे भर्ती कराने की कोशिश करूंगी ।

9. वह काम कब शुरू करेंगे ?

10. वह लड़की नई मोटर चलाएगी ।

G.  Translate orally:

1. It's very hot here nowadays.

2. It will be very hot here.

3. How long will it be very hot here?

4. How long will it be cold here?

5. It will be cold here for a month.

6. It was cold here for a month.

7. It was cold here until the end of June.

8. It may be cold here until the end of June.

H.  Translate orally:

1. It's raining.

2. It will rain tomorrow.

3. It rained yesterday.

4. It snowed yesterday.

5. It was snowing yesterday.

6. It was snowing in Kashmir.

7. It began to snow in Kashmir.

8. It kept on snowing in Kashmir.

9. It kept on snowing till March.

10. It kept on snowing till the beginning of March.


## REVIEW V

A. Substitute orally in the sentences below the Hindi equivalent of the English given:

1. गांव यहां से ----- मील है ।

| | |
|---|---|
| fifty | forty-eight |
| fifty-five | thirty-eight |
| twenty-five | thirty-three |
| fifty-nine | twenty-seven |
| fifty-one | sixty-seven |
| sixty-nine | seventy |
| thirty-one | forty-seven |
| sixty-six | forty-five |
| sixty-three | forty-four |
| fifty-three | twenty-four |
| fifty-six | nineteen |
| sixty-eight | |

2. ----- यह किताब पढ़ी ।

| | |
|---|---|
| I | you (familiar) |
| he | nobody |
| we | she |
| who | you (polite) |
| they | Mr. Sharma |
| somebody | my brother |

3. मेरी इच्छा ----- है ।

| | |
|---|---|
| to speak Hindi | to return home |
| to study Hindi | to see a village |
| to go to Agra | to meet your father |
| to build a house | to learn Indian dancing |
| to build a new house | to finish this book |

4. मैंने ----- बारे में पढ़ा है ।

| | |
|---|---|
| that hotel | the schools in Poona |
| the bazaar in Agra | Indian weather |
| Nagpur oranges | Indian films |
| the stores in Kanpur | that accident |
| the Indian cities | the Indian languages |

5. ----- बहुत समय हुआ ।

since I came to India

since he saw a Hindi film

since it has rained

since we finished our work

since they built their house

since we began to speak Hindi

since I lived in Kashmir

since he worked in Agra

6. ----- कि हिन्दी फ़िल्में लम्बी होती हैं ।

is it true                    we have heard

did you know                  my sister wrote me

I think                       he didn't know

he told me                    she didn't tell me

7. मैंने सोचा कि शायद आप ----- ।

might like to see a Hindi film

might like to go to India

might want to go to Poona

might read this book

might stay with me

might drive the car

might want to drive the car

might be able to drive the car

8. हमें ----- की ज़रूरत पड़ेगी ।

some laborers

some more books

how many books

at least a thousand bricks

one more room

some special materials

a long holiday

some writing materials

another Hindi dictionary

sixty rupees more

327

9. ----- मुफे यह जगह पसन्द नहीं ।

       on account of the weather

       on account of the cold

       on account of the heat

       on account of the rains

       on account of the darkness

       on account of the fog

       on account of the people

       on account of the roof

10. वह ----- बाहर जाने वाला है ।

| | |
|---|---|
| on Tuesday | for how long |
| on Friday | for a few weeks |
| in a week | for a year |
| in a month | for a month |
| in an hour | during the vacation |
| in a few hours | during the coming vacation |
| in a few days | |

11. ----- आप कहां जाएंगे ?

| | |
|---|---|
| during the vacation | in the North of India |
| during the coming vacation | in the South of India |
| | in the western part of this state |
| next year | |
| in the eastern part of this state | |

12. उसे ----- बहुत दिलचस्पी है ।

       in seeing Indian movies

       in dancing

       in singing

in learning Hindi

in learning new languages

in visiting a new country

in going to the North of this country

in meeting new people

C. Transform the following sentences according to the model given:

मैं गांव जा रहा हूं । ----- मैं गांव जाने वाला हूं ।

1. वह दरवाज़ा बन्द कर रहा है ।

2. वह पत्र लिख रही है ।

3. नौकर अपना काम पूरा कर रहा है ।

4. वे लड़के समाचार पत्र पढ़ रहे हैं ।

5. वह दुकान खोल रहा है ।

6. लड़कियां नाचना सीख रही हैं ।

7. पानी बरस रहा है ।

8. वे मकान बनाना शुरू कर रहे हैं ।

9. वह यात्रा के लिए टिकट ख़रीद रहा है ।

10. वे लड़के गाना गा रहे हैं ।

D. Transform the following sentences according to the model given:

मैंने यह किताब पढ़नी चाही ----- लेकिन मैं अभी तक नहीं पढ़

थी ।                                     पाया ।

1. उसने एक नया मकान बनाना चाहा था ।

2. उसने उत्तरी भारत की यात्रा करनी चाही थी ।

3. हमने आपकी मां से मिलना चाहा था ।

4. उन्होंने एक भारतीय गांव देखना चाहा था ।

5. मैंने उसे भारतीय ऋतुओं के बारे में बताना चाहा था ।

6. मैंने भारत लौटना चाहा था ।

7. उसने मोटर चलाना सीखना चाहा था ।

8. उसने भारत के लोगों के बारे में जानना चाहा था ।

E. Transform the following sentences with करना constructions to होना constructions according to the model given:

मैं यह किताब पसन्द करता हूं ----- मुझे यह किताब पसन्द है ।

1. वह यहां का मौसम पसन्द करता है ।

2. लड़के नाच गाना पसन्द करते हैं ।

3. क्या तुम सुबह घूमना पसन्द करते हो ?

4. क्या आप गांव वालों से मिलना पसन्द नहीं करते ?

5. क्या आपका भाई यहां रहना पसन्द नहीं करता ?

6. क्या आप इस समय अपनी पत्नी का इंतज़ार कर रहे हैं ?

7. वह अपने भाई का इंतज़ार कर रहा था ।

8. उसने कल मेरा इंतज़ार किया ।

9. क्या आप इस समय अपनी पत्नी की प्रतीक्षा कर रहे हैं ?

10. उसने कल मेरी प्रतीक्षा की ।

11. वह अपने भाई की प्रतीक्षा कर रहा था ।

12. हम गांव देखने जाने का इरादा कर रहे हैं ।

13. क्या आप भारत लौटने का इरादा कर रहे हैं ?

14. क्या उसने एक नया मकान बनाने का इरादा किया ?

15. मैं भारत जाने का विचार कर रहा हूं ।

16. वह इसी मकान में रहने का विचार कर रहा था ।

17. उसने उत्तरी भारत का दौरा करने का विचार किया ।

18. वह गर्मियों में इसी शहर में रुकने का विचार कर रहा है ।

F. Transform the following sentences according to the
model given:

अगले हफ़्ते में फल ख़रीदूंगा ----- पिछले हफ़्ते मैंने फल ख़रीदे ।

1. अगले हफ़्ते डाक्टर नई दवाएं देगा ।

2. अगले हफ़्ते में अपने पत्नी को पत्र लिखूंगा ।

3. अगले हफ़्ते में यह किताब पढ़ूंगा ।

4. अगले हफ़्ते में यह किताब पढ़ने की कोशिश करूंगा ।

5. अगले हफ़्ते हम कुछ नया सामान लेंगे ।

6. अगले हफ़्ते वह अपनी लड़की को स्कूल में भर्ती कराएगा ।

7. अगले हफ़्ते वह अपना दफ़्तर बन्द करेगा ।

8. अगले हफ़्ते में दुकान पर ख़बर भेज दूंगा ।

9. अगले हफ़्ते में गाड़ी चलाना सीखूंगा ।

10. अगले हफ़्ते में इसे अपनी यात्रा के बारे में बताऊंगा ।


G.  Translate orally:

1.  What are you going to do during the coming
    vacation?

2.  What did you do during the vacation?

3.  What did you do at that time?

4.  What did he do at that time?

5.  What did he do on Wednesday?

6.  I don't know what he did on Wednesday.

7.  I don't know where he is going.

8.  I don't know where he went.

9.  I don't know what he said.

10.  What did he say?

11.  What did he say about the vacation?

12.  What did they say about the vacation?


H.  Translate orally:

1.  The office will be closed on Saturday.

331

2. The office will be closed on Friday.

3. The school will be closed on Friday

4. The school will remain open on Friday

5. The school remained open on Friday.

6. The school remained open in the rainy season.

7. They built the school in the rainy season.

8. Somebody built the school in the rainy season.

9. Who built the school in the rainy season?

10. Will they build a school in the rainy season?

11. Will they keep on building the school in the rainy season?

12. Will they be able to build the school in the rainy season?

I. Translate orally:

1. I haven't seen a Hindi film yet.

2. He hasn't seen a Hindi film yet.

3. He has often seen a Hindi film.

4. He is going to see a Hindi film.

5. He is going to see an Indian village.

6. He intends to see an Indian village.

7. He intends to study Hindi.

8. He intended to study Hindi.

9. He intended to write his wife.

10. He intended to bring his wife.

11. He made arrangements to bring his wife.

12. He will make arrangements to bring his wife.

J. Translate orally:

1. It doesn't get as cold here as in the northern part of your country.

2. It doesn't get as cold here as in the western part of your country.

3. It doesn't get as hot here as in the western part of your country.

4. It doesn't get as hot here as in India.

5. It doesn't rain as much here as in India.

6. It doesn't rain as much here as in the East.

7. It doesn't snow as much here as in the East.

8. It doesn't snow as much here as in the South.

9. The days are not as long here as in the North.

10. The days are not as long here as he said.

11. This book is not as interesting as he said.

12. Hindi is not as easy as he said.

K. Conversation:

1. A declines B's invitation to go to see an Indian movie and explains that he has seen one and didn't like it. A further tells that what he didn't like was that it was very long, was difficult to understand and had a lot of singing and dancing and was not very interesting.

2. A has just returned from a trip to India. B, who has never been to India, asks him about the Indian seasons. A gives a brief description of Indian seasons and tells B how they differ from the seasons in their own country.

3. A plans to take a trip to the northern part of India and asks his friend B, who has been in the North, to give him some helpful tips about the climate, people, speech and such things. B tells A briefly about his experiences in the North and how different and interesting they were.

4. A tells his secretary to make arrangements for a trip he wants to take in South India. The secretary asks when and how he is going, and asks for the details of the trip and the arrangements to be

made and goes off to do what is necessary.

5.  A drives out to an Indian village. On his way, he
    sees that they are putting up a building. Out of
    curiousity he stops and talks to the man in charge
    of the construction. A finds out that they are
    building a school for the children of the neigh-
    boring villages and also inquires about the way
    they are building it, the materials they are using
    and such things.

6.  A visits a village school in India. During the
    visit he talks to the principal of the school,
    and they talk about the differences between the
    Indian and American schools. They discuss the
    number of children in the schools, the languages
    of instruction, how far the children come to
    school, etc.

7.  A tells his friend B about how he got held up the
    night before while returning from Ajmer because of
    the storm and the rains. B asks some questions
    and A gives a detailed account of the weather the
    night before and of his difficulties in coming
    back.

8.  A spends an evening at a party to which he is
    invited. Next morning he tells his colleague B
    in the office about the party and how much he en-
    joyed the dancing, singing and meeting people.

# LESSON XXI

## Conversation -- Holi

### RAM DAS

| | |
|---|---|
| होली | Holi |
| क्या आप होली की छुट्टियों में कहीं बाहर जा रहे हैं ? | Are you going away anywhere during the Holi vacation? |

### BILL

| | |
|---|---|
| अमरीका | America |
| त्योहार | festival |
| मैं जब अमरीका में था तो मैंने भारतीय त्योहारों के बारे में पढ़ा था । | When I was in America, I read about Indian festivals. |
| रुक कर | staying |
| मनाना | to observe, celebrate |
| मनाई जाती है | is observed, is celebrated |
| मैं यहां रुक कर देखना चाहता हूं कि भारत में होली कैसे मनाई जाती है । | I want to stay here and see how Holi is celebrated in India. |

### RAM DAS

| | |
|---|---|
| यह तो बहुत अच्छा है । | That is fine. |
| नगर | city |
| इस नगर की होली है भी बहुत प्रसिद्ध । | The Holi celebration of this city is very well known. |

BILL

हां, यह तो मैंने भी सुना है ।

Yes, I have also heard about it.

कृपया

kindly

कृपया मुझे बताइए कि यहां लोग होली कैसे मनाते हैं ।

Please tell me how people celebrate Holi here.

RAM DAS

मुहल्ला

locality

हर

every

हर एक

every one, each

इकट्ठा होना

to gather

जमा रहना

to be piled up

आम तौर पर होली के दिन, रात को हर एक मुहल्ले में सभी लोग एक जगह इकट्ठा होते हैं, जहां पहले से बहुत सी लकड़ी आदि जमा रहती है ।

Generally, on the day of Holi, all the people in every locality gather at a particular place in the evening where previously a lot of wood, etc. has been piled up.

बजाना

to play (a musical instrument)

शुभ

auspicious

मुहूर्त

moment

जलाना

to set fire to, to burn

लोग वहां पहले गाते-बजाते हैं और तब शुभ मुहूर्त में होली जलाते हैं ।

People sing and play musical instruments, and then at an auspicious moment they

336

set fire to the pile of
wood.

NUMERALS

| | | |
|---|---|---|
| इकहत्तर | (ikhattar, ik-hattar) | seventy-one |
| बहत्तर | (bahattar) | seventy-two |
| तिहत्तर | (tihattar) | seventy-three |
| चौहत्तर | (cauhattar) | seventy-four |
| पचहत्तर | (pachattar) | seventy-five |
| छिहत्तर | (chihattar) | seventy-six |
| सतहत्तर | (sassattar, sat-hattar) | seventy-seven |
| अठहत्तर | (aThattar) | seventy-eight |
| उन्नासी उन्यासी | (unnaasii, unyaasii) | seventy-nine |
| अस्सी | | eighty |

GRAMMAR

1. <u>New Nouns</u>

<u>Masc. I</u>

मुहल्ला    locality

<u>Masc. II</u>

अमरीका (no pl.) America

त्योहार       festival

नगर          city

मुहूर्त        moment

<u>Fem. I</u>

होली    Holi

<u>Fem. II</u>

मुहूर्त       moment

2. <u>New Verbs</u>

मनाना    to observe, to celebrate

बजाना    to play (a musical instrument)

337

जलाना      to set fire to, to burn

जमाना      to pile up

2.1 <u>New Compound Verbs</u>

   <u>Type I</u>

जमा रहना         to be piled up

   <u>Type II</u>

इकट्ठा होना      to gather

3. <u>New Adjectives in</u> -aa

इकट्ठा         gathered

4. <u>Passive</u>

Hindi has a complete passive conjugation for transitive verbs. The verb to be conjugated is put in the perfect form and the verb जाना is used as an auxiliary. The auxiliary may appear in any form of the conjugation just as in the English passive the auxiliary "to be" may be in any form. The main verb in the perfect will have the usual agreement of the perfect.

| Present | <u>Active</u>: | मैं यह फल खरीदता हूं । |
|---|---|---|
| Imperfect | | I buy this fruit. |
| | <u>Passive</u>: | यह फल खरीदा जाता है । |
| | | This fruit is bought. |
| Past | <u>Active</u>: | मैं यह फल खरीदता था । |
| Imperfect | | I used to buy this fruit. |
| | <u>Passive</u>: | यह फल खरीदा जाता था । |
| | | This fruit used to be bought. |

338

| | | |
|---|---|---|
| Perfect | Active: | मैंने यह फल ख़रीदा । |
| | | I bought this fruit. |
| | Passive: | यह फल ख़रीदा गया । |
| | | This fruit was bought. |
| Present Perfect | Active: | मैंने यह फल ख़रीदा है । |
| | | I have bought this fruit. |
| | Passive: | यह फल ख़रीदा गया है । |
| | | This fruit has been bought. |
| Past Perfect | Active: | मैंने यह फल ख़रीदा था । |
| | | I had bought this fruit. |
| | Passive: | यह फल ख़रीदा गया था । |
| | | This fruit had been bought. |
| Future | Active: | मैं यह फल ख़रीदूंगा । |
| | | I will buy this fruit. |
| | Passive: | यह फल ख़रीदा जाएगा । |
| | | This fruit will be bought. |
| Optative | Active: | क्या मैं यह फल ख़रीदूं ? |
| | | Should I buy this fruit? |
| | Passive: | क्या यह फल ख़रीदा जाए ? |
| | | Should this fruit be bought? |
| Present Progressive | Active: | मैं यह फल ख़रीद रहा हूं । |
| | | I am buying this fruit. |
| | Passive: | यह फल ख़रीदा जा रहा है । |
| | | This fruit is being bought. |
| Past Progressive | Active: | मैं यह फल ख़रीद रहा था । |
| | | I was buying this fruit. |

339

Passive: यह फल खरीदा जा रहा था ।

This fruit was being bought.

चाहिए     Active: मुझे यह फल खरीदना चाहिए ।

construction     I should buy this fruit.

Passive: यह फल खरीदा जाना चाहिए ।

This fruit should be bought.

The passive construction is most likely to be used in the above sentences when the person who performs the action is not stated. In those cases where the passive is used and the performer of the action is stated, the performer is expressed by using the postposition के द्वारा.

| | |
|---|---|
| मैंने कल फल खरीदे । | I bought fruit yesterday. |
| कल फल खरीदे गए । | The fruit was bought yesterday. |
| कल मेरे द्वारा फल खरीदे गए । | The fruit was bought by me yesterday. |

The first of these sentences is the most common one when the performer is expressed, although the third is possible. The second is the normal expression when the performer is not expressed.

| | |
|---|---|
| भारत में होली कैसे मनाई जाती है ? | How is Holi celebrated in India? |
| यहां क्या काम किया जाता है ? | What kind of work is done here? |
| हिन्दी कैसे लिखी जाती है ? | How is Hindi written? |

340

| | |
|---|---|
| कहा गया है कि ----- | It has been said that ... |
| उसके बारे में बहुत सी बातें सुनी गई हैं । | Many things have been heard about him. |
| लड़कों को भारत के बारे में बताया जा रहा है । | The boys are being told about India. |
| उसे हर महीने कितने रुपए दिए जाते हैं ? | How many rupees are given to him every month? (How much does he earn per month?) |
| यह कमीज़ इसी दुकान से ली गई थी । | This shirt was bought from this store. |
| सुना गया है ----- | It has been heard that ... |

Note that in compounds of the काम करना type (i.e., those compounds of Type II which have a noun as the first element of the compound), the first element of the compound acts as the subject of the passive construction and the verb agrees with it.

<u>Active</u>:  मैं उसकी प्रतीक्षा करता हूं ।

I am waiting for him.

<u>Passive</u>:  उसकी प्रतीक्षा की जाती है ।

He is being waited for (lit.: his waiting for is being done).

<u>Active</u>:  मैं उसके ठहरने का इंतज़ाम कर रहा हूं ।

I am making arrangements for his stay.

<u>Passive</u>:  उसके ठहरने का इंतज़ाम किया जा रहा है ।

Arrangements for his stay are being made.

341

# 5. Past Participle

Hindi forms the past participle by adding either कर or के to the stem of the verb. The form with कर is the one most frequently used, except that the verb करना always forms the past participle by adding के e.g.,

| | |
|---|---|
| जा कर | having gone |
| खरीद कर | having bought |
| पढ़ कर | having read |
| कर के | having done |

In Hindi this past participle is used to make a clause subordinate to a main verb where the time of the participle is previous to the time of the main verb. It is used where English may use similar constructions, or where English uses two main verbs.

| | |
|---|---|
| मैं यहां रुक कर देखना चाहता हूं । | Having stayed here I want to see... (I want to stay here and see...). |
| मैं बाज़ार जाकर कुछ कपड़े लाऊंगा । | Having gone to the bazaar, I will bring some clothes back (I'll go to the store and bring...). |
| मेरा नया घर देखकर वह बहुत खुश हुआ । | Having seen my new house, he was very pleased. |

The Hindi construction with कर may also equate with an English clause beginning with "after."

| | |
|---|---|
| आगरे से आकर वह मुझसे | He met me after he returned |

मिला ।                          from Agra.

## 6. होली

The word होली in Hindi, besides referring to the
celebration of Holi in general, may also refer to any
part of the ceremony or activities by themselves.
Thus:

| | |
|---|---|
| होली मनाना | to celebrate Holi |
| होली खेलना | to play Holi; i.e., to throw colored water at people in the celebration of Holi. |
| होली जलाना | to burn Holi; i.e., to burn a bonfire in celebrating Holi. |
| होली इकट्ठा करना<br>होली जमा करना | to collect Holi; i.e., to collect the wood for the Holi bonfire. |
| होली मिलना | to meet Holi; i.e., to embrace people in the celebration of Holi or to visit people on the occasion of Holi. |

## 7. मुहूर्त

In Hindi the word मुहूर्त is used to mean "moment"
only in the sense of an auspicious or inauspicious
moment determined astrologically.

| | |
|---|---|
| शुभ मुहूर्त में<br>अच्छे मुहूर्त में | at an auspicious moment |
| अशुभ मुहूर्त में<br>बुरे मुहूर्त में | at an inauspicious moment |

## EXERCISES

A. Substitute orally in the sentences below the Hindi equivalent of the English given:

1. इसे ख़रीदने में ----- रुपए लगते हैं ।

| | |
|---|---|
| seventy-five | seventy-six |
| fifty-five | thirty-six |
| seventy-nine | seventy-one |
| sixty-nine | eighty |
| seventy-two | seventy |
| seventy-eight | seventy-three |
| seventy-seven | sixty-three |
| sixty-seven | seventeen |
| seventy-four | fifty-four |
| forty-four | forty-nine |

2. एक नया घर ----- ।

is being built

was built last year

was being built last year

has been built

will be built next year

had been built

may be built

344

should be built

has to be built

can be built

3. होली मार्च में * ----- ।

is celebrated

will be celebrated

is being celebrated

has been celebrated

was celebrated

used to be celebrated

may be celebrated

should be celebrated

4. मैं ----- घर गया ।

having seen his new house

having read a book

having celebrated Holi

having played Holi

having written a letter

having finished the work

having met my brother at the station

having waited for an hour

having stayed for half an hour

5. यह (masc.) ----- ।

----------
* According to the Hindu calendar, Holi is on the last
  full moon day of the Hindu year, which usually falls
  in the latter part of February or the first three
  weeks of March.

is celebrated          is said

is read                is understood

is written             is told

is heard               is burnt

6. यह किताब ----- ।

was being read         will be written

was being written      will be read

was being bought       has been read

was being brought      had been written

7. मैं जानना चाहता हूं कि होली ----- मनाई जाती है ।

how                    in what country

where                  at what time

when                   in which part of India

why                    by whom

8. ----- आपने क्या किया ?

after studying         about driving a car

before studying        on account of the fog

besides studying       for your children


B.  Transform the following sentences according to the
model given, omitting the performer of the action:

लड़का किताब ख़रीद रहा है । ----- किताब ख़रीदी जा रही है ।

1. धोबी मेरे कपड़े ला रहा है ।

2. लोग त्योहार मना रहे हैं ।

3. लोग लकड़ी जला रहे हैं ।

4. डाक्टर दवाएं दे रहे हैं ।

5. नौकर काम कर रहा है ।

6. मैं मोटर चला रहा हूं ।

C. Transform the following sentences according to the model given, omitting the performer of the action:

मैंने होली मनाई । ----- होली मनाई गई ।

1. मैंने उसकी बात सुनी ।

2. मैंने कुछ किताबें ख़रीदीं ।

3. मैं उसके भाई से मिला ।

4. उसने स्कूल में आगरे के बारे में बताया ।

5. उसने क्या कहा ?

6. मैंने उसके भाई को पहचाना ।

7. उन्होंने मुझे एक किताब भेजी ।

8. क्या आपने समाचार पत्र पढ़ा ?

D. Transform the following sentences according to the model given, omitting the performer of the action and retaining the tense of the original sentence:

मैंने एक किताब लिखी । ----- एक किताब लिखी गई ।

1. वह किताब पढ़ रहा है ।

2. वह मोटरवाले का इंतज़ार कर रहा था ।

3. मुझे उस भारतीय ऋतुओं के बारे में बताना चाहिए ।

4. उन्होंने अक्टूबर में त्योहार मनाया ।

5. लोगों ने होली कैसे मनाई थी ?

6. वे लड़कों को स्कूल में भर्ती कराएंगे ।

7. क्या गर्मियों में मज़दूर मकान बनाएं ?

8. हम कुटिटयों का इंतज़ाम कर रहे हैं ।

9. क्या उसने एक घर बनाया है ?

10. क्या उसने किताब जला दी ?

E. Translate orally:

1. All the people gather where the festival will be celebrated.

347

2. All the people gather when the festival is celebrated.

3. All the people gather because the festival is being celebrated.

4. All the people, by whom the festival is celebrated, gather.

5. All the people gather at the place where the festival is celebrated.

6. All the people gather at the place near which the festival is celebrated.

F. Translate orally:

1. This book was written in September.

2. This book will be written in September.

3. This book will be finished in September.

4. This book will be finished by the end of March.

5. This house will be finished by the end of March.

6. The house will be built by the end of March.

7. The house was built by the end of March.

8. The house was built by the beginning of June.

G. Translate orally:

1. The letter was written in the evening.

2. The letter was written at an auspicious moment.

3. The letter was written at that time.

4. The book was read at that time.

5. The book will be read at that time.

6. The book will be read on Thursday.

7. The book will be read next month.

8. This book has been read by many people.

# LESSON XXII

## Conversation -- Holi (continued)

### RAM DAS

| | |
|---|---|
| रंग | color |
| खेलना | to play |
| रंग खेलना | to throw colored water |
| इसके बाद दो दिनों तक लोग एक दूसरे से रंग खेलते हैं । | After this, people throw colored water at each other for two days. |

### BILL

| | |
|---|---|
| कैसा रंग ? | What colors (do they throw)? |

### RAM DAS

| | |
|---|---|
| लाल | red |
| हरा | green |
| पीला | yellow, orange |
| नीला | blue |
| सभी तरह का --- लाल, हरा, पीला, नीला --- किसी भी तरह का । | All kinds of colors -- red, green, yellow, blue -- any kind. |
| अबीर | red powder |
| गुलाल | pink powder |
| लगाना | to rub |
| इसके अलावा लोग एक दूसरे पर अबीर गुलाल आदि भी लगाते हैं । | Besides this, people rub powders of various colors on each other's faces. |

349

| | |
|---|---|
| आनन्द | joy, pleasure |
| आम तौर पर बच्चों को रंग | Generally, the children |
| खेलने में बड़ा आनन्द मिलता | enjoy throwing colored |
| है । | water very much. |
| पिचकारी | syringe |
| भरना | to fill |
| सारा | whole |
| खड़ा | standing |
| डालना | to drop |
| रंग डालना | to throw or shoot |
| | colored water |
| वे पिचकारियों में रंग भरे सारे | They stand on the street all |
| दिन सड़कों पर खड़े रहते हैं | day filling syringes with |
| और लोगों पर रंग डालते हैं । | colored water and shoot it |
| | at people. |

BILL

| | |
|---|---|
| बुरा | bad |
| मानना | to think, consider |
| बुरा मानना | to take offense |
| क्या लोग बुरा नहीं मानते ? | Don't people take offense? |

RAM DAS

| | |
|---|---|
| डलवाना | to let throw |
| जी नहीं, लोग बड़ी खुशी से | No, people allow the |
| रंग डलवाते हैं । | children to throw color |
| | on them with great pleasure. |
| प्रेम | love, affection, joy |
| पुराना | ancient, old |

350

| | |
|---|---|
| दुश्मनी | enmity |
| बुराई | grievance |
| भूलना | to forget |
| भूल जाना | to forget |

होली के इन दो दिनों में लोग एक दूसरे से बड़े प्रेम से मिलते हैं, और पुरानी दुश्मनी और बुराई भूल जाते हैं ।

During these two days of Holi, people are glad to see each other and forget old enmities and grievances.

| | |
|---|---|
| मेला | fair, gathering of people |

आम तौर पर दूसरे या तीसरे दिन शाम को एक जगह बड़ा मेला लगता है ।

Generally on the second or third day there is a gathering of people at a particular place.

| | |
|---|---|
| गला | neck |
| गले मिलना | to embrace |

वहां शहर के सभी लोग इकट्ठा होते हैं और एक दूसरे से गले मिलते हैं ।

There all the people of the city gather and embrace each other.

इस त्योहार को लोग बड़े आनन्द से मनाते हैं ।

People enjoy celebrating this festival.

| | |
|---|---|
| स्वयम, स्वयं | self |

यह आप स्वयं देखेंगे ही ।

You will see it yourself.

BILL

जी हां, मैं देखूंगा ही नहीं, आप लोगों के साथ होली

Yes, I will not only watch it, I will celebrate Holi

351

खेलूंगा मी ।                         with you (all).

## ADDITIONAL VOCABULARY

| | |
|---|---|
| काला | black |
| सफ़े द | white |
| बैंगनी | purple |
| ब्राउन | brown |
| भूरा | gray |
| खुद | self |

## NUMERALS

| | |
|---|---|
| इक्यासी | eighty-one |
| बयासी | eighty-two |
| तिरासी | eighty-three |
| चौरासी | eighty-four |
| पचासी | eighty-five |
| छियासी | eighty-six |
| सत्तासी | eighty-seven |
| अट्ठासी | eighty-eight |
| नवासी | eighty-nine |
| नब्बे | ninety |

## GRAMMAR

1. <u>New Nouns</u>

<u>Masc. I</u>

| | | | |
|---|---|---|---|
| मेला | fair, gathering of people | पिचकारी | syringe |
| गला | neck | दुश्मनी | enmity |
| | | बुराई | grievance |

<u>Fem. I</u>

352

| Masc. II | | Fem. II | |
|---|---|---|---|
| रंग | color | अबीर | red powder |
| गुलाल | pink powder | | |
| आनन्द | joy, pleasure | | |
| प्रेम | love, affection, joy | | |

## 2. New Verbs

| | |
|---|---|
| खेलना | to play |
| लगाना | to rub |
| भरना | to fill |
| डालना | to drop |
| मानना | to think, consider |
| डलवाना | to let throw |
| भूलना | to forget |

### 2.1 New Compound Verbs

#### Type I

| | |
|---|---|
| भूल जाना | to forget |

#### Type II

| | |
|---|---|
| बुरा मानना | to take something ill |
| गले मिलना | to embrace |

## 3. New Adjectives in -aa

| हरा | green | खड़ा | standing |
|---|---|---|---|
| पीला | yellow, orange | बुरा | bad |
| नीला | blue | पुराना | old |
| सारा | whole | भूरा | gray |
| काला | black | | |

353

## 4. Perfect Participle

Hindi has a perfect participle which may appear in one of two forms:

1. The perfect form of the verb itself, e.g., किया, किए, की.

2. The perfect form of the verb followed by the perfect form of the verb होना e.g., किया हुआ, किए हुए, की हुई.

The perfect participle may be used as an adjective modifying the following noun and then it agrees with the noun in number and gender.

| | |
|---|---|
| उसका खरीदा (हुआ) कपड़ा मुझे बहुत पसंद है । | I like the cloth bought by him very much. |
| उसके खरीदे (हुए) फल मीठे नहीं हैं । | The fruit, bought by him, isn't sweet. |
| उसकी दी (हुई) किताब मैंने पढ़ ली है । | I have read the book given by him (the book he gave to me). |
| मैंने राम की लिखी (हुई) किताबें पढ़ी हैं । | I have read the books written by Ram. |

A second usage of the perfect participle is as an adverb, not modifying a following noun, in which case the participle is always in the oblique -ee form.

| | |
|---|---|
| वे पिचकारियों में रंग भरे (हुए) सारे दिन सड़कों पर खड़े रहते हैं । | They stand on the street all day filling syringes with colored water. |

354

वह मेज़ पर बैठे (हुए) पत्र लिख रहा है ।　　He is writing a letter sitting at the table.

लोग अच्छे कपड़े पहने (हुए) होली के मेले में गए ।

People went to the Holi gathering wearing good clothes.

The people, putting on their good clothes, went to the Holi gathering.

The implication of the perfect participle is that although the act expressed by it may have started earlier than the time expressed by the main verb, it continues during the time of the main verb. This may be compared with the use of the past participle which implies an action that is completed before the time of the main verb.

वह अच्छे कपड़े पहन कर होली के मेले में गया ।

Having put on his good clothes, he went to the Holi gathering.

वह अच्छे कपड़े पहने हुए होली के मेले में गया ।

He went to the Holi gathering wearing good clothes.

5. "Oneself"

The Hindi form स्वयं or खुद is used as a reflexive pronoun for all persons and numbers, i.e., they may mean "myself," "yourself," "himself" etc.

यह आप स्वयं देखेंगे ही ।　　You will see it yourself.

उसने स्वयं ही यह बताया था ।　　He told that himself.

उसने खुद कुछ नहीं खरीदा ।     He didn't buy anything
                              himself.

6.  "Not only ... but also"

Where English uses the construction "not only ...
but also," Hindi uses for the "not only" ही नहीं and for
the "but also" either भी or बल्कि ---- भी or वरन् -----
भी. The ही नहीं will always appear at the end of the
first clause. In the latter part, if either बल्कि or
वरन् is used, it will occur at the beginning of the
clause, and भी, whether used by itself or with बल्कि or
वरन्, will appear at the end.

मैं भारत जाऊंगा ही नहीं,      I will not only go to India,
वहां पढ़ूंगा भी ।               but I will also study
                              there.

मैं देखूंगा ही नहीं, (वरन्) आप   I will not only watch, but
लोगों के साथ होली खेलूंगा       I will celebrate Holi
भी ।                          with you.

मैं कपड़ा देखूंगा ही नहीं,       I will not only look at the
(बल्कि) खरीदूंगा भी ।           cloth, but I will also
                              buy it.

7.  Color Terms

The basic colors of the spectrum are not viewed in
Hindi quite the same way as they are in English.  Thus
the single term पीला is used both for those things
which may be called "yellow" in English and for those
things which may be called "orange."  In Hindi various

356

shades of brown are likely to be referred to as लाल,
पीला or sometimes by the English borrowing ब्राउन
"brown."  Other important colors are:

|  |  |
|---|---|
| बैंगनी | purple |
| सफ़ेद | white |
| काला | black |
| भूरा | gray |

8.  "To enjoy"

As an equivalent of the English verb "to enjoy,"
Hindi may use either आनन्द मिलना or आनन्द आना.  With
both these verbal expressions, the person who enjoys
something is in the dative case.

बच्चों को रंग खेलने में बड़ा
आनन्द मिलता है ।
बच्चों को रंग खेलने में बड़ा
आनन्द आता है ।
} The children enjoy throwing colored water very much.

राम को पढ़ने में बहुत आनन्द
मिलता है ।
राम को पढ़ने में बहुत आनन्द
आता है ।
} Ram enjoys reading.

A. Substitute orally in the sentences below the Hindi
equivalent of the English given:

1. उसके घर का रंग ----- है ।

| | |
|---|---|
| green | black |
| blue | gray |
| yellow | red |
| white | brown |
| purple | |

2. आगरा यहां से ----- मील है ।

| | |
|---|---|
| how many | seventy-four |
| ninety | eighty-two |
| eighty-six | forty-two |
| eighty-three | seventy-two |
| seventy-three | eighty-five |
| eighty-eight | fifty |
| twenty-eight | twenty-five |
| eighty-nine | seventy-five |
| sixty-nine | eighty-one |
| seventy-nine | seventy-one |
| eighty-seven | fifty-one |
| twenty-seven | eighty |
| eighty-four | seventy |

3. वह ----- कमीज़ पहने हुए है ।

| | |
|---|---|
| white | blue |
| green | gray |
| black | purple |

red                    orange

yellow

4. ----- किताबें मुझे पसन्द नहीं हैं ।  (use the perfect parti-
                                        ciple form of the
                                        verb)

bought by him          told by you

brought by you         written by you

given by you           read by him

5. मैं भारत जाऊंगा ही नहीं ----- ।

            but I will also live there

            but I will also live there for some time

            but I will also study Hindi there

            but I will also celebrate Indian festivals

            but I will also meet the Indian villagers

            but I will also visit Indian villages

            but I will also put on Indian clothes

            but I will also speak Hindi

            but I will also learn Indian singing and
               dancing

            but I will also try to learn an Indian
               language

6. ----- वह कहां गया ?    (use the past participle form
                            of the verb)

            having put on good clothes

            having celebrated Holi

            having seen an Indian movie

            having burned the wood

            having heard Indian songs

            having played the musical instruments

having built a new house

7. क्या वह मेरी बात का ----- ?

    takes offense

    will take offense

    can take offense

    will not take offense

    can't take offense

    was taking offense

8. लड़कों को ----- बहुत आनन्द मिलता है ।

    in throwing colored water

    in rubbing colored powders

    in celebrating Holi

    in gathering the wood for Holi

    in setting fire to the Holi wood

    in going to the fair

    in playing musical instruments

    in visiting new places

9. वे एक दूसरे से ----- ।

    throw colored water

    are glad to see

    talk in Hindi

    talk in their native language

    embrace at the fair

    learn how to sing

10. ये कपड़े ----- हैं ।

    old                new              good

bad                    quite new              quite old

B. Transform the following sentences according to the
model given, omitting the performer of the action and
retaining the tense of the original sentence:

वह घर बनाता है । ----- घर बनाया जाता है ।

1. लड़कों ने गुलाल लगाया ।

2. लोग होली जला रहे हैं ।

3. बच्चे होली पर रंग खेलेंगे ।

4. लड़का पिचकारी भर रहा है ।

5. औरतों ने मेरी बात मान ली है ।

6. क्या वे पैदल जाने वालों पर रंग डालेंगे ?

7. लोग होली जलाते समय गाते-बजाते है ।

8. मैं उसकी बात नहीं भूल सकता ।

9. क्या बच्चे नए कपड़े पहनें ?

10. उसे रंगों के नाम जानने चाहिए ।

11. क्या वह मेले के बारे में बता रहा था ?

12. लड़के स्कूल में हिन्दी बोलते थे ।


C. Transform the following sentences according to the
model given:

मैं कुछ फल ख़रीद रहा था । ----- मैंने कुछ फल ख़रीदे ।

1. बच्चे रंग डाल रहे थे ।

2. क्या आप उनकी बातों का बुरा मान रहे थे ?

3. वे गाने-बजाने की कोशिश कर रहे थे ।

4. लोग होली खेल रहे थे ।

5. सभी लोग ख़ुशी से रंग डलवा रहे थे ।

6. वे सभी लोगों से बड़ी ख़ुशी से बात कर रहे थे ।

7. मैं उन्हें भारतीय त्योहारों के बारे में बता रही थी ।

8. क्या आप उनकी बात समझ रहे थे ?

9.लड़के स्कूल में हिन्दी बोल रहे थे ।

10.क्या आप उसे पहचान रहे थे ?

D.  Transform the following sentences according to the model given:

वह अस्पताल गया और दवा ----- वह अस्पताल जाकर दवा लाया ।

लाया ।

1.उसने कुछ कपड़े ख़रीदे और वह घर वापस आया ।

2.वह बाज़ार गया और राम से मिला ।

3.उन्होंने गाया-बजाया और होली जलाई ।

4.राम ने मेरी बात मानी और कुछ कपड़े ख़रीदे ।

5.मैंने कपड़े पहने और मेले में गया ।

6.लड़के पार्क गए और खेलने लगे ।

7.राम ने टेलीफ़ोन किया और अपना काम पूरा किया ।

8.उसने मेला देखा और बहुत खुश हुआ ।

E.  Translate orally:

1.  People throw colored water at each other.

2.  People are throwing colored water at each other.

3.  People threw colored water at each other.

4.  People kept throwing colored water at each other.

5.  Colored water was thrown.

6.  Colored water was thrown by children.

7.  The colored water was being thrown by the children.

8.  The children enjoy throwing colored water.

9.  Children like to throw colored water.

10. The children intend to throw colored water at each other.

F. Translate orally:

1. They forget old enmities.

2. He forgot the old enmities.

3. He forgot his old friends.

4. He forgets his old friends.

5. He forgets his books.

6. He forgot to bring his books.

7. He forgot to meet his friend.

8. He forgot where he was going.

9. He forgot to write his parents.

10. He forgot when they were coming.

G. Translate orally:

1. He not only went there, but he also stayed there.

2. He not only went there, but he also worked there.

3. He not only lived there, but he also worked there.

4. He not only lives there, but he also works there.

5. He not only lives on the street, but he also works there.

6. He not only reads books, but writes them too.

7. He not only reads Hindi, but he writes Hindi too.

8. He not only writes Hindi, but he speaks Hindi too.

9. He not only speaks English, but he speaks Hindi too.

10. He not only speaks Hindi, but he keeps on speaking Hindi continuously.

363

H. Translate orally:

1. He reads books.

2. He doesn't read books.

3. He never reads books.

4. Sometimes he reads books.

5. Somebody is reading this book.

6. Nobody is reading this book.

7. Somebody read this book.

8. Who read this book?

9. He reads nothing.

10. Nothing was read in the class.

I. Translate orally:

1. They met each other.

2. They work for each other.

3. They sent letters to each other.

4. They saw each other's houses.

5. They throw colored water at each other.

6. The children played with each other.

Conversation -- Visit to a Historical Site

JOHN

| | |
|---|---|
| अजन्ता | Ajanta |
| ऐलोरा | Ellora |
| अगले हफ़्ते में अजन्ता और ऐलोरा देखने जाना चाहता हूं । | I want to visit (to go and see) Ajanta and Ellora next week. |
| बार | times |
| चुकना | to finish |
| मैंने सुना है कि आप कई बार ये जगहें देखने जा चुके हैं । | I have heard that you have already visited these places many times. |
| सहायक | helper, helpful |
| ख़ास | important, special |
| कृपया मुझे यात्रा में सहायक ख़ास ख़ास बातें बताइए । | Please tell me anything that may be important and helpful for the trip. |

SHIVA LAL

| | |
|---|---|
| आप पहले अजन्ता जाना चाहते हैं या ऐलोरा ? | Do you want to go to Ajanta first or to Ellora? |

JOHN

| | |
|---|---|
| जहां जाने में सुविधा हो । | Wherever it's convenient to go (first). |
| अधिक | more, much |

मैंने सुना है कि यहां से पहले
ऐलोरा जाने में अधिक
आसानी होती है ।

I have heard that it's
easier to go to Ellora
first from here.

SHIVA LAL

हां, यह सच है ।

Yes, that's true.

औरंगाबाद

Aurangabad

आप यहां से पहले औरंगाबाद
जाएं ।

You should go to Aurangabad
from here first.

औरंगाबाद आप रेल से जा
सकते हैं ।

You can go to Aurangabad by
train.

औरंगाबाद एक बड़ा शहर है ।

Aurangabad is a big city.

खाना

to eat

पीना

to drink

वहां आप को ठहरने और
खाने-पीने की सुविधा
रहेगी ।

You will have (more) facil-
ities for board and
lodging there.

वहीं से आप ऐलोरा जा
सकते हैं ।

From there you can go to
Ellora.

टैक्सी

taxi

आपको बसें भी मिलेंगी और
टैक्सियां भी ।

You will get busses as well
as taxis.

जो भी चाहें, ले लें ।

Take whatever you want.

JOHN

क्या ऐलोरा वहां से बहुत
पास है ?

Is Ellora very near (to
Aurangabad)?

SHIVA LAL

जी हां, केवल सोलह मील

Yes, it's only sixteen

366

| | |
|---|---|
| है । | miles |
| रास्ता | way, road |
| दौलताबाद | Daulatabad |
| और हां, जब ऐलोरा जाएं, तो रास्ते में दौलताबाद में रुकना न भूलें । | And moreover, when you go to Ellora, don't forget to stop in Daulatabad on the way. |
| किला | fort |
| दौलताबाद में एक बहुत पुराना किला है । | There is a very old fort in Daulatabad. |
| प्रसन्न | pleased |
| विश्वास | belief, faith |
| मुझे विश्वास है कि आप उसे देखकर प्रसन्न होंगे । | I believe that you will enjoy seeing it. |

JOHN

| | |
|---|---|
| उचित | proper |
| अगर मैं दौलताबाद रुकना चाहूं, तब तो शायद टैक्सी करना ही उचित होगा । | If I want to stop in Aurangabad, then it will be better to take a taxi. |

SHIVA LAL

| | |
|---|---|
| सलाह | advice |
| जी हां, मेरी सलाह तो टैक्सी के लिए ही होगी । | Yes, I would advise you to take a taxi. |

JOHN

| | |
|---|---|
| महंगा | expensive |
| क्या टैक्सी बहुत महंगी होगी ? | Will the taxi be very expensive? |

367

विशेष        especially

जी नहीं, विशेष महंगी नहीं    No, it won't be especially

होगी ।           expensive.

यदि          if

सरकारी       governmental

निजी          private

सस्ता        cheap

यदि आप वहां के सरकारी   If you hire a taxi from the

बस-स्टेशन से टैक्सी किराए   government bus station

पर लेंगे, तो वह निजी    there, it will certainly

टैक्सियों से सस्ती ही पड़ेगी ।   be cheaper than private

                taxis.

दौलताबाद में क्या देखने   What places are worth

योग्य है ?        seeing in Daulatabad?

वास्तव       reality

हिन्दू        Hindu

राजा         king

बनवाना      to have made

दौलताबाद में एक किला है,   There is a fort in Daulata-

जो वास्तव में एक हिन्दू    bad which a Hindu king

राजा ने बनवाया था ।    had really had built.

शताब्दी       century

यह किला दसवीं शताब्दी में   This fort was built in the

बना था ।       tenth century.

देवगिरि — Devagiri

कहलाना — to be called

उस समय इस प्रदेश का नाम देवगिरि था और यह किला देवगिरि का किला कहलाता था । — At that time, this region was called Devagiri and this fort was called Devagiri fort.

सदी — century

मुसलमान — Muslim

अधिकार — authority

कुछ सदियों बाद इस किले पर मुसलमानों का अधिकार हो गया । — A few centuries later, this fort came under the authority of the Muslims.

स्थान — place

बदलना — to change

उस समय इस स्थान का नाम बदलकर दौलताबाद कर दिया गया । — At that time, the name of this place was changed to Daulatabad.

कला — art

नमूना — example

यह किला हिन्दुओं की किले बनाने की कला का बड़ा अच्छा नमूना है । — This fort is a good example of the art of fort-building of the Hindus.

ऐतिहासिक — historical

महत्व — importance

मस्जिद — mosque

दर्शनीय — worth seeing

इसके अलावा यहां एक ऐतिहासिक — Besides this, there is a

| | |
|---|---|
| महत्व की मस्जिद भी है, जो दर्शनीय है । | mosque of historical importance here, which is worth seeing. |

| | |
|---|---|
| औरंगाबाद से दौलताबाद कितनी दूर है ? | How far is it from Auranga-bad to Daulatabad? |

SHIVA LAL

| | |
|---|---|
| यही कोई चार मील के लगभग । दौलताबाद में ये जगहें देखने के बाद आप ऐलोरा जाएं । | Oh, about four miles. After visiting these places in Daulatabad, you should go to Ellora. |

ADDITIONAL VOCABULARY

| | | |
|---|---|---|
| इक्यानवे | | ninety-one |
| बानवे | | ninety-two |
| तिरानवे | | ninety-three |
| चौरानवे | | ninety-four |
| पच्चानवे | (paccaanawee) | ninety-five |
| पंचानवे | (pãcaanawee) | |
| छानवे | | ninety-six |
| सत्तानवे | (sattaanawee, santaanawee) | ninety-seven |
| अट्ठानवे | (aTThaanawee, aNThaanawee) | ninety-eight |
| निन्यानवे | | ninety-nine |
| सौ | | hundred |
| मन्दिर | | temple |

# GRAMMAR

1. **New Nouns**

   **Masc. I**

   रास्ता    way, road

   किला    fort

   राजा    king

   नमूना    example

   **Masc. II**

   बार NP    times

   सहायक    helper

   विश्वास    belief, faith

   उचित NP    proper

   वास्तव NP    reality

   राजा    king

   हिन्दू    Hindu

   मुसलमान    Muslim

   अधिकार    authority

   महत्व NP    importance

   मन्दिर    temple

   **Fem. I**

   टैक्सी    taxi

   शताब्दी    century

   सदी    century

   **Fem. II**

   सलाह    advice

   कला    art

   मस्जिद    mosque

2. **New Verbs**

   चुकना    to finish

   खाना    to eat

   पीना    to drink

   बनवाना    to have built

   कहलाना    to be called

   बदलाना    to change

3. **New Adjectives in -aa**

   महंगा    expensive

   सस्ता    cheap

371

# 4. Causative Verbs

Many verbs in Hindi will have three separate forms in a set. Each member of the set will have a complete inflection, e.g., बनना "to become," "to be made," बनाना "to make," बनवाना "to cause to make," each with a complete inflection. To have names for each member of the set, the first form will be called the Basic Form, e.g., बनना , the second will be called the First Causative, e.g., बनाना, and the third member of the set will be called the Second Causative, e.g., बनवाना .

## 4.1 Forms of Causatives

For most verbs, the stem of the First Causative may be formed from the stem of the Basic Form by adding -aa-, and the stem of the Second Causative can be formed from the stem of the Basic Form by adding -waa-.

| | | | | | |
|---|---|---|---|---|---|
| बनना | bannaa | बनाना | banaanaa | बनवाना | banwaanaa |
| सुनना | sunnaa | सुनाना | sunaanaa | सुनवाना | sunwaanaa |
| मिलना | milnaa | मिलाना | milaanaa | मिलवाना | milwaanaa |
| करना | karnaa | कराना | karaanaa | करवाना | karwaanaa |
| रुकना | ruknaa | रुकाना | rukaanaa | रुकवाना | rukwaanaa |
| लिखना | likhnaa | लिखाना | likhaanaa | लिखवाना | likhwaanaa |
| ठहरना | Thahrnaa | ठहराना | Thahraanaa | ठहरवाना | Thahrwaanaa |
| लगना | lagnaa | लगाना | lagaanaa | लगवाना | lagwaanaa |
| पहुंचना | pahũcnaa | पहुंचाना | pahũcaanaa | पहुंचवाना | pahũcwaanaa |
| पढ़ना | paRhnaa | पढ़ाना | paRhaanaa | पढ़वाना | paRhwaanaa |

| | | | | | |
|---|---|---|---|---|---|
| लौटना | lauTnaa | लौटाना | lauTaanaa | लौटवाना | lauTwaanaa |
| रखना | rakhnaa | रखाना | rakhaanaa | रखवाना | rakhwaanaa |
| चलना | calnaa | चलाना | calaanaa | चलवाना | calwaanaa |
| बचना | bacnaa | बचाना | bacaanaa | बचवाना | bacwaanaa |
| गिरना | girnaa | गिराना | giraanaa | गिरवाना | girwaanaa |
| बजना | bajnaa | बजाना | bajaanaa | बजवाना | bajwaanaa |
| जलना | jalnaa | जलाना | jalaanaa | जलवाना | jalwaanaa |
| जमना | jamnaa | जमाना | jamaanaa | जमवाना | jamwaanaa |
| भरना | bharnaa | भराना | bharaanaa | भरवाना | bharwaanaa |

In a two syllable stem ending in a short vowel -a-
followed by a single consonant, the vowel -a- will be
lost in the spoken form of the First Causative according to the rules previously discussed in Lesson VIII:11
although the written form will not be affected.

| | | |
|---|---|---|
| बदलना | बदलाना | बदलवाना |
| badalnaa | badlaanaa | badalwaanaa |
| समझना | समझाना | समझवाना |
| samajhnaa | samjhaanaa | samajhwaanaa |

For some verbs besides the addition of -aa- and
-waa- to form the causatives, the stem vowel of the
Basic Form is also changed as follows:

| | | |
|---|---|---|
| -ee- | becomes | -i- |
| -ii- | becomes | -i- |
| -oo- | becomes | -u- |
| -uu- | becomes | -u- |
| -aa- | becomes | -a- |

| देखना | दिखाना | दिखवाना |
|---|---|---|
| deekhnaa | dikhaanaa | dikhwaanaa |
| खेलना | खिलाना | खिलवाना |
| kheelnaa | khilaanaa | khilwaanaa |
| सीखना | सिखाना | सिखवाना |
| siikhnaa | sikhaanaa | sikhwaanaa |
| बोलना | बुलाना | बुलवाना |
| boolnaa | bulaanaa | bulwaanaa |
| भूलना | भुलाना | भुलवाना |
| bhuulnaa | bhulaanaa | bhulwaanaa |
| मानना | मनाना | मनवाना |
| maannaa | manaanaa | manwaanaa |

Some verbs show an irregular form either of the stem or of the causative suffix.

| पीना | पिलाना | पिलवाना |
|---|---|---|
| piinaa | pilaanaa | pilwaanaa |
| खाना | खिलाना | खिलवाना |
| khaanaa | khilaanaa | khilwaanaa |
| देना | दिलाना | दिलवाना |
| deenaa | dilaanaa | dilwaanaa |
| छूटना | छोड़ना | छुड़वाना |
| chuuTnaa | chooRnaa | chuRwaanaa |
| बैठना | बिठाना | बिठलाना |
| baiThnaa | biThaanaa | biThlaanaa |
| देखना | दिखाना | दिखलाना |
| deekhnaa | dikhaanaa | dikhlaanaa |

One verb uses a suppletive form for the causatives:

पढ़ना paRnaa    डालना Daalnaa    डलवाना Dalwaanaa

Some other verbs show only two forms:

| | | | |
|---|---|---|---|
| कहना | kahnaa | कहलाना | kahlaanaa |
| लेना | leenaa | लिवाना | liwaanaa |
| लाना | laanaa | लिवाना | liwaanaa |
| भेजना | bheejnaa | भिजवाना | bhijwaanaa |
| नाचना | naacnaa | नचवाना | nacwaanaa |
| बीतना | biitnaa | बिताना | bitaanaa |

The list of the verbs above is not complete but includes the most useful forms from the ones you have met so far.


## 4.2 Use of Causatives

Many of the Basic Forms above have a meaning that is either intransitive or passive or both. For these verbs the First Causative is always transitive and the Second Causative is causative in meaning. This type of verb set will be referred to as Type A.

बनना      बनाना        बनवाना

to become,     to make      to cause to make
   to be made

रुकना      रुकाना        रुकवाना

to stop (Intr.)   to stop (Trans.)   to cause to stop

कूटना      छोड़ना        छुड़वाना

to leave       to leave      to cause to
   (Intr.)       (Trans.)      leave, to allow
                                 to leave

ठहरना      ठहराना        ठहरवाना

to stay (Intr.)   to stop (Trans.)   to cause to stop
   to stop    "

बचना      बचाना        बचवाना

to be saved,     to save,       to cause to save,
   to be          to avoid       to cause to
   avoided                             avoid

| बैठना | बिठाना | बिठलाना |
|---|---|---|
| to sit | to set | to cause to set |

| पहुंचना | पहुंचाना | पहुंचवाना |
|---|---|---|
| to reach | to send | to cause to send |

| लौटना | लौटाना | लौटवाना |
|---|---|---|
| to return (Intr.) | to return (Trans.) | to cause to return |

| चलना | चलाना | चलवाना |
|---|---|---|
| to go, to move (Intr.) | to drive, to move (Trans.) | to cause to drive, to cause to move |

| लगना | लगाना | लगवाना |
|---|---|---|
| to cost, to take (time), to be applied | to spend (money), to spend (time), to apply | to cause to spend (money), to cause to spend (time), to cause to apply |

| गिरना | गिराना | गिरवाना |
|---|---|---|
| to fall | to drop | to cause to drop |

| बजना | बजाना | बजवाना |
|---|---|---|
| to be played (music) | to play (music) | to cause to play (music) |

| बजना | बजाना | बजवाना |
|---|---|---|
| to ring (Intr.) | to ring (Trans.) | to cause to ring |

| जलना | जलाना | जलवाना |
|---|---|---|
| to burn (Intr.) | to burn (Trans.) | to cause to burn |

| जमना | जमाना | जमवाना |
|---|---|---|
| to be collected, to freeze (Intr.) | to collect, to freeze (Trans.) | to cause to collect, to cause to freeze |

| पड़ना | डालना | डलवाना |
|---|---|---|
| to fall | to drop | to cause to drop, to allow to drop |

| बदलना | बदलाना | बदलवाना |
|---|---|---|
| to change (Intr.) | to change (Trans.) | to cause to change |

Examples:

| | |
|---|---|
| यह घर पिछले साल बना था । | This house was built last year. |
| उसने पिछले साल अपना घर बनाया । | He built this house last year (i.e., he built it himself). |
| उसने पिछले साल अपना घर बनवाया । | He had his house built last year (i.e., he got somebody else to do it). |
| मोटर ठीक नहीं चलती । | The car doesn't run well. |
| वह मोटर नहीं चलाता । | He doesn't drive a car. |
| वह अपने मित्र से मोटर चलवाता है । | He gets his friend to drive the car. |
| गाड़ी पांच बजे स्टेशन से छूटी । | The train left the station at five o'clock. |
| गाड़ी ने पांच बजे स्टेशन छोड़ा । | The train left the station at five o'clock |
| उसने अपनी किताबें घर में छोड़ीं । | He left his books in school. |
| नौकर से धोबी के यहां कपड़े छुड़वा दीजिए । | Please get the servant to leave the clothes at the |

377

dhobi's.

Many verbs have a Basic Form which, unlike those of the preceding list, is transitive in meaning. For these verbs the First Causative has a causative meaning, and the Second Causative form usually has a causative meaning too and is used as an alternative of the First Causative, but may occasionally be used in a double causative meaning. This type of verb-set will be referred to as Type B.

| सुनना | सुनाना | सुनवाना |
|---|---|---|
| to hear | to tell | to cause to tell |
| मिलना | मिलाना | मिलवाना |
| to meet | to introduce | to cause to introduce |
| देखना | दिखाना | दिखलाना, दिखवाना |
| to see | to show | to show, to cause to show |
| देना | दिलाना | दिलवाना |
| to give | to cause to give | to cause to give |
| करना | कराना | करवाना |
| to make, to do | to cause to make, to cause to do | to cause to make, to cause to do |
| लिखना | लिखाना | लिखवाना |
| to write | to cause to write | to cause to write |
| सीखना | सिखाना | सिखवाना |
| to learn | to teach, to train | to cause to teach, to cause to train |
| समझना | समझाना | समझवाना |
| to understand | to explain | to cause to explain |

| पढ़ना | पढ़ाना | पढ़वाना |
|---|---|---|
| to read, to study, to learn | to teach | to cause to teach |
| बोलना | बुलाना | बुलवाना |
| to speak | to call, to invite | to cause to call, to cause to invite |
| रखना | रखाना | रखवाना |
| to put, to place | to cause to put, to cause to place | to cause to put, to cause to place |
| मानना | मनाना | मनवाना |
| to agree to, to consider | to persuade, to celebrate | to cause to persuade, to cause to celebrate |
| खेलना | खिलाना | खिलवाना |
| to play | to cause to play, to allow to play | to cause to play, to allow to play |
| भूलना | भुलाना | भुलवाना |
| to forget | to cause to forget | to cause to forget |
| खाना | खिलाना | खिलवाना |
| to eat | to feed, to serve food | to cause to feed, to cause to serve food |
| पीना | पिलाना | पिलवाना |
| to drink | to cause to drink, to water (animals) | to cause to cause to drink, to get somebody to serve somebody else water |
| भरना | भराना | भरवाना |
| to fill | to cause to fill | to cause to fill |

नाचना        नचाना        नचवाना

to dance       to cause to       to cause to
                 dance              dance

Examples:

| | |
|---|---|
| मैंने वह किला देखा है । | I have seen that fort. |
| मेरे मित्र ने मुझे वह किला दिखाया । | My friend showed me that fort. |
| मेरे मित्र ने मुझे वह किला दिखलाया । | |
| मैंने उसकी बात सुनी । | I heard what he said. |
| मैंने उसे अपनी यात्रा के बारे में सुनाया । | I told him about my trip. |
| मैंने उसे अपने मित्र से अमरीका के बारे में सुनवाया । | I had my friend tell him about America. |
| लड़के हिन्दी पढ़ते हैं । | The students study Hindi. |
| मैं राम से लड़कों को हिन्दी पढ़वाता हूँ । | I get Ram to teach the students Hindi. |
| वह लड़कों को हिन्दी पढ़ाता है । | He teaches the students Hindi. |

Some verbs of this type have only a Basic Form and
a First Causative Form that are used with any con-
siderable frequency.

| | | | |
|---|---|---|---|
| लेना | to take | लिवाना | to cause to take |
| लाना | to bring | लिवाना | to cause to bring |
| कहना | to say, to tell | कहलाना | to cause to say, to cause to tell |
| भेजना | to send | भिजवाना | to cause to send |
| गाना | to sing | गवाना | to cause to sing |

Any of the verbs of either Type A or Type B that is used in a causative sense, i.e., to get somebody to do something, will express the somebody by using either the postposition से or the postposition के द्वारा.

| | |
|---|---|
| उसने अपने मित्र से (के द्वारा) मोटर चलवाई । | He got his friend to drive the car. |
| मैंने उसे अपने मित्र से (के द्वारा) इसके बारे में सुनवाया । | I had my friend tell him about it. |
| मैं राम से (के द्वारा) लड़कों को हिन्दी पढ़वाता हूं । | I get Ram to teach the students Hindi. |

## 4.3 Compound Causatives

Verbs compounded with होना and करना function like the type listed above where the compound with होना acts as the basic verb, the compound with करना acts as the first causative, and the compound with कराना or करवाना acts as the second causative.

| | |
|---|---|
| स्कूल पांच बजे बन्द होता है । | The school closes at five o'clock. |
| उसने पांच बजे स्कूल बन्द किया । | He closed the school at five o'clock. |
| उसने पांच बजे स्कूल बन्द करवाया | He got the school closed at five o'clock. |

## 5. चुकना

The verb चुकना may be used by itself in the meaning "to run out of."

| | |
|---|---|
| मेरे पैसे चुक गए हैं । | My money has run out (I |

381

have run out of money).

This verb may also be used with a dependent verb in the stem form, in which case it means "to finish doing something" or "to have already done something."

वह यह किताब पढ़ चुका है ।                He has finished reading
                                         this book.

वह यह किताब कब पढ़ चुकेगी ?              When will she finish read-
                                         ing this book?

वह इस समय तक खाना खा                      He finishes eating by this
  चुकता है ।                              time.

आप कई बार ये जगहें देखने                  You have already visited
  जा चुके हैं ।                           these places many times.

In English the verb "finish" may take a noun as direct object, "he finished the book," or be used with a dependent verb, "he finished reading the book." In Hindi चुकना in the meaning "finish" may be used only with a dependent verb, and ख़तम करना may be used with a noun as a direct object.

वह किताब पढ़ चुका ।  ⎫
उसने किताब ख़तम की ।  ⎬   He finished the book.
                     ⎭

The verb चुकना is not used with a ने construction.

6. अधिक

The word अधिक "much," "more," may be used in the same constructions in which ज्यादा occurs.

यहां से ऐलोरा जाने में अधिक              From here it's easier to go
  (ज्यादा) आसानी होती है ।               to Ellora.

382

यह बहुत अधिक (ज़्यादा) है ।
{ That's too much.
  That's a lot. }

7. "Near" and "far"

English uses "near to" but "far from." In Hindi the postposition से is used both with दूर "far" and पास "near."

ऐलोरा औरंगाबाद से पास है ।    Ellora is near to Aurangabad.

ऐलोरा आगरे से दूर है ।    Ellora is far from Agra.

8. विश्वास

The form विश्वास "belief," "faith," is used where English uses the verb "to believe." The subject of the English verb is in the dative form in Hindi.

मुझे विश्वास है कि ---    I believe that ...

This form is also the equivalent of the English "to have faith in," "to believe in." If the thing believed in is a person or a god, it will be expressed by the postposition पर or में. Otherwise, the thing believed in is expressed by a का construction.

मुझे राम पर (में) विश्वास है ।
{ I have faith in Ram (a person).
  I have faith in Ram, the god. }

उसे अपनी पत्नी पर (में) विश्वास है ।    He has faith in his wife.

उसे इस बात का विश्वास    He has faith in the fact

383

है कि ---           that....

उसे मेरी बात का विश्वास      He had faith in what I
था ।               said.

The forms विश्वास होना, विश्वास करना and विश्वास कराना (करवाना) will form a set of verbs, respectively Basic, First Causative and Second Causative.

उसने मेरी बात का विश्वास     He believed in what I said.
किया ।

9. उचित

The form उचित होना "to be better" expresses the person involved in the dative case or by a के लिए construction.

टैक्सी करना उचित होगा ।      It will be better to take
                          a taxi.

उसके लिए इस स्कूल में पढ़ना    It will be better for him
उचित होगा ।           to study in this school.

10. सलाह

The form सलाह may be used with होना as an equivalent of the English verb "to advise." When followed by a कि clause, the verb of the कि clause is likely to be in optative. The person to whom the advice is given will be in either the dative case or will be expressed by the postposition के लिए.

(आपको) मेरी सलाह है कि      I advise you to go to the
आप डाक्टर के यहां जाएं ।     doctor.

## 11. "To hire, to rent"

The expression किराए पर लेना may mean either "to hire or to rent from somebody."

| | |
|---|---|
| उसने टैक्सी किराए पर ली । | He hired a taxi. |
| मैंने उनसे मकान किराए पर लिया । | I rented a house from him. |

The expression किराए पर देना also means "to hire out" or "to rent to somebody else."

| | |
|---|---|
| मैंने उनको मकान किराए पर दिया । | I rented a house to him. |

To express "to hire a taxi, to take a taxi," it is also possible to use टैक्सी करना.

| | |
|---|---|
| उसने टैक्सी की । | He took (hired) a taxi. |
| मैंने होटल के लिए टैक्सी की । | I took a taxi to the hotel. |

## EXERCISES

A. Substitute orally in the sentences below the Hindi equivalent of the English given:

1. अजन्ता वहां से ----- है ।

| | |
|---|---|
| very near | ninety-one miles |
| very far | eighty-one miles |
| how far | forty-one miles |
| one hundred miles | ninety-six miles |
| ninety-three miles | ninety-eight miles |
| ninety-nine miles | eighty-eight miles |
| eighty-nine miles | eighty-six miles |

385

| | |
|---|---|
| ninety-five miles | eighty-seven miles |
| fifty-five miles | ninety-seven miles |
| seventy-five miles | ninety miles |
| eighty-five miles | eighty miles |
| eighty-four miles | eighty-three miles |
| ninety-four miles | five hundred miles |
| ninety-two miles | one thousand miles |
| eighty-two miles | only seventy-nine miles |

2. आप ----- भारत गए हैं ।

| | |
|---|---|
| how many times | twice |
| many times | three times |
| once | |

3. शायद वहां रुकने में आपको ----- हो ।

| | |
|---|---|
| convenient | inconvenient |
| easy | more convenient |
| difficult | less difficult |

4. क्या ये चीज़ें बहुत ----- नहीं हैं ?

| | |
|---|---|
| good | new |
| bad | cheap |
| old | expensive |

5. इसके बाद उस देश पर ----- का अधिकार हो गया ।

| | |
|---|---|
| Hindus | a Hindu king |
| Muslims | a Muslim king |
| a king | my parents |

6. उसने ----- विश्वास किया ।

| | |
|---|---|
| in Ram | in what he said |

386

in his children      in my work

in his advice       in Hindus

7. ----- राम पर विश्वास है ।

     I                       he

     we                   the King

     they                the boys

8. क्या वह ----- किराए पर लेगा ?

     a taxi            a room in that hotel

     a house          a car

     a room           an office

9. क्या इस समय ----- देखना मेरे लिए उचित होगा ?

     a historical site     a mosque

     a village           an old temple

     a small village     a new country

     a fort              an Indian fair

     a temple

10. वह ----- है ।

        is driving a car

        is stopping the car

        is stopping his car in the road

        is returning the car to him

11. उसने उससे कुछ पैसा ----- ।

     caused to save      caused to take

     caused to give      caused to send

12. मैं लड़कों को ----- ।

     will persuade

will invite

will explain Indian dancing

will show the temple

will teach

13. क्या आप ----- ?

finished reading

finished drinking

finished eating

finished singing

finished dancing

finished playing Holi

finished celebrating the festival

finished seeing the temple

finished sending his things

finished buying some clothing

finished taking a trip

B. Transform the following sentences according to the model given, retaining the tense of the original:

लड़का पत्र लिखता है । ----- लड़का पत्र लिखाता है ।

1. उसने मेरी बात सुनी ।

2. क्या आप किला देखेंगे ?

3. मैं यात्रा का इंतज़ाम कर रहा हूं ।

4. हम भारतीय भाषाएं सीख रहे थे ।

5. क्या आप अंग्रेज़ी की किताबें समझ सकते हैं ?

6. वह हिन्दी पढ़ता है ।

7. लड़के ने कपड़े कहां रखे ?

8. लड़कियां स्कूल में नाचती हैं ।

9. वह ऊनी कपड़े ले रहा था ।

10. वह मुफ़्त बीस रुपए भेज रहा है ।

C. Transform the following sentences according to the model given, retaining the tense of the original, and supplying a third person singular subject:

घर बन रहा है । ----- वह घर बना रहा है ।

1. गाड़ी सड़क पर रुकेगी ।

2. मेरी छोटा भाई मोटर में बैठ रहा है ।

3. लकड़ी कहां जलेगी ?

4. सामान सड़क के किनारे पड़ा है ।

5. मोटर चलती है ।

6. किताब दीवाल से गिरी ।

7. क्या बज रहा है ?

8. होली में लोगों पर गुलाल लगती है ।

9. इसमें कितना पैसा लगता है ?

10. गाड़ी प्लेटफ़ार्म पर ठहरती है ।

11. कितने रुपए बचे थे ?

12. कितना समय बीता ?

D. Transform the following sentences to sentences with चुकना constructions according to the model given:

क्या आपने पत्र लिखा ? ----- जी हां, मैं पत्र लिख चुका ।

1. क्या आपने त्यौहार मनाया ?

2. क्या आपने पानी पिया ?

3. क्या आपने नया मकान बनवाया ?

4. क्या आपने सूती कपड़े पहने ?

5. क्या आपने हिन्दी की किताबें जमा कीं ?

6. क्या आप मन्दिर गए ?

7. क्या आपने काश्मीर यात्रा का इंतज़ाम किया ?

8. क्या आपने हिन्दू मन्दिर देखे ?

9. क्या आपने इस काम में बहुत समय लगाया ?

10. क्या आपने होली खेली ?

E.  Translate orally:

    1.  I'm going to Ajanta.

    2.  Do you want to go to Ajanta too?

    3.  Do you want to go to Ajanta first or to Ellora?

    4.  I have to go to Ajanta first.

    5.  I am thinking of going to Ajanta next week.

    6.  I have heard that he is going to Ajanta next week.

    7.  I have heard that maybe he will go to Ajanta.

    8.  He told me that it's easier to go to Ajanta first.

    9.  You can go to Aurangabad by train.

   10.  Aurangabad is near to Ajanta.

F.  Translate orally:

    1.  There is a fort in Daulatabad.

    2.  The fort was built in the tenth century.

    3.  The fort was built by a Hindu king.

    4.  A Hindu king had the fort in Daulatabad built.

    5.  This fort is called Devagiri fort.

    6.  This fort used to be called Devagiri fort.

    7.  Devagiri is the name of a place near the fort.

    8.  The Muslims changed the name of this place.

G.  Translate orally:

    1.  The car runs.

390

2.  He drives the car.

3.  The car is running.

4.  He is driving the car.

5.  Yesterday the car ran well.

6.  Yesterday he drove the car for an hour.

7.  The car stopped.

8.  He stopped the car.

9.  I saw the Agra fort.

10. They showed me the Agra fort.

Conversation -- A Lecture

### HARI LAL

| | |
|---|---|
| कालेज | college |
| क्या अभी कालेज से आ रहे हो ? | Are you coming from classes right now? |

### DEVI PRASAD

| | |
|---|---|
| क्लास | class |
| लाइब्रेरी | library |
| हां, क्लास तो समय से ही ख़तम हो गया था, पर मैं उसके बाद लाइब्रेरी चला गया था । | Yes, the class finished on time, but after that I went to the library. |
| निकलना | to be published |
| कुछ हाल में ही निकली किताबें लाना चाहता था । | I wanted to get some recently published books. |
| पुस्तकालय | library |
| आ गई होंगी | must have come |
| सोचता था कि पुस्तकालय में आ गई होंगी, पर लगता है कि अभी नहीं आईं । | I thought that they must have arrived at the library, but it seems that they haven't come yet. |
| बेकार | unemployed |
| बेकार में | in vain, uselessly |
| बरबाद होना | to be wasted |
| बेकार में ही इतना वक़्त बरबाद हो गया । | A lot of time was wasted to no purpose. |

392

| जल्दी करना | to hurry |
|---|---|
| भाषण | speech, lecture |
| चूकना | to miss |
| अब मुझे जल्दी करनी होगी, मैं आज शाम का भाषण नहीं चूकना चाहता । | Now I'll have to hurry because I don't want to miss this afternoon's lecture. |

HARI LAL

| कौन सा भाषण ? | Which lecture? |
|---|---|

DEVI PRASAD

| प्रोफेसर | professor |
|---|---|
| प्रोफेसर आप्टे का भाषण । | Professor Apte's lecture. |
| क्या तुम्हें पता नहीं है ? | Don't you know about it? |
| ख्याल | idea, thought |
| जानते होगा | must know |
| मेरा ख्याल था कि तुम इसके बारे में जानते होगे । | I thought that you must know about it. |

HARI LAL

| नहीं, प्रो० आप्टे कौन हैं ? | No, who is Professor Apte? |
|---|---|

DEVI PRASAD

| बम्बई | Bombay |
|---|---|
| विश्वविद्यालय | university |
| राजनीति | politics |
| विज्ञान | science |
| विभाग | department |
| अध्यक्ष | head, chairman |

393

| | |
|---|---|
| माना हुआ | recognized |
| विद्वान | scholar |
| प्रो० आप्टे बम्बई विश्वविद्यालय में राजनीति विज्ञान विभाग के अध्यक्ष हैं और एक माने हुए विद्वान हैं । | Professor Apte is the Head of the Political Science Department at the University of Bombay and is a recognized scholar. |
| व्याख्यान | lecture |
| वे पिछले वर्ष भी यहां व्याख्यान देने आए थे । | He came here last year to give a lecture. |
| सुना होगा | must have heard |
| तुमने उस समय उनका भाषण तो सुना ही होगा । | You certainly must have heard his lecture at that time. |

HARI LAL

| | |
|---|---|
| नहीं, मैं उस समय बाहर गया होऊंगा । | No, I must have been away at that time. |
| उनका भाषण किस विषय पर है ? | What's the subject of his lecture? |

DEVI PRASAD

| | |
|---|---|
| आम | general, common |
| चुनाव | election |
| राजनीतिक | political |
| दल | party, group |
| असर | influence |
| पिछले भारतीय आम चुनाव का राजनीतिक दलों पर असर । | The influence of the last Indian general election |

व्याख्यान अच्छा होना चाहिए ।

on the political parties.
The lecture should be good.

पुस्तक

book

हाल में ही उनकी एक नई पुस्तक भी भारतीय आम चुनावों के बारे में निकली है ।

Recently, a new book of his about the Indian general elections has been published.

जिक्र करना

to mention

क्लास में प्रो॰ शर्मा उसका जिक्र कर रहे थे ।

Professor Sharma mentioned it in the class.

### HARI LAL

क्या प्रो॰ आप्टे केवल इस भाषण के लिए ही बम्बई से आने वाले हैं ?

Is Professor Apte coming from Bombay just for this lecture?

### DEVI PRASAD

मुझे ठीक ठीक पता नहीं है ।

I don't really know.

### HARI LAL

हालांकि

although

तैयारी

preparation

हालांकि मुझे कल के क्लास के लिए तैयारी करनी थी, पर मैं भी भाषण सुनने चला चलूंगा ।

Although I had some home work for tomorrow's class, nevertheless I'll go with you to hear the lecture too.

किस समय है यह भाषण ?

What time is the lecture?

## DEVI PRASAD

| | |
|---|---|
| यूनियन | Union |
| हाल | hall |
| शाम साढ़े सात बजे, यूनियन हाल में । | At half past seven, in the Students' Union. |
| नहीं तो | otherwise |
| भीड़ | crowd |
| हमें समय से कुछ पहले चलना होगा, नहीं तो भीड़ की वजह से जगह न मिलेगी । | We will have to go a little ahead of time, otherwise we won't get a place on account of the crowd. |
| सफल | impressive, fruitful |
| वक्ता | speaker |
| वे बड़े सफल वक्ता हैं । | He is a very impressive speaker. |

## HARI LAL

| | |
|---|---|
| चल देना | to set out |
| ठीक है, तब हम लोग सात बजे चल देंगे । | Fine, then we'll start at seven o'clock. |
| अच्छा ? | O.K.? |

## ADDITIONAL VOCABULARY

| | | | |
|---|---|---|---|
| दिल्ली, देहली | Delhi | बंगाल | Bengal |
| मद्रास | Madras | गुजरात | Gujarat |
| कलकत्ता | Calcutta | महाराष्ट्र | Maharashtra |
| इतिहास | history | पंजाबी | Panjabi |
| भूगोल | geography | गुजराती | Gujarati |

| गणित | mathematics | बंगाली | Bengali |
|---|---|---|---|
| समाज | society | रानी | queen |
| साहित्य | literature | नौकरानी | female servant |
| अमरीकन | American | धोबिन | washerwoman |
| अंग्रेज़ | Englishman | मज़दूरिन | female worker |
| पंजाब | Panjab | | |

## GRAMMAR

### 1. New Nouns

| Fem. I | | Fem. II | |
|---|---|---|---|
| लाइब्रेरी | library | पुस्तक | book |
| राजनीति | politics | भीड़ | crowd |
| तैयारी | preparation | यूनियन | union |
| दिल्ली, देहली | Delhi | मज़दूरिन | female worker |
| रानी | queen | धोबिन | washerwoman |
| नौकरानी | female servant | | |

#### Masc. I

| | |
|---|---|
| वक्ता | speaker |
| कलकत्ता | Calcutta |

| Masc. II | | Masc. II | |
|---|---|---|---|
| कालेज | college | हाल | hall |
| क्लास | class | इतिहास | history |
| पुस्तकालय | library | भूगोल | geography |
| भाषण | speech, lecture | गणित | mathematics |
| प्रोफ़ेसर | professor | समाज | society |
| ख्याल | idea, thought | साहित्य | literature |

| | | | |
|---|---|---|---|
| विश्वविद्यालय | university | अमरीका | American |
| विज्ञान | science | अंग्रेज़ | Englishman |
| विभाग | department | बंगाल | Bengal |
| अध्यक्ष | head, chairman | पंजाब | Panjab |
| विद्वान | scholar | गुजरात | Gujarat |
| व्याख्यान | lecture | महाराष्ट्र | Maharashtra |
| चुनाव | election | पंजाबी | Panjabi |
| दल | party, group | गुजराती | Gujarati |
| असर | influence | बंगाली | Bengali |
| ज़िक्र | mention | | |

## 2. New Verbs

| | 1st Causative | 2nd Causative |
|---|---|---|
| निकलना | निकालना | निकलवाना |
| to be published, to come out, to go out | to publish, to let go | to cause to publish, to cause to let go |
| चूकना | चुकाना | |
| to miss | to cause to miss | |

## 2.1 New Compound Verbs

### Type I

चल देना

to set out

### Type II

| बरबाद होना | बरबाद करना |
|---|---|
| to be wasted | to waste |
| जल्दी होना | जल्दी करना |
| to be in a hurry | to hurry |

398

| जिक्र होना | जिक्र करना |
|---|---|
| to be mentioned | to mention |
| असर होना | असर करना |
| to influence | to influence |
| ख्याल होना | ख्याल करना |
| to think | to think |

## 3. Future

Hindi has a Future Imperfect, Future Perfect, and
Future Progressive parallel to the Present and Past
Imperfect, Present and Past Perfect, and the Present
and Past Progressive. This tense is formed by adding
the Future of होना to the Imperfect, Perfect, and
Progressive respectively.

|  | Imperf. | Perf. | Progr. |
|---|---|---|---|
| Pres. | देखता है | देखा है | देख रहा है |
| Past | देखता था | देखा था | देख रहा था |
| Future | देखता होगा | देखा होगा | देख रहा होगा |

These tenses are classified as Future, since they
are formed with the Future of होना . The meaning of
these tenses is one of certainty rather than of futuri-
ty and is the equivalent of the use of English "must"
expressing certainty rather than obligation.

| Future Imperf. | देखता होगा | must see |
|---|---|---|
| Future Perf. | देखा होगा | must have seen |
| Future Progr. | देख रहा होगा | must be seeing |

किताबें इस समय तक पुस्तकालय    The books must have arrived

| | |
|---|---|
| में आ गई होंगी । | in the library by this time. |
| तुम इसके बारे में जानते होंगे । | You must know about that. |
| तुमने उनका भाषण सुना होगा । | You must have heard his lecture. |
| मैं उस समय बाहर गया होऊंगा । | I must have been away at that time. |
| अभी वह पुस्तकालय में काम कर रहा होगा । | He must be working in the library right now. |

Note the contrast in the following sentences:

| | |
|---|---|
| वह पुस्तकालय में काम करता होगा, क्योंकि मैंने उसे वहां देखा है । | He must work in the library because I have seen him there. |
| उसे पुस्तकालय में काम करना पड़ता है (चाहिए, है) । | He must (has to) work in the library (i.e., he needs the money). |

## 4.  Vocabulary

### 4.1 विश्वविधालय

The form विधालय is used by itself referring to any kind of school.  When the form विश्व "all," "universal" is used with विधालय , it refers to a university.

### 4.2 आम  and ख़ास

The form आम "general," "common" contrasts in meaning with the form ख़ास "special" and forms a similar adverb as follows:

| | |
|---|---|
| ख़ास तौर पर | especially |

400

आम तौर पर         generally, usually

## 5. Adjective Formation

From some nouns adjectives are formed by the addition of -iiy or -ik. In the latter case there is sometimes a change in the stem as follows:

| | | |
|---|---|---|
| -i, -ii, -ee | changes to | -ai |
| -u, -uu, -oo | changes to | -au |
| -a | changes to | -aa |

Some adjectives of these two types are the following:

| | | | |
|---|---|---|---|
| भारत | India | भारतीय | Indian |
| गणित | mathematics | गणितीय | mathematical |
| देश | country | देशीय | indigenous |
| इतिहास | history | ऐतिहासिक | historical |
| भूगोल | geography | भौगोलिक | geographical |
| राजनीति | politics | राजनीतिक | political |
| समाज | society | सामाजिक | social |
| साहित्य | literature | साहित्यिक | literary |
| विज्ञान | science | वैज्ञानिक | scientific |
| दिन | day | दैनिक | daily |
| सप्ताह | week | साप्ताहिक | weekly |
| मास | month | मासिक | monthly |
| वर्ष | year | वार्षिक | yearly |

## 6. Verbs with होना

Note the constructions used with the following verbs compounded with होना and करना :

भाषण में उसके नाम का      His name was mentioned at

जिक्र हुआ ।               the lecture.

401

| | |
|---|---|
| प्रो॰ शर्मा ने उसका ज़िक्र किया । | Professor Sharma mentioned him. |
| लड़कों पर भाषण का असर हुआ । | The lecture influenced the children. |
| चुनाव ने राजनीतिक दलों पर असर नहीं किया । | The election did not influence the political parties. |
| मेरा समय बरबाद हुआ । | My time was wasted. |
| उसने मेरा समय बरबाद किया । | He wasted my time. |
| मुझे जाने की जल्दी है । | I am in a hurry to leave. |
| लड़के जाने की जल्दी कर रहे हैं । | The boys are in a hurry to leave. |
| मेरा ख्याल कलकत्ता जाने का है । | I am thinking of going to Calcutta. |
| मैं मद्रास जाने का ख्याल कर रहा हूं । | I am thinking of going to Madras. |

The form ख्याल may replace विचार in any construction in which the latter occurs, which implies that in negative constructions, where English makes the verb "to think" negative, Hindi puts the negative in the subordinate clause.

| | |
|---|---|
| मेरा ख्याल है कि उसने यह किताब नहीं लिखी है । | I don't think he wrote this book. |

## 7.  Professional Names

Many professional names and other group names, such as प्रोफ़ेसर, डाक्टर, विद्वान, नौकर, मज़दूर, हिन्दू, मुसलमान are inflected as Masc. Type II nouns, but may refer to

402

either a man or a woman; in the latter case, the
adjective or verb will show feminine agreement.

डाक्टर शर्मा व्याख्यान दे          Doctor Sharma (a woman) is
रही है ।                                        giving a lecture.
नौकर हमारे घर का काम           The servant (a woman) does
करती है ।                                    our housework.

This is regularly true of the names of nationali-
ties, e.g.,

मैं बहुत से बंगालियों से          I have met a lot of Bengalis.
मिला हूं ।

Some professional names have a special feminine
form, e.g., रानी "queen," धोबिन "washerwoman," नौकरानी
"female servant," मज़दूरिन "female worker."

8. Abbreviations

Where in English an abbreviated form is written
with a period after the form (Mr., U.S.A., etc.), Hindi uses the symbol ० instead of a period.

प्रो०                                         professor
डा०                                         doctor

Generally speaking, Hindi forms abbreviations by
one of two different systems.

1. A form may be abbreviated by writing the first
syllable of the word instead of the whole word. This
is comparable to one type of English abbreviation,
except that the first syllable, not the first letter,
is used.

| | |
|---|---|
| प्रो० | professor |
| डा० | doctor |
| उ० ना० तिवारी | U.N. Tiwari |
| उदय नारायण तिवारी | |
| रा० कु० शर्मा | R.K. Sharma |
| राम कुमार शर्मा | |
| उ० प्र० | U.P. |
| उत्तर प्रदेश | |
| रु० | Rs. |
| रुपया, रुपए | rupee, rupees |
| पै० | pice |
| पैसा, पैसे | |
| ई० | A.D. |
| ईसवी | of Jesus |
| ई० पू० | B.C. |
| ईसा पूर्व | Before Jesus |

2. Basically the second type of abbreviation is based on an English abbreviation which is composed of the first letter of each word. The Hindi abbreviation is then written the way the English abbreviation would be pronounced. A good example of this is the abbreviation for the State of Uttar Pradesh, which is abbreviated in English as U.P. This abbreviation would be spoken in English as "yuu pii" (following our transcription) and is then written in Hindi by the symbols you would expect for this pronunciation, यू० पी०

यू० एस० ए०                    U.S.A.

| | |
|---|---|
| संयुक्त राज्य अमरीका | |
| यू० के० | U.K. |
| संयुक्त राज्य | United Kingdom |
| यू० एन० | U.N. |
| संयुक्त राष्ट्रसंघ | United Nations |
| यू० एस० एस० आर० | U.S.S.R. |
| सोवियत यूनियन | |
| बी० ए० | B.A. |
| एम० ए० | M.A. |
| पी-एच० डी० | |
| पी० एच० डी० | Ph.D. |
| जी० टी० रोड | G.T. Road |
| | Grand Trunk Road |

EXERCISES

A. Substitute orally in the sentences below the Hindi equivalent of the English given:

1. क्या आपने ----- के बारे में भी पढ़ा है ?

| | |
|---|---|
| the Englishmen | the villagers |
| the Americans | the Indian villagers |
| the Indians | the ancient Hindu kings |
| the Bengalis | the old temples |
| the Gujaratis | the old Indian temples |
| the Panjabis | the Indian women |
| the Hindus | the Indian people |
| the Muslims | this country |
| the Hindu kings | America |

|                    |                        |
| ------------------ | ---------------------- |
| the Muslim kings   | Calcutta               |
| the Indian kings   | the Indian cities      |
| the Hindu queens   | the western countries  |

2. उनकी ----- जानकारी बहुत अच्छी है ।

| historical   | mathematical |
| ------------ | ------------ |
| geographical | social       |
| literary     | political    |
| scientific   |              |

3. लड़के इस समय ----- ।

must be studying

must be writing

must be playing

must be celebrating the festival

must be singing

must be working

must be hurrying for the lecture

must be returning from India

must be taking a trip

must be walking

4. मेरा ख्याल था कि आपने इस ----- पत्र के बारे में सुना होगा ।

| daily   | literary   |
| ------- | ---------- |
| weekly  | political  |
| yearly  | social     |
| monthly | scientific |

5. इस समय वहां ----- ।

| must be raining | must be hot |
| --------------- | ----------- |

406

must be snowing          must be cold

6. आप लोगों ने इस के बारे में ----- ।

must have heard          must have known

must have read           must have told him

must have thought        must have explained to him

7. वह कल सुबह ----- ।

must have gone           must have met his son

must have come           must have been here

must have come back      must have stayed here

8. प्रोफ़ेसर को ----- कुछ किताबें चाहिए ।

recently published       recently written

recently arrived         recently bought

9. क्या आप पर ----- का कोई असर हुआ ?

that lecture             that book

that dance               that election

that singing             that speaker

10. क्या आपने भारतीय ----- भी देखे हैं ?

schools                  libraries

colleges                 cities

universities             villages

11. उस कालेज में ----- काम करते हैं ।

many scholars

many well-known scholars

many literary scholars

many recognized scholars

many recognized literary scholars

407

many American scholars

some English scholars

12.आप वहां ----- पहुंच गए थे ।

a little ahead of time

an hour ahead of time

much ahead of time

how long ahead of time

13.उन्होंने कल ----- का जिक्र किया था ।

you

your book

your recently published book

your books

your trip

your Indian trip

your lecture

your film

your art

your literary books

your ideas

14.मुझे ----- की जल्दी है ।

to leave

to go to Bengal

to visit Delhi

to return to America

to listen to the lecture

to finish building the house

408

15. उनका भाषण ----- पर है ।

        Indian political parties

        American literature

        American elections

        Indian general elections

        ancient Indian history

        ancient Indian art

        history of Indian art

        western society

        Indian languages

        Indian festivals

        Indian schools and colleges

        Indian cities

B.  Transform the following sentences according to the model given:

किताबें आईं । ----- किताबें आई होंगी ।

1. क्लास समय से ख़तम हो गया ।

2. वह मेरे भाई से मिली ।

3. वह यहां पिछले साल आया ।

4. मैंने उनका भाषण सुना ।

5. भारत के बारे में एक नई किताब निकली ।

6. उन्होंने कुछ रुपए बचाए ।

7. उन्होंने उनको लाल किला दिखलाया ।

8. वह बम्बई में रहा ।

C.  Transform the following sentences from the Present Perfect to the Future Imperfect according to the model given:

मैंने यह किताब पढ़ी है । ----- आपको यह किताब पढ़ना चाहिए ।

1. मैंने दिल्ली का लाल किला देखा है ।

2. मैंने नई हिन्दी फ़िल्म देखी है ।

3. मैंने एक नया मकान ख़रीदा है ।

4. मैंने हिन्दी बोलना सीखा है ।

5. मैं उसकी बहिन से मिला हूं ।

6. मैंने उनका भाषण सुना है ।

7. मैंने उन्हें अजन्ता के बारे में बताया है ।

8. मैं भारत लौटा हूं ।

D.  Translate orally:

1.  The Red Fort is in Delhi.

2.  When you are in Delhi you should see the Red
    Fort.

3.  Near the Red Fort is the Pearl ( मोती ) Mosque.

4.  The Pearl Mosque is of great historical im-
    portance.

5.  You should visit the Pearl mosque in Delhi too.

6.  Muslims go to mosques.

7.  Hindus go to temples.

8.  In India there are many temples, especially in
    South India.

E.  Translate orally:

1.  You must know about it.

2.  He must have known about it.

3.  She must have heard the lecture.

4.  He must be a recognized scholar.

5.  You must have met Professor Apte.

6.  They must be studying in the library.

7.  We must have read his new book.

8. He must be giving a lecture right now.

9. He must have mentioned your name in the class.

10. You must have done your homework.

F. Translate orally:

1. He speaks English.

2. They were speaking Panjabi.

3. She must speak Marathi.

4. Bengalis usually speak Bengali.

5. Do you speak Gujarati too?

6. People in Maharashtra speak Marathi.

7. Indians speak many Indian languages.

8. I have learnt to speak Hindi.

G. Translate orally:

1. Professor Apte is the head of our department.

2. There are a lot of scholars in this department.

3. Professor Apte teaches Indian history.

4. He has recently published a book on Indian history.

5. The recently published book on Indian literature interests me very much.

6. Many scholars have written about Indian geography.

7. Few Americans have read about Marathi literature.

8. To understand India, you must study Indian history.

REVIEW VI

A. Substitute orally in the sentences below the Hindi equivalent of the English given:

1. इस कमरे का मासिक किराया ----- है ।

| | |
|---|---|
| how much | hundred rupees |
| very much | ninety rupees |
| very little | twenty-five rupees |
| seventy rupees | fifty rupees |
| seventy-five rupees | fifty-five rupees |
| eighty-five rupees | forty-five rupees |
| eighty rupees | sixty rupees |
| ninety-five rupees | how many rupees |

2. बम्बई यहां से ----- है ।

| | |
|---|---|
| how far | seventy-nine miles |
| very far | sixty-nine miles |
| very near | eighty-seven miles |
| seventy-two miles | seventy-seven miles |
| eighty-two miles | seventy-six miles |
| ninety-two miles | ninety-six miles |
| ninety-nine miles | eighty-six miles |
| eighty-nine miles | eighteen miles |

3. यह मोटर इस समय तक ----- चल चुकी है ।

| | |
|---|---|
| seventy-one miles | ninety-four miles |
| ninety-one miles | seventy-four miles |
| seventy-three miles | eighty-four miles |
| eighty-three miles | one hundred miles |
| ninety-three miles | one thousand miles |

412

| eighty-one miles | seven hundred miles |
| eighty-eight miles | three thousand miles |
| seventy-eight miles | many thousand miles |
| ninety-eight miles | how many miles |

4. क्या आप की लड़की को ----- कपड़े पसन्द हैं ?

| green | black |
| brown | gray |
| red | white |
| yellow | purple |
| blue | |

5. भारत के ----- बहुत से प्रसिद्ध ऐतिहासिक स्थान हैं ।

| in the northern part | in the eastern part |
| in the western part | in the southern part |

6. इस देश के ----- कई विश्वविधालय हैं ।

| in the South | in the West |
| in the North | in the East |

7. ----- के बारे में आपका क्या विचार है ?

| Bengalis | Gujaratis |
| Hindus | Indians |
| Muslims | Americans |
| Panjabis | Englishmen |

8. वे सारे दिन ----- खड़े रहते हैं ।

on the streets
on the roofs
on the roofs of their houses
in front of their houses

413

in front of their stores

outside

9. क्या आपने कालेज में ----- के बारे में पढ़ा है ?

Indian elections

Indian villages

Indian festivals

American elections

Indian political parties

ancient Indian history

American literature

Hindu kings

Muslim festivals

the historical sites of India

Indian temples

Muslim mosques

Indian seasons

Indian scholars

10. वे वहां जाएंगे ही नहीं ----- ।

but will also study there

but will also give a lecture there

but will also live there for a year

but will also see the historical sites

but will also talk with the professors

but will also visit his old friends

but will also spend all his vacation there

but will also teach American history there

but will also work in the university library
there

414

but will also celebrate Holi there

but will also play with the children there

11. क्या यह मकान ----- हैं ?

| | |
|---|---|
| good | expensive |
| bad | private |
| old | governmental |
| new | cheap |

12. ----- वह अपने माता-पिता से मिलने गया ।   (use a past
                                           participle form)

having eaten

having drunk water

having hired a taxi

having put on his best clothes

having returned from the North

having celebrated Holi

having called on the telephone

having seen a movie

having enrolled his son in the school

having closed his store

having walked in the park

having told me about it

13. धोबी के यहां से कपड़े ----- ।

| | |
|---|---|
| are brought | are being brought |
| were brought | were being brought |
| have been brought | should be brought |
| had been brought | can be brought |
| will be brought | could be brought |

415

14. क्या आप ----- भूल गए ?

       how to write Hindi

       to stop at Aurangabad

       to hire a taxi

       to see the temple on your way

       to go to hear the lecture

       what he said

       the time of his lecture

       the way to the Union Hall

15. अगर मैं आगरे में रहना चाहूं, ----- ।

       then it will be better to rent a house

       then it will be better to stay in a hotel

       then it will be better to learn Hindi

       then it will be better to study in Agra

       then it will be better to work there

       then it will be better to take the car with me

16. वे मन्दिर ----- हैं ।

       very well-known

       worth seeing

       from the eighth century

       good examples of Hindu art

       of historical importance

       ancient

17. लड़कों ने स्कूल में ----- ।

       must have learnt Hindi

       must have talked in Hindi

must have spoken in Hindi

must have written Hindi

must have studied Hindi

must have heard Hindi

must have heard his lecture

must have seen movies

18. लड़के इस समय ----- ।

must be celebrating the festival

must be throwing colored water

must be eating

must be collecting old books

must be making arrangements to go to Bombay

must be studying Indian art

must be hearing a political lecture

must be going to the fair

must be working in the library

must be waiting for the train

B. Transform the following sentences according to the model given:

अमरीका में कौन सी भाषा ----- अमरीका में अंग्रेज़ी बोली
बोली जाती है ?                  जाती है ।

1. भारत में कौन सी भाषाएं बोली जाती हैं ?

2. बंगाल में कौन सी भाषा बोली जाती है ?

3. पंजाब में कौन सी भाषा बोली जाती है ?

4. गुजरात में कौन सि भाषा बोली जाती है ?

5. महाराष्ट्र में कौन सि भाषा बोली जाती है ?

6. बम्बई में कौन सी भाषाएं बोली जाती हैं ?

7.यू० पी० में कौन सी भाषा बोली जाती है ?

8.कलकत्ता में कौन सी भाषा बोली जाती है ?

9.नई दिल्ली में कौन सी भाषाएं बोली जाती हैं ?

10.उत्तरी भारत में कौन सी भाषाएं बोली जाती हैं ?

C. Transform the following sentences from active to passive according to the model given:

लोग यहां बंगाली बोलते हैं । ----- यहां बंगाली बोली जाती है ।

1.वे विश्वविधालय में राजनीति पढ़ते थे ।

2.उन्होंने मेरी यात्रा का इंतज़ाम किया ।

3.सरकार ने पिछले साल आम चुनाव कराए ।

4.वे गणित के बारे में बात कर रहे थे ।

5.वे भारतीय त्योहारों के बारे में भाषण देंगे ।

6.प्रोफ़ेसर ने क्लास में गुजरात का ज़िक्र किया ।

7.हमें होली मनानी चाहिए ।

8.हिन्दुओं ने पांचवीं शताब्दी में बहुत से मन्दिर बनाए ।

D. Transform the following sentences according to the model given:

कपड़ा, जो उसने ख़रीदा, मुझे ----- उसका ख़रीदा कपड़ा मुझे
पसन्द है ।                         पसन्द है ।

1.भाषण, जो उन्होंने कल दिया था, भारतीय राजनीति पर
था ।

2.किताब, जो उसने मुझे दी थी, मैंने पढ़ ली है ।

3.पुस्तकें, जो हाल में ही निकली हैं, बहुत सस्ती हैं ।

4.किला, जो आठवीं सदी में बनाया गया था, दिल्ली के पास
है ।

5.फल, जो उसने खाए, मीठे न थे ।

6.मकान, जो उसने किराए पर लिया, सफ़ेद रंग का है ।

7.नगर, जो मैंने भारत में देखे, बहुत बड़े हैं ।

8.किताबें, जो राम ने लिखी हैं, बहुत मुश्किल हैं ।

E.  Transform the following sentences according to the model given, retaining the tense of the original:

वह कल पांच बजे खाना खाएगा ----- वह कल पांच बजे खाना खा

चुकेगा ।

1.वह कल एक हिन्दू मन्दिर देखेगी ।

2.उसने पिछले साल हिन्दी में एक किताब लिखी थी ।

3.वह आम तौर पर सात बजे खाना खाता है ।

4.वह दो बजे अपना व्याख्यान खतम करता था ।

5.प्रोफ़ेसर ने भूगोल पर किताब लिखी है ।

6.आप ने इस समय तक अपना काम किया होगा ।

7.वह अपनी यात्रा के बारे में जल्दी बताएगा ।

8.उसने घर खरीदने के लिए पैसे बचाए ।

F.  Transform the following sentences according to the model given:

उसने लाल किला देखा है । ----- उसने लाल किला देखा होगा ।

1.उसने होली का त्योहार मनाया है ।

2.आपने भारतीय चुनावों के बारे में पढ़ा है ।

3.प्रोफ़ेसर हिन्दी साहित्य के बारे में बता रहे हैं ।

4.वे लोग बंगाली बोल रहे हैं ।

5.उसने अजन्ता जाने के लिए टैक्सी किराए पर की है ।

6.उनके व्याख्यान ने लड़कों पर बड़ा असर किया है ।

7.लड़के वहां अपना समय बरबाद कर रहे में ।

8.वह पिछले हफ़्ते बम्बई गया था ।

G.  Translate orally:

1.  I went to the library.

2. After that I went to the library.

3. I went to the library before class.

4. I went to the library to get a book.

5. I went to the library to read a book.

6. I went to the library to do some homework for class.

7. I went to the library to do some homework for Monday's class.

8. I should go to the library to read some books.

H.  Translate orally:

1. He came here last year to give a lecture.

2. He comes here every year to give a lecture.

3. He will come here to give the annual lecture.

4. He will come tomorrow to give the weekly lecture.

5. Have you heard his lecture?

6. You must hear his lecture tomorrow evening.

7. You must have heard his lecture last month.

8. I have heard that his lecture is good.

I.  Translate orally:

1. Will the lecture be on time?

2. He came on time.

3. They came a little ahead of time.

4. They will have to go a little ahead of time.

5. They will have to go a little ahead of time, otherwise they will not get a seat.

6. They will have to go a little ahead of time, otherwise they will miss their train.

7. I will have to go a little ahead of time, otherwise the train may leave.

8.  She will have to go much ahead of time in order
    to get a seat.


J.  Conversation:

1.  A wants to visit the Red Fort in Delhi.  His
    friend B  takes him around and tells him various
    important details about the Fort, viz., when it
    was built, by whom, etc.  A thanks B for showing
    him around.

2.  A has just returned from a trip to Ajanta and
    Ellora.  His elder brother B  has never been to
    either one of these places and asks him about how
    he travelled, where he stayed, what places he went
    to, and what he saw.  A gives his brother a short
    account of his trip and tells him all the histori-
    cal facts he knows about the places he visited.

3.  A and B are students in an Indian university and
    are classmates.  On their way back home from the
    school, they discuss their classes, fields of
    study, professors, and other things of mutual in-
    terest.

4.  A is in a book store and sees a recent publication
    about Indian elections.  He asks B, who is with
    him, if he knows anything about the book or its
    author.   B tells A that the book was mentioned in
    his class and that he has read other books by the
    same author and that it should be good.  A decides
    to buy the book.

5.  A goes to India and visits his old classmate B in
    Delhi.  B tells his friend  A  about the various
    languages, nationalities and states in India,
    differences of climate in the various parts of the
    country, and other things of general interest about
    the people.

6.  A has recently come back from a trip to some big
    Indian cities like Calcutta, Bombay, Madras, Kan-
    pur, and Delhi, etc., and tells his wife about the
    trip, the things and places he liked and he didn't
    like.

7.  A wants to find out about a lecture to be held
    that evening.  He asks his roommate B if he knows
    about the lecture.  B has all the information and
    tells A about the place, time and topic of the
    lecture, and also what he knows about the speaker.

421

8.  A, an American, is a student at an Indian university. Before the Holi vacation, he asks his Indian friend B about the Holi festival. B gives a full account of how Holi is celebrated by Hindus in North India.

9.  A, an American, goes to see B, a professor in an Indian university, and tells him that he has been sent to him by his teacher in the United States. B asks A about when he came to India, what he has studied in the United States, what he is interested in studying while in India, and where he is staying. B also asks A, if he can do anything for him. A thanks B and leaves.

10. A goes to a book store in Delhi and asks for some books on Indian literature and history. The clerk at the store shows him some books he thinks are good and some books which have recently been published. A looks them over and buys some of them. A pays for the books, tells his address to the clerk, and asks him to send them to his house.

APPENDIX

## 1. Nouns

Nouns may be subdivided into two classes, masculine and feminine, on the basis of adjective and verb agreement with the nouns. Nouns are inflected for two cases and two numbers, nominative singular, oblique singular, nominative plural and oblique plural.

Masculine nouns are subdivided into two classes on the basis of their inflection as follows:

| Masc. Type I | | Masc. Type II |
|---|---|---|
| Nom. Sg. | लड़का | घर |
| Obl. Sg. | लड़के | घर |
| Nom. Pl. | लड़के | घर |
| Obl. Pl. | लड़कों | घरों |

All Masculine Type I nouns end in -aa, but not all nouns that end in -aa belong to this class, although the majority do.

Feminine nouns may likewise be subdivided into two classes by inflection as follows:

| Fem. Type I | | Fem. Type II |
|---|---|---|
| Nom. Sg. | लड़की | चीज़ |
| Obl. Sg. | लड़की | चीज़ |
| Nom. Pl. | लड़कियां | चीज़ें |
| Obl. Pl. | लड़कियों | चीज़ों |

All Feminine Type I nouns end in -ii or in -i, although the latter are few in number, and most nouns that end in -ii or -i are Fem. Type I. In Fem. Type I nouns, an -ii is always replaced by -iy before the endings -ãã and -õõ. In Fem. Type II a -uu is always replaced by -uv before the endings -ẽẽ and -õõ.

All Hindi nouns belong to one of the four inflectional types listed above, and there are no irregular forms from the point of view of the written form. There are a few irregularities from the point of view of the spoken form. Thus the oblique plural form

423

गांवों is normally pronounced the same way as the nominative singular form गांव although it may be distinguished from the nominative form in very careful speech as g̃ãw̃õõ.

## 2. Adjectives

Adjectives may be subdivided into two groups, those that end in -aa or -ãã and all others. Those that do not end in -aa or -ãã are not inflected at all. Those that end in -aa or -ãã are inflected for case, number and gender as follows:

|          | Masc. | Fem. |
|----------|-------|------|
| Nom. Sg. | बड़ा   | बड़ी   |
| Obl. Sg. | बड़े   | बड़ी   |
| Nom. Pl. | बड़े   | बड़ी   |
| Obl. Pl. | बड़े   | बड़ी   |

Adjectives may be used as nouns. When so used, adjectives in -aa or -ãã have the inflection of Masc. Type I nouns when referring to masculine things, and the inflection of Fem. Type I nouns when referring to feminine things, thus अच्छे "the good (men)" and अच्छियां "the good (women)." In this use adjectives that do not end in -aa or -ãã have the inflection of Masc. Type II nouns and Fem. Type II nouns respectively.

## 3. Pronouns

For the most part, pronouns have a fuller inflection than nouns, since some have four oblique forms, and some have three oblique forms as well as a nominative form. One oblique form is used with the postposition nee and is called here the nee-form. A second is used where a noun would be used with the postposition koo and is called the dative or the koo-form. A third is used where a noun would be used with the postposition

424

kaa and is called the kaa-form. The fourth is used with any other postposition and is called the see-form.

The personal pronouns of the first and second persons are the pronouns having five forms as follows:

|  | 1st Per.Sg. | 1st Per.Pl. | 2nd Per.Pl. |
|---|---|---|---|
| Nom. | मैं | हम | तुम |
| nee-form | मैंने | हमने | तुमने |
| koo-form | मुझे, मुझको | हमें, हमको | तुम्हें, तुमको |
| see-form | मुझसे | हमसे | तुमसे |
| kaa-form | मेरा | हमारा | तुम्हारा |

The pronouns that have four forms do not distinguish the see-form and the kaa-form, i.e., the same form is used with any following postposition except nee or koo. The following pronouns, given with a following postposition, belong to this group:

|  | 3rd Per.Sg. proximate | 3rd Per.Pl.proximate |
|---|---|---|
| Nom. | यह | ये |
| nee-form | इसने | इन्होंने |
| koo-form | इसे, इसको | इन्हें, इनको |
| see-form | इससे | इनसे |

|  | 3rd Per.Sg. distant | 3rd Per. Pl. distant |
|---|---|---|
| Nom. | वह | वे |
| nee-form | उसने | उन्होंने |
| koo-form | उसे, उसको | उन्हें, उनको |
| see-form | उससे | उनसे |

|  | relative pron. Sg. | relative pron. Pl. |
|---|---|---|
| Nom. | जो | जो |
| nee-form | जिसने | जिन्होंने |
| koo-form | जिसे, जिसको | जिन्हें, जिनको |

425

see-form     जिससे                  जिनसे

|  | interrog. pron. Sg. | interrog. pron. Pl. |
|---|---|---|
| Nom. | कौन | कौन |
| nee-form | किसने | किन्होंने |
| koo-form | किसे, किसको | किन्हें, किनको |
| see-form | किससे | किनसे |

The pronouns in this group यह, वह, जो and कौन may be used as adjectives, in which case they have only two forms, a nominative and an oblique. The nominative of the adjective is always the same as the nominative of the pronoun, and the oblique of the adjective is always the same as the see-form of the pronoun, as follows:

| Nom. | यह | ये | वह | वे | जो | जो | कौन | कौन |
|---|---|---|---|---|---|---|---|---|
| Obl. | इस | इन | उस | उन | जिस | जिन | किस | किन |

The pronouns क्या "what," and कोई "someone" have only two forms, nominative and oblique:

| Nom. | क्या | कोई |
|---|---|---|
| Obl. | किस | किसी |

The oblique forms are used with all postpositions although since क्या is inanimate in reference, it is not ever used with को.

The pronouns आप "you (polite)" and कुछ "some" have only a single form used as nominative and also used with any following postposition.

426

## 4. Verbs

The verb होना is the only verb in Hindi that has a simple present form and a simple past form. Their inflection is as follows:

| Simple Present | | Simple Past | |
|---|---|---|---|
| 1st Per Sg. | हूँ | Masc. Sg. | था |
| 3rd Per. Sg. | है | Masc. Pl. | थे |
| 1st,3rd Per.Pl. | हैं | Fem. Sg. | थी |
| 2nd Per. Pl. | हो | Fem. Pl. | थीं |

As examples of verb inflection two verbs are given, होना because it has a number of irregular forms, and देखना because it is completely regular. In the following table the forms of these verbs are cited in the 3rd Per. Sg. Masc. form to illustrate the system of tense forms.

| Infin. | होना | देखना |
|---|---|---|
| Stem | हो | देख |
| Imper. (familiar) | हो | देखो |
| Imper. (polite) | होइए | देखिए |
| Past Participle | हो कर | देख कर |
| Perfect Participle | हुआ | देखा हुआ |
| Optative | हो | देखे |
| Future | होगा | देखेगा |
| Imperfect | होता | देखता |
| Pres. Imperf. | होता है | देखता है |
| Past Imperf. | होता था | देखता था |
| Future Imperf. | होता होगा | देखता होगा |

427

| | | |
|---|---|---|
| Perfect | हुआ | देखा |
| Pres. Perfect | हुआ है | देखा है |
| Past Perfect | हुआ था | देखा था |
| Future Perfect | हुआ होगा | देखा होगा |
| Pres. Progressive | हो रहा है | देख रहा है |
| Past Progressive | हो रहा था | देख रहा था |
| Future Progressive | हो रहा होगा | देख रहा होगा |

The imperative forms हो and होइए exist but are re-placed by the imperative forms of रहना, रहो and रहिए .

## 4.1 Inflection

The infinitive, the imperfect and the perfect forms show the following adjective type of inflection:

| | | | |
|---|---|---|---|
| Infinitive | Masc. Sg. Nom. | होना | देखना |
| | Masc. Sg. Obl. | होने | देखने |
| | Masc. Pl. | होने | देखने |
| | Fem. Sg. | होनी | देखनी |
| | Fem. Pl. | होनीं | देखनीं |
| Imperfect | Masc. Sg. | होता | देखता |
| | Masc. Pl. | होते | देखते |
| | Fem. Sg. | होती | देखती |
| | Fem. Pl. | होतीं | देखतीं |
| Perfect | Masc. Sg. | हुआ | देखा |
| | Masc. Pl. | हुए | देखे |
| | Fem. Sg. | हुई | देखी |
| | Fem. Pl. | हुईं | देखीं |

428

The Fem. Pl. form is always replaced by the Fem.
Sg. form if some other part of the verb phrase indi-
cates plurality. The result of this restriction is that
the Imperfect and Perfect, when used with the Present,
Past and Future auxiliaries, will never be used in the
Fem. Pl. form. The particle गा shows the same adjectives inflection but, since it never occurs alone,
never shows a Fem. Pl. form.

| | |
|---|---|
| Masc. Sg. | गा |
| Masc. Pl. | गे |
| Fem. Sg. | गी |

The optative shows the following inflection:

| | | |
|---|---|---|
| 1st Per. Sg. | होऊं, हूं | देखूं |
| 3rd Per. Sg. | हो | देखे |
| 1st, 3rd Per. Pl. | हों, होएं | देखें |
| 2nd Per. Pl. | हो | देखो |

All other tense forms are combinations of the
forms whose inflection is given above. It may be
noted that all the perfect tense forms of those transitive verbs that take a subject expressed by ने will
occur only in the third person.

4.2  Irregularities

Relatively few verbs in Hindi have irregular forms.
Apart from the verb होना , the forms of which are given
above, most irregularities are restricted to the verbs
देना, लेना, जाना and करना .

The following irregularities occur:

429

|  | Infin. | Imper. (polite) |
|---|---|---|
| Imperative (polite) | देना | दीजिये or दीजिए |
|  | लेना | लीजिये or लीजिए |
|  | करना | कीजिये or कीजिए |
|  | पीना | पीजिये or पीजिए |

|  | Infin. | Optative |  |  |  |
|---|---|---|---|---|---|
| Optative | देना | दूँ | दे | दें | दो |
|  | लेना | लूँ | ले | लें | लो |

| | Infin. | Perfect | | | |
|---|---|---|---|---|---|
| Perfect | देना | दिया | दिये, दिए | दी | दीं |
|  | लेना | लिया | लिये, लिए | ली | लीं |
|  | जाना | गया | गये, गए | गयी, गई | गयीं, गईं |
|  | करना | किया | किये, किए | की | कीं |
|  | पीना | पिया | पिये, पिर | पी | पीं |

The last verb illustrates two consistent irregularities:

1. All verbs with a stem ending in -ii will not add an extra -ii to form the feminine of the perfect, and the stem will end in -i in the Masc. Sg. and Masc. Pl.

2. All verbs with a stem ending in -a, -aa, or -ii will add -y before an ending -aa; thus गया, आया and पिया . Those with a stem ending in -a or -aa will have alternative spellings for the Masc. Pl., Fem. Sg., and Fem. Pl. of the Perfect, and those with a stem ending in -ii will have alternative spellings for the Masc. Pl. of the Perfect.

## 4.3 Passive

Hindi has a complete passive inflection using the verb जाना as an auxiliary with the perfect form of the verb that is passive. The passive forms of the verb देखना in the 3rd Per. Sg. Masc. are as follows:

| | |
|---|---|
| Infinitive | देखा जाना |
| Stem | देखा जा |
| Optative | देखा जाए |
| Future | देखा जाएगा |
| Imperfect | देखा जाता |
| Pres. Imperf. | देखा जाता है |
| Past Imperf. | देखा जाता था |
| Future Imperf. | देखा जाता होगा |
| Perfect | देखा गया |
| Pres. Perfect | देखा गया है |
| Past Perfect | देखा गया था |
| Future Perfect | देखा गया होगा |
| Pres. Progressive | देखा जा रहा है |
| Past Progressive | देखा जा रहा था |
| Future Progr. | देखा जा रहा होगा |

The imperative and participle forms have been omitted from the list because they would only very rarely occur. Their form is, however, regular.

## 4.4 Continuative

Hindi has a complete continuative inflection using the verb रहना as an auxiliary and the Imperfect of the verb being inflected. Without giving the complete system, a couple of forms will illustrate the system.

| | | |
|---|---|---|
| Infinitive | देखते रहना | to keep on seeing |
| Pres. Imperf. | देखता रहता है | (he) keeps on seeing |
| Pres. Perf. | देखता रहा है | (he) has kept on " |

431

Note that when the Imperfect is followed by the Infinitive of रहना, it is invariably in the oblique form देखते , but otherwise it is regularly inflected.


## VOCABULARY

In the vocabulary the gender of nouns is indicated. The inflection of nouns and the conjugation of verbs can be more readily found in the appendix and therefore are omitted from the vocabulary.

The Hindi-English section of the vocabulary is alphabetized according to the standard Hindi order. This should cause no difficulty to the student, except for the following three cases:

1. A long nasalized vowel.

A long nasalized vowel is alphabetized immediately after the equivalent long vowel when this vowel is not followed by anything, but before the long vowel when it is followed by any other vowel or consonant. Thus मा will occur before माँ-but माँ- will occur before माइ- or माक-.

2. A short vowel followed by a nasal consonant plus consonant.

As mentioned in the text, all such words may be written either with an anusvāra (˙) or with a nasal consonant joined to the following consonant. In the vocabulary, for the sake of consistency all such forms will be written with anusvāra. For these forms the

432

principle of alphabetization is the same as for the
long nasalized vowels, i.e., म will occur before मन्द-,
but मन्द- will occur before मइ- or मक- .

3. Consonant clusters that are written in देवनागरी
with separate consonant symbols but excluding those that
are written with a हलन्त under the first consonant and
also excluding those written with a vowel symbol joined
to the consonant. These combinations are alphabetized
as if the first consonant were followed by the vowel a
even though there is no a vowel in the pronunciation.
Thus बनना will occur before बनाना .

## HINDI-ENGLISH

अ

अंग्रेज़ Englishman

अंग्रेज़ी f., English

अंतर m., difference

अंतर्देशीय inland

  अंतर्देशीय पत्र inland letter

अंदर in, inside

अंधेरा m., darkness

अकेला alone

अक्टूबर October

अक्सर often, usually

अगर if

अगला next

अगस्त August

अच्छा good; O.K., alright

अजंता Ajanta

अजमेरी of Ajmer

अट्ठाइस twenty-eight

अट्ठानवे ninety-eight

अट्ठावन fifty-eight

अट्ठासी eighty-eight

अठारह eighteen

अठहत्तर seventy-eight

अड़तालीस forty-eight

अड़तीस thirty-eight

अड़सठ sixty-eight

अधिक more, much

अधिकार m., authority

अध्यक्ष m., head, chairman

अपना one's

अप्रैल April

अफ़सोस m., sorrow

अब now

अबीर m., red powder

अभी now (emphatic)

अमरीकन American

अमरीका America

अरे oh!

अवश्य certainly

असर m. influence

असर करना to influence

असर होना to influence

असुविधा f., inconvenience

अस्पताल m., hospital

अस्सी eighty

## आ

आखिर m., end

आगरा m., Agra

आज today

आजकल nowadays

आज्ञा f., permission

आठ eight

आठवां eighth

आदमी m., man

आदि et cetera

आनंद m., joy, pleasure

आनंद आना to enjoy

आनंद मिलना to enjoy

आना to come

आप you (polite)

आम general, common

आम तौर पर generally, usually

आवश्यक necessary

आवश्यकता need, necessity

आसपास m., vicinity

के आसपास about, approximately

आसमान m., sky

आसानी f., ease

आशा f., hope

## इ

इंतज़ाम m., arrangement

इंतज़ाम करना to arrange, make arrangements

इंतज़ाम होना to be arranged

इंतज़ार m., waiting

इंतज़ार करना to wait for

इंतज़ार होना to wait for

इकट्ठा gathered

इकतालीस forty-one

इकतीस thirty-one

इकसठ sixty-one

इकहत्तर seventy-one

इक्कीस twenty-one
इक्यानवे ninety-one
इक्यावन fifty-one
इक्यासी eighty-one
इच्छा f., desire
   इच्छा करना to want to
   इच्छा होना to want to
इतवार Sunday
इतिहास m., history
इधर this way, here
इरादा m., intention
   इरादा करना to intend
   इरादा होना to intend
इसलिए therefore

ई
ईंट f., brick

उ
उचित proper
उतना as
उत्तर m., north
उत्तरी northern
उनचास forty-nine
उनतालीस thirty-nine
उनतीस twenty-nine
उनसठ fifty-nine
उनहत्तर sixty-nine
उन्नासी seventy-nine

उन्नीस nineteen
उन्यासी seventy-nine

ऊ
ऊनी woolen

ऋ
ऋतु f., season

ए
एक one
   एक ही the same
एहवांस m., advance

ऐ
ऐतिहासिक historical
ऐलोरा, एलोरा Ellora
ऐसा so, such

ओ
ओर f., direction

औ
और and, else
   और कुछ something else
औरंगाबाद Aurangabad
औरत f., woman

क
कंपनी f., company
कई many
कठिन difficult
कठिनाई f., difficulty
कपड़ा m., cloth

कपड़े clothes

कब when

कभी sometimes

कभी नहीं never

कम little, less

कम से कम at least

कमरा m., room

कमीज़ f., shirt

करना to do, make

करवाना to cause to make

कराना to get done, made

कल yesterday, tomorrow

कलकत्ता Calcutta

कला f., art

कष्ट m., trouble,
        inconvenience

कहना to say, tell

कह देना to tell

कहलाना to be called

कहाँ where

कहीं somewhere

कहीं नहीं nowhere

का of

कानपुर Kanpur

काफ़ी enough, quite

काम m., work

काम करना to work

कारण m., reason

कार्ड m., card, postcard

काला black

कालेज m., college

काश्मीर Kashmir

कि that

कितना how, how much

किताब f., book

किधर where

किनारा m., edge, bank

किराया m., rent; fare

किला m., fort

कुछ some

कुमारी Miss

कुल in all

कृपया kindly

कृपा f., kindness

के अलावा besides

के द्वारा by

के पहले before

के पास at, which

के बाद after

के बारे में about, concerning

के बाहर outside of

के लिए for

केवल only

के साथ with

के सामने in front of

कैसा what kind; how

को to

कोई any, some

कोठी f., house

कोशिश f., attempt

  कोशिश करना to try

कोहरा m., fog

कौन who, what, which

  कौन सा what kind of

क्या what, interrogative

      particle

क्यों why

क्लास m., class

ख

खड़ा standing

ख़तम end

  ख़तम करना to finish

  ख़तम होना to be finished

ख़बर f., news, information

ख़राब bad

ख़रीदना to buy

खाना to eat

ख़ाली empty

ख़ास special, important

  ख़ास तौर पर specially

खिड़की f., window

खिलवाना to cause to feed;

    to cause, allow to play

खिलाना to feed, serve food;

    to cause, allow to play

ख़ुद self

खुला open

  खुला रहना to be open,

              remain open

ख़ुशी f., pleasure, happiness

खेलना to play

ख़्याल m., idea, thought

ग

गणित m., mathematics

गणितीय mathematical

गर्मी f., heat, hot season

गला m., neck

  गले मिलना to embrace

गवाना to cause to sing

गांव m., village

गाड़ी f., train

गाना m., song, singing

गाना to sing

गारा m., mortar

गिरना to fall

  बरफ़ गिरना to snow

गिरवाना to cause to drop

गिराना to drop

गुजरात Gujarat
गुजराती Gujarati
गुरुवार Thursday
गुलाल m., pink powder
ग्यारह eleven

घ

घंटा m., hour
घर m., house
घूमना to walk

च

चउवन fifty-four
चतुर skillful
चलना to go
  चल देना to start off
चलवाना to cause to drive
चलाना to drive
चले जाना to go away
चवालीस forty-four
चार four
चालीस forty
चाहना to want
  चाहिए should
चीज़ f., thing
चुकना to finish
चुकाना to cause to miss
चुनाव m., election
चूकना to miss

चूना m., lime
चोट f., injury
चौंतीस thirty-four
चौंसठ sixty-four
चौथा fourth
चौदह fourteen
चौबीस twenty-four
चौरानवे ninety-four
चौरासी eighty-four
चौवन fifty-four
चौहत्तर seventy-four

छ

छत f., roof
छत्तीस thirty-six
छप्पन fifty-six
छब्बीस twenty-six
छयालीस forty-six
छह six
छानवे ninety-six
छाया gathered
छियासी eighty-six
छिहत्तर seventy-six
छुट्टी f., vacation
छुड़वाना to cause to leave
छूटना to leave (intr.)
छोटा little, younger
छोड़ना to leave (trans.)

438

क़्यासठ sixty-six

**ज**

जगह f., place

जनवरी January

जब when

जमना to be collected

जमवाना to cause to collect

जमाना to pile up, collect

  जमा रहना to be piled up

ज़रा a little

ज़रूर certainly

ज़रूरत f., need, necessity

ज़रूरी important

जलना to burn (intr.)

जलवाना to cause to burn

जलाना to bury (trans.),
     set fire to

जल्दी soon

  जल्दी करना to be in a hurry

  जल्दी होना to be in a hurry

जाड़ा m., cold season

जानकारी f., knowledge
     information

जानना to know

जाना to go

  आ जाना to come

  चले जाना to go away

ले जाना to take

ज़िक्र करना to mention

ज़िक्र होना to be mentioned

जितना as

जी particle of respect

जी नहीं no

जी हां yes

ज़ुकाम m., cold

जुलाई July

जून June

जैसा as

जो which

जोड़े pair

ज़्यादा much, more

**ट**

टकराना to run into

  टकरा जाना to run into

टिकट m., stamp; ticket

टेलीफ़ोन m., telephone

टेलीफ़ोन करना to call on
     the telephone

टैक्सी f., taxi

**ठ**

ठंड f., cold season

ठंडक f., cold season

ठहरना to wait, stay;
     to stop (intr.)

439

ठहरवाना to cause to stop

ठहराना to stop (trans.)

ठीक right

## ह

हबल double

हलवाना to let throw

हाक्टर m., doctor

हालना to throw

हिक्शनरी f., dictionary

हेढ़ one and a half

## ढ

ढाई two and a half

## त

तक to, as far as; until

तथा and

तब then

तब तो then

तबादला m., transfer

तबियत f., condition,health

तमी just then

तरफ़ f., side, direction

तरह f., kind, sort

तितालीस forty-three

तिरपन fifty-three

तिरसठ sixty-three

तिरानवे ninety-three

तिरासी eighty-three

तिहत्तर seventy-three

तीन three

तीस thirty

तीसरा third

तीसरा पहर late afternoon

तुम्हारा your (familiar)

तुम्हीं you (emphatic)

तूफ़ानी stormy

तेइस twenty-three

तेज़ strong, sharp, fast

तेज़ी f., speed

तेज़ी से fast

तेरह thirteen

तैंतीस thirty-three

तैयार ready

तैयारी f., preparation

त्योहार m., festival

## थ

थोड़ा little

## द

दक्षिण south

दक्षिणी southern

दफ़्तर m., office

दर्जन m., dozen

दर्जा m., class, grade

दर्शनीय worth seeing

दल m., party, group

दवा f., medicine

दवाख़ाना m., doctor's office

दस ten

दाईं right (direction)

दाम m., price

दावत f., dinner

दिखलाना to show

दिखवाना to show

दिखाना to show

दिन m., day

दिलचस्पी f., interest

दिलवाना to cause to give

दिलाना to cause to give

दिल्ली Delhi

दिसम्बर December

दीवाल f., wall

दुकान f., shop, store

दुर्घटना f., accident

दुश्मनी f., enmity

दूर far

दूसरा second

देखना to see, look at

   देख लेना to take a look

देना to give

   दे देना to give

देर f., delay, duration

देवगिरि Devagiri

देश m., country

देशीय indigenous

देहली Delhi

दैनिक daily

दो two

दोपहर f., noon

दौरा m., tour

दौलताबाद Daulatabad

घ

घन्यवाद thanks, thank you

धूप f., sunshine

धोबिन f., washerwoman

धोबी m., washerman

न

नंबर m., number

न not; isn't it

नगर m., town, city

नचवाना to cause to dance

नचाना to cause to dance

नब्बे ninety

नमस्ते hello! Hindu greeting

नमूना m., example

नया new

नरसों two days before yesterday, two days after tomorrow

नवम्बर November

नवासी eighty-nine

441

नहीं not

नहीं तो otherwise

नागपुर Nagpur

नागपुरी from Nagpur

नाच m., dance

नाचना to dance

नाम m., name

नाम लिखाना to enroll

निकलना to be published

निकलवाना to cause to publish

निकालना to publish; to let go

निजी private

निन्यानवे ninety-nine

निश्चय m., certainty

नींव f., foundation

नीला blue

ने subject marker with perfect forms of transitive verbs

नौ nine

नौकर m., servant

नौकरानी f., female servant

## प

पंजाब Panjab

पंजाबी Panjabi

पंद्रह fifteen

पचपन fifty-five

पचहत्तर seventy-five

पचास fifty

पचासी eighty-five

पचानवे, पच्चानवे ninety-five

पच्चीस twenty-five

पड़ना to fall; to have to, must; to be, remain

पड़ जाना to get involved in

पड़ोस m., neighborhood

पढ़ना to read, study

पढ़वाना to cause to teach

पढ़ाई f., study, instruction

पढ़ाना to teach

पता m., address

पता m., knowledge, awareness

पता होना to know, be aware

पति m., husband

पत्नी f., wife

पत्र m., letter

अंतर्देशीय पत्र inland letter

हवाई पत्र air letter

पर on, at; but

442

परसों the day before yesterday, the day after tomorrow

परिवार m., family

पश्चिम m., west

पश्चिमी western

पसंद pleasing

पसंद करना to like

पसंद होना to like

पहचानना to recognize

पहनना to put on

पहर m., part of day

पहला first

पहले early, earlier

के पहले before

से पहले before

पहुंचना to reach, arrive

पहुंच जाना to reach, arrive

पहुंचवाना to cause to send

पहुंचाना to send

पांच fine

पाना to find; to get to

पानी m., water

पार्क m., park

पार्टी f., party

पास near

के पास at, with; near

पास m., pass

पास करना to pass

पिचकारी f., syringe

पिछला last, previous

पिता m., father

पिलवाना to cause to drink

पिलाना to cause to drink

पीना to drink

पीला yellow, orange

पुराना old, ancient

पुस्तक f., book

पुस्तकालय m., library

पूना Poona

पूरा full, complete

पूरा करना to complete

पूरा होना to be completed

पूर्व, पूरब m., east

पूर्वी eastern

पैंट trousers

पैंतालीस forty-five

पैंतीस thirty-five

पैंसठ sixty-five

पैदल on foot

पैसा m., pice; money

पोस्टकार्ड m., postcard

पौन three quarters

443

पौने less one quarter
प्रतीक्षा f., waiting
  प्रतीक्षा करना to wait for
  प्रतीक्षा होना to wait for
प्रदेश m., state, province
प्रसन्न pleased
प्रसिद्ध famous
प्रार्थना f., request
प्रेम m., love, affection
प्रोफ़ेसर m., professor
प्लेटफ़ार्म m., platform

फ

फ़रवरी February
फल pl., fruit
फिर then; again
फिर भी however
फ़िल्म f., film

ब

बंगाल Bengal
बंगाली Bengali
बंद करना to close
  बंद होना to be closed
बंबई Bombay
बचना to be saved
  बच जाना to be saved
बचना to be left
  बच रहना to be left

बचवाना to cause to save
बचाना to save
बच्चा m., child
बजा m., o'clock
बजना to be played; to ring
  (intr.)
बजवाना to cause to play,
  cause to ring
बजाना to play (an instru-
  ment); to ring (trans.)
बड़ा big; older
बताना to tell
  बता देना to tell
बत्तीस thirty-two
बदलना to change (intr.)
बदलवाना to cause to change
बदलाना to change (trans.)
बनना to be made, done; to
  become
बनवाना to get made
बनाना to make, build
बनियाइन f., undershirt
बयालीस forty-two
बयासी eighty-two
बरबाद करना to waste
  बरबाद होना to be wasted
बरसना to rain

बरसात f., rainy season

बराबर continuously

बर्फ़, बरफ़ f., snow, ice

बल्कि but

बस f., bus

   बस-स्टाप m., bus stop

बहत्तर seventy-two

बहिन f., sister

बहुत very

बाइस twenty-two

बाईं left (direction)

बाज़ार m., bazaar

बात f., thing, affair

बाद after

बादल m., cloud

बानवे ninety-two

बाप m., father

बार m., times

बारह twelve

बावन fifty-two

बासठ sixty-two

बाहर out, outside

बिठलाना to cause to set

बिठाना to set

बीतना to pass, be spent

   बीत जाना to pass, be

      spent

बीमार sick, ill

बीस twenty

बुख़ार m., fever

बुधवार Wednesday

बुरा bad

   बुरा मानना to take offense

बुराई f. grievance

बुलवाना to cause to call

बुलाना to call

बृहस्पतिवार Thursday

बेकार unemployed

   बेकार में in vain, uselessly

बैंगनी purple

बैठना to sit down

बोलना to speak

ब्राउन brown

ब्रेक m., brake

म

मरना to fill

मरपूर filled

मरवाना to cause to fill

मराना to cause to fill

भर्ती f., admission

   भर्ती कराना to get admitted

भाई m., brother

भाग m., part

भारत m., India

भारतीय Indian

भाषण m., speech, lecture

भाषा f., language

भिजवाना to cause to send

भी too, also

भीड़ f., crowd

भूगोल m., geography

भूरा gray

भूलना to forget

　भूल जाना to forget

भुलवाना to cause to forget

भुलाना to cause to forget

भेजना to send

　भेज देना to send

भौगोलिक geographical

म

मंगलवार Tuesday

मई May

मकान m., house

मज़दूर m., worker, laborer

मज़दूरिन f., female worker

मज़दूरी f., wages

मतलब m., meaning

मद्रास Madras

मनवाना to cause to
　　celebrate

मनाना to observe,
　　celebrate

मनीआर्डर m., money order

मराठी f., Marathi

मशहूर famous

महंगा expensive

महत्व m., importance

महाराष्ट्र Maharashtra

महीना m., month

मां f., mother

माता f., mother

मातृभाषा f., mother tongue

मानना to think, consider

मार्ग m., road, street

मार्च March

मालूम m., awareness,
　　knowledge

　मालूम होना to know

मास m., month

मासिक monthly

मित्र m., friend

मिनट f., minute

मिलना to be available,
　　get; meet

मिलवाना to cause to intro-
　　duce

मिलाना to introduce

मीठा sweet

446

मील m., mile

मुसलमान m., Muslim

मुश्किल difficult

मुसीबत f., trouble

मुहल्ला m., locality

मुहूर्त f., moment

में in

मेरा my

मेला m., fair,
गैदरिंग of people

मेहरबानी f., kindness;
thank you

मैं I

मोज़ा m., sock

मोटर f., car

मोटरवाला m., driver

मौसम m., weather, season

य

यदि if

यह this

यही this (emphatic)

यही कोई about

यहां here

यहीं here (emphatic)

या or

यात्रा f., trip

यूनियन f., union

ये these

योग्य competent

र

रंग m., color

रंग खेलना to throw colored
water

रंग डालना to throw colored
water

रखना to put

रखवाना to cause to put

रखाना to cause to put

रहना to stay, live; to be;
to keep on

रहा here is

राजनीति f., politics,
political science

राजनीतिक political

राजा m., king

रात f., night

रानी f., queen

रास्ता m., way, road

रुकना to stop (intr.);
to stay, wait

रुकवाना to cause to stop

रुकाना to stop (trans.)

रुपया m., rupee

रुमाल m., handkerchief

447

रेलगाड़ी f., train

रेशमी silk

रोज़ m., day

## ल

लंबा long

लकड़ी f., wood

लगना to cost; to seem

लगभग about, approximately

लगवाना to cause to spend

लगाना to rub; to spend

लड़का m., boy, son

लड़की f., girl, daughter

लाइब्रेरी f., library

लाना to bring

लाल red

लिखना to write

लिख लेना to write down

लिखवाना to cause to write

लिखाना to cause to write

लिफ़ाफ़ा m., envelope

लिवाना to cause to take, bring

लू f., hot wind

लेकिन but

लेना to take; buy

ले लेना to take

ले जाना to take

लोग m., people

लोहा m., iron, steel

लौटना to return (intr.)

लौटवाना to cause to return

लौटाना to return (trans.)

## व

वक्त m., time

वक्त से (पर) on time

वक्ता m., speaker

वजह f., reason, cause

की वजह से on account of

वरन but

वर्ष m., year

वर्षगांठ f., birthday

वह he, she, it, that

वही that (emphatic)

वहां there

वहीं there (emphatic)

वापस back

वापस आना to come back

वार्षिक yearly

वाला of, connected with

वास्तव m., reality

विचार m., thought, idea

विचार करना to think of

विचार होना to think of

विज्ञान m., science

विद्यालय m., school

विद्वान m., scholar

विभाग m., department

विशेष especially

विश्व all, universal

विश्वविद्यालय m., university

विश्वास m., belief, faith

विषय m., subject

वैज्ञानिक scientific

वैसा as

व्याख्यान m., lecture

व्यापार m., business

श

शताब्दी f., century

शनिचर Saturday

शनिवार Saturday

शब्द m., word

शब्दकोष m., dictionary

शर्मा Sharma

शहर m., city

शाम f., evening

शायद perhaps

शुक्रवार Friday

शुभ auspicious

शुरू beginning

शुरू करना to begin

शुरू होना to begin

श्री Mr.

श्रीमती Mrs.

श्रीमान् Mr.

स

संतरा m., orange

सकना to be able

सच true

सचमुच really

सड़क f., street, road

सड़सठ sixty-seven

सतहत्तर seventy-seven

सत्तर seventy

सत्ताइस twenty-seven

सत्तानवे ninety-seven

सत्तावन fifty-seven

सत्तासी eighty-seven

सत्रह seventeen

सदी f., century

सप्ताह m., week

सफल impressive; fruitful

सफ़ेद white

सब all

समी all

समझना to understand

समझवाना to cause to
explain

समझाना to explain

449

समय m., time
समय से (पर) on time
समाचार m., news
समाचार पत्र m., newspaper
समाज m., society
सरकारी governmental
सरल easy, simple
सर्टिफ़िकेट m., certificate
सलाह f., advice
सवा plus one quarter
सस्ता cheap
सहायक m., helper, helpful
साठ sixty
साढ़े plus one half
सात seven
सातवां seventh
साथ along
साथ देना to accompany
साप्ताहिक weekly
सामने in front
सामने से from in front
सामाजिक social
सामान m., materials
सारा whole
साल m., year
सावधानी f., caution
साहब m., sir, gentleman

साहित्य m., literature
साहित्यिक literary
सिंगिल single
सिखवाना to cause to teach
सिखाना to teach
सितम्बर September
सिनेमा m., movie
सीखना to learn
सीधे straight ahead
सीमेंट f., cement
सुनना to hear, listen
सुनवाना to cause to tell
सुनाना to tell
सुबह f., morning
सुविधा f., convenience
सूती cotton
से from, with; than
से पहले before
सेल्स मैनेजर m., sales manager
सैंतालीस forty-seven
सैंतीस thirty-seven
सोचना to think
सोमवार Monday
सोलह sixteen
सौ hundred
स्कूल m., school
स्टेशन m., station

450

स्थान m., place

स्वयम्, स्वयं self

ह

हज़ार m., thousand

हफ़्ता m., week

हमारा our

हमेशा always

हर every

  हर एक each

हरा green

हवा f., wind, air

हवाई air

  हवाई पत्र air letter

हाल m., recent time; situation

  हाल में recently

हाल m., hall

हालचाल m., welfare

हालांकि although

हिंदी f., Hindi

हिंदू m., Hindu

ही (emphatic particle)

होटल m., hotel

होना to be, become

होली f., Holi, a Hindu festival

## ENGLISH - HINDI

A

(be) able सकना

about के आसपास, के बारे में, यही कोई, लगभग

accident, f. दुर्घटना

accompany साथ देना

(on) account of की वजह से

address, m. पता

admission, f. भर्ती

(get) admitted भर्ती कराना

advance, m. एडवांस

advice, f. सलाह

affair, f. बात

affection, m. प्रेम

after बाद, के बाद

afternoon, m. तीसरा पहर

again फिर

Agra, m. आगरा

air हवाई

  air letter हवाई पत्र

Ajanta अजंता

alone अकेला

all सब, सभी, विश्व

  in all कुल

451

along साथ

alright अच्छा

also भी

although हालांकि

always हमेशा

America, m. अमरीका

American अमरीकन

ancient पुराना

and और, तथा

any कोई

approximately के आसपास,
लगभग

April अप्रैल

arrange इंतज़ाम करना

be arranged इंतज़ाम होना

arrangement, m. इंतज़ाम

arrive पहुंचना, पहुंच जाना

art, f. कला

as वैसा, जैसा, उतना, जितना

at पर, के पास, में

attempt, f. कोशिश

August अगस्त

Aurangabad औरंगाबाद

auspicious शुभ

authority, m. अधिकार

(be) available मिलना

(be) aware पता होना

awareness, m. पता, मालूम

B

back वापस

come back वापस आना

bad बुरा, ख़राब

bank, m. किनारा

bazaar, m. बाज़ार

be होना, रहना

become होना, बनना

before के पहले, से पहले

begin शुरू करना, शुरू होना

beginning शुरू

belief, m. विश्वास

Bengal बंगाल

Bengali बंगाली

besides के अलावा

big बड़ा

birthday, f. वर्षगांठ

black काला

blue नीला

Bombay बंबई

book, f. किताब, पुस्तक

boy, m. लड़का

brake, m. ब्रेक

brick, f. ईंट

bring लाना

cause to bring लिवाना

452

brother, m. भाई

brown ब्राउन

build बनाना

burn (intr.) जलना

    (trans.) जलाना

  cause to burn जलवाना

bus, f. बस

  bus stop, m. बस स्टाप

business, m. व्यापार

but लेकिन, बल्कि, वरन, पर

buy ख़रीदना, लेना

by के द्वारा

C

Calcutta कलकत्ता

call बुलाना

  be called कहलाना

  cause to call बुलवाना

car, f. मोटर

card, m. कार्ड

cause, f. वजह

caution, f. सावधानी

celebrate मनाना

  cause to celebrate
    मनवाना

cement, f. सीमेंट

century, f. शताब्दी, सदी

certainly अवश्य, ज़रूर

certainty, m. निश्चय

certificate, m. सर्टिफ़िकेट

chairman, m. अध्यक्ष

change (intr.) बदलना

    (trans.) बदलाना

  cause to change बदलवाना

cheap सस्ता

child, m. बच्चा

city, m. नगर, शहर

class, m. दर्जा, क्लास

close बंद करना

  be closed बंद होना

cloth, m. कपड़ा

  clothes कपड़े

cloud, m. बादल

cold, m. ज़ुकाम

  cold season, m. जाड़ा,
     f. ठंड, ठंडक

collect जमाना

  be collected जमना

  cause to collect जमवाना

college, m. कालेज

color, m. रंग

come आना, आ जाना

  come back वापस आना

common आम

company, f. कंपनी

competent योग्य

complete पूरा करना

  be completed पूरा होना

complete पूरा

concerning के बारे में

condition, f. तबियत

connected with वाला

consider मानना

continuously बराबर

convenience, f. सुविधा

cost लगना

cotton सूती

country, m. देश

crowd, f. भीड़

      D

daily दैनिक

dance, m. नाच

dance नाचना

  cause to dance नचाना, नचवाना

darkness, m. अंधेरा

daughter, f. लड़की

Daulatabad दौलताबाद

day, m. दिन, रोज़

December दिसंबर

delay, f. देर

Delhi दिल्ली, देहली

department, m. विभाग

desire, f. इच्छा

Devagiri देवगिरि

dictionary, m. शब्दकोश, डिक्शनरी

difference, m. अंतर

difficult मुश्किल, कठिन

difficulty, f. कठिनाई

dinner, f. दावत

direction, f. तरफ़, ओर

do करना

  cause to do करवाना

  get done कराना

doctor, m. डाक्टर

doctor's office, m. दवाख़ाना

double डबल

dozen, m. दर्जन

drink पीना

  cause to drink पिलाना, पिलवाना

drive चलाना

  cause to drive चलवाना

driver, m. मोटरवाला

drop गिराना

  cause to drop गिरवाना

duration, f. देर

## E

each हर एक

early पहले

ease, f. आसानी

east, m. पूरब, पूर्व

eastern पूर्वी

easy सरल

eat खाना

edge, m. किनारा

eight आठ

eighteen अठारह

eighth आठवां

eighty अस्सी

  81 इक्यासी

  82 बयासी

  83 तिरासी

  84 चौरासी

  85 पचासी

  86 क्ियासी

  87 सत्तासी

  88 अट्ठासी

  89 नवासी

election, m. चुनाव

eleven ग्यारह

Ellora ऐलोरा

else और

embrace गले मिलना

empty ख़ाली

end, m. आखिर, ख़तम

English अंग्रेज़ी

Englishman अंग्रेज़

enjoy आनंद आना, आनंद मिलना

enmity, f. दुश्मनी

enough काफ़ी

enroll नाम लिखना

envelope, m. लिफ़ाफ़ा

especially विशेष

et cetera आदि

evening, f. शाम

every हर

example, m. नमूना

expensive महंगा

explain समझाना

  cause to explain

  समझवाना

## F

fair, m. मेला

faith, m. विश्वास

fall पड़ना, गिरना

family, m. परिवार

famous प्रसिद्ध, मशहूर

far दूर

  as far as तक

fare, m. किराया

fast तेज़ी से

father, m. पिता, बाप

February फ़रवरी

feed खिलाना

    cause to feed खिलवाना

festival, m. त्योहार

fever, m. बुखार

fifteen पंद्रह

fifty पचास

    51 इक्यावन

    52 बावन

    53 तिरपन

    54 चौवन, चउवन

    55 पचपन

    56 छप्पन

    57 सत्तावन

    58 अट्ठावन

    59 उनसठ

fill भरना

    cause to fill भरवाना
        भराना

filled भरपूर

film, f. फ़िल्म

find पाना

finish ख़तम करना, चुकना

    be finished ख़तम होना

first पहला

five पांच

fog, m. कोहरा

(on) foot पैदल

for के लिए, को

forget भूलना

    cause to forget भुलवाना,
    भुलाना

fort, m. किला

forty चालीस

    41 इकतालीस

    42 बयालीस

    43 तितालीस

    44 चवालीस

    45 पेंतालीस

    46 छयालीस

    47 सेंतालीस

    48 अड़तालीस

    49 उनचास

foundation, f. नींव

four चार

fourteen चौदह

fourth चौथा

Friday शुक्रवार

friend, m. मित्र

from से

(in) front सामने

    from in front सामने से

fruit, pl. फल

fruitful सफल

full पूरा

### G

gathered इकट्ठा, कट्ठा

general आम

  generally आम तौर पर

gentleman, m. साहब

geographical भौगोलिक

geography, m. भूगोल

get मिलना

girl, f. लड़की

give देना, दे देना

  cause to give दिलाना, दिलवाना

go जाना

  go away चले जाना

good अच्छा

governmental सरकारी

grade, m. दर्जा

gray भूरा

green हरा

grievance, f. बुराई

group, m. दल

Gujarat गुजरात

Gujarati गुजराती

### H

(plus one) half साढ़े

hall, m. हाल

handkerchief, m. रुमाल

happiness, f. खुशी

have to पड़ना, होना

he वह

health, f. तबियत

hear सुनना

heat, f. गर्मी

hello! नमस्ते

helper, m. सहायक

helpful सहायक

here यहां, यहीं, इधर

  here is रहा

Hindi हिन्दी

Hindu, m. हिन्दू

historical ऐतिहासिक

history, m. इतिहास

Holi, (a Hindu festival) f. होली

hope, f. आशा

hospital, m. अस्पताल

hot गरम

  hot season, f. गर्मी

hotel, m. होटल

hour, m. घंटा

house, m. घर, मकान,
    f. कोठी

how कितना, कैसा
  how much कितना

however फिर भी

hundred सौ

hurry जल्दी करना, जल्दी
  होना

husband, m. पति

### I

I मैं

ice, f. बरफ़, बर्फ़

idea, m. ख़्याल, विचार

if यदि, अगर

ill बीमार

importance, m. महत्त्व

important ख़ास, ज़रूरी

impressive सफल

in में, अंदर

inconvenience, m. कष्ट
    f. असुविधा

India, m. भारत

Indian भारतीय

indigenous देशीय

influence, m असर
  influence असर करना,
  असर होना

information, m. ख़बर
    f. जानकारी

injury, f. चोट

inland अंतर्देशीय

inland letter अंतर्देशीय पत्र

inside अंदर

instruction, f. पढ़ाई

intend इरादा करना, इरादा
  होना

intention, m. इरादा

interest, f. दिलचस्पी

introduce मिलाना
  cause to introduce
  मिलवाना

(get) involved पड़ जाना

iron, m. लोहा

### J

January जनवरी

joy, m. आनंद

July जुलाई

June जून

### K

Kanpur कानपुर

Kashmir काश्मीर

keep on रहना

kind, f. तरह

kindly कृपया

kindness, f. मेहरबानी,
कृपा
king. m. राजा
know जानना, पता होना,
मालूम होना
knowledge, f. जानकारी
m. पता, मालूम

## L

laborer, m. मज़दूर
language, f. भाषा
last पिछला
learn सीखना
leave (intr.) छूटना
(trans.) छोड़ना
cause to leave छुड़वाना
lecture, m. भाषण, व्याख्यान
left (direction) बाईं
to be left बच रहना,
बचना
less कम
letter, m. पत्र
air letter हवाई पत्र
inland letter अंतर्देशीय
पत्र
library, m. पुस्तकालय
f. लाइब्रेरी
like पसंद करना, पसंद होना

lime, m. चूना
listen सुनना
literary साहित्यिक
literature, m. साहित्य
little कम, थोड़ा, छोटा
a little ज़रा
live रहना
locality, m. मुहल्ला
long लंबा
look at देखना
take a look देख लेना
love, m. प्रेम

## M

Madras मद्रास
Maharashtra महाराष्ट्र
make करना, बनाना
cause to make करवाना
get made कराना, बनवाना
be made बनना
man, m. आदमी
many कई
Marathi, f. मराठी
March मार्च
materials, m. सामान
mathematical गणितीय
mathematics, m. गणित
May मई

459

meaning, m. मतलब

medicine, f. दवा

meet मिलना

mention ज़िक्र करना

   to be mentioned ज़िक्र होना

mile, m. मील

minute, f. मिनट

Miss कुमारी

miss चुकना

   cause to miss चुकाना

moment, f. मुहूर्त

Monday सोमवार

money पैसे, रुपए

money order, m. मनीआर्डर

month, m. महीना, मास

monthly मासिक

more ज़्यादा, अधिक

morning, f. सुबह

mortar, m., गारा

mother, f. माता, मां

mother tongue, f. मातृभाषा

movie, m. सिनेमा

Mr. श्री, श्रीमान्

Mrs. श्रीमती

much ज़्यादा, अधिक

Muslim, m. मुसलमान

must पड़ना

my मेरा

N

Nagpur नागपुर

   from Nagpur नागपुरी

name, m. नाम

near पास, के पास

necessary आवश्यक, ज़रूरी

necessity, f. आवश्यकता, ज़रूरत

neck, m. गला

need, f. आवश्यकता, ज़रूरत

neighborhood, m. पड़ोस

never कभी नहीं

new नया

news, f. ख़बर   m. समाचार

newspaper, m. समाचार पत्र

next अगला

night, f. रात

nine नौ

nineteen उन्नीस

ninety नब्बे

   91 इक्यानवे

   92 बानवे

   93 तिरानवे

   94 चौरानवे

   95 पच्चानवे, पंचानवे

96 छानवे

97 सत्तानवे

98 अट्ठानवे

99 निन्यानवे

noon, f. दोपहर

north, m. उत्तर

northern उत्तरी

not न, नहीं

November नवम्बर

now अब, अभी

nowadays आजकल

nowhere कहीं नहीं

number, m. नंबर

O

observe मनाना

o'clock, m. बजा

October अक्टूबर

of का

(take) offense बुरा मानना

office, m. दफ़्तर

often अक्सर

oh! अरे

old पुराना

older बड़ा

on पर

one एक

one's अपना

only केवल

open खुला

  be open खुला रहना

or या

orange, m. संतरा

orange (color) पीला

otherwise नहीं तो

our हमारा

out बाहर

outside बाहर

P

pair जोड़े

Panjab पंजाब

Panjabi पंजाबी

park, m. पार्क

part, m. भाग

party, f. पार्टी   m. दल

pass, m. पास

  pass पास करना

pass (time) बीतना, बीत जाना

people, m. लोग

perhaps शायद

permission, f. आज्ञा

pice, m. पैसा

pink powder, m. गुलाल

place, f. जगह   m. स्थान

platform, m. प्लेटफ़ार्म

play खेलना

  cause to play खिलाना

  खिलवाना

play (instrument) बजाना

  be played बजना

  cause to play बजवाना

pleased प्रसन्न

pleasing पसंद

pleasure, m. आनंद

  f. खुशी

political राजनीतिक

political science

  f. राजनीति

politics, f. राजनीति

Poona पूना

postcard, m. पोस्टकार्ड,

  कार्ड

preparation, f. तैयारी

previous पिछला

price, m. दाम

private निजी

professor, m. प्रोफ़ेसर

proper उचित

province, m. प्रदेश

publish निकालना

  be published निकलना

  cause to publish
  निकलवाना

purple बैंगनी

put रखना

  cause to put रखाना, रखवाना

  put on पहनना

Q

(three) quarters पौन

  less one quarter पौने

  plus one quarter सवा

queen, f. रानी

quite काफ़ी

R

rain बरसना

rainy season, f. बरसात

reach पहुंचना, पहुंच जाना

read पढ़ना, पढ़ लेना

ready तैयार

reality, m. वास्तव

really सचमुच

reason, f. वजह  m. कारण

recently हाल में

recent time, m. हाल

recognize पहचानना

red लाल

red powder, m. अबीर

rent, m. किराया

request, f. प्रार्थना

return (intr.) लौटना

462

(trans.) लौटाना    second दूसरा

cause to return लौटवाना    see देखना

right ठीक, (direction) दाईं    seem लगना

ring (intr.) बजना    self खुद, स्वयम्, स्वयं

     (trans.) बजाना    send भेजना, भेज देना, पहुंचाना

cause to ring बजवाना    cause to send भिजवाना,

road, m. रास्ता, मार्ग    पहुंचवाना

     f. सड़क    September सितम्बर

roof, f. छत    servant, m. नौकर

room, m. कमरा    female servant, f. नौकरानी

rub लगाना    set बिठाना

run into टकराना, टकरा    cause to set बिठलाना

जाना    seven सात

rupee, m. रुपया    seventeen सत्रह

     S    seventh सातवां

sales manager, m. सेल्स मैनेजर    seventy सत्तर

same एक ही    71 इकहत्तर

Saturday शनीचर, शनिवार    72 बहत्तर

save बचाना    73 तिहत्तर

be saved बचना, बच जाना    74 चौहत्तर

cause to save बचवाना    75 पचहत्तर

say कहना    76 छिहत्तर

scholar, m. विद्वान    77 सतहत्तर

school, m. स्कूल, विद्यालय    78 अठहत्तर

science, m. विज्ञान    79 उन्यासी

scientific वैज्ञानिक    Sharma शर्मा

season, m. मौसम    f. ऋतु    she वह

shirt, f. कमीज़

shop, f. दुकान

should चाहिए

show दिखाना, दिखलाना, दिखवाना

sick बीमार

side, f. तरफ़

silk रेशमी

simple सरल

sing गाना

  cause to sing गवाना

single सिंगिल

sir, m. साहब

sister, f. बहिन

sit down बैठना

situation, m. हाल

six छह

sixteen सोलह

sixty साठ

  61 इकसठ

  62 बासठ

  63 तिरसठ

  64 चौंसठ

  65 पैंसठ

  66 छ्यासठ

  67 सड़सठ

  68 अड़सठ

  69 उनहत्तर

skillful चतुर

sky, m. आसमान

snow, f. बर्फ़, बरफ़

snow बरफ़ गिरना

so ऐसा

social सामाजिक

society, m. समाज

sock, m. मोज़ा

some कुछ, कोई

something else और कुछ

sometimes कभी

somewhere कहीं

son, m. लड़का

song, m. गाना

soon जल्दी

sorrow, m. अफ़सोस

sort, f. तरह

south, m. दक्षिण

southern दक्षिणी

speak बोलना

speaker, m. वक्ता

special ख़ास

  specially ख़ास तौर पर

speech, m. भाषण

speed, f. तेज़ी

spend लगाना

be spent (time) बीतना,
बीत जाना

cause to spend लगवाना

stamp, m. टिकट

standing खड़ा

start off चल देना

state, m. प्रदेश

station, m. स्टेशन

stay ठहरना, रहना, रुकना

steel, m. लोहा

stop (intr.) ठहरना, रुकना
(trans.) ठहराना, रुकाना

cause to stop ठहरवाना,
रुकवाना

store, f. दुकान

stormy तूफ़ानी

straight ahead सीधे

street, m. मार्ग f. सड़क

strong तेज

study पढ़ना

study, f. पढ़ाई

subject, m. विषय

such ऐसा

Sunday इतवार

sunshine, f. घूप

sweet मीठा

syringe, f. पिचकारी

T

take लेना, ले लेना, लेजाना

cause to take लिवाना

taxi, f. टैक्सी

teach पढ़ाना, सिखाना

cause to teach पढ़वाना,
सिखवाना

telephone, m. टेलीफ़ोन

call on the telephone
टेलीफ़ोन करना

tell कहना, कह देना, बताना,
बता देना, सुनाना

cause to tell सुनवाना

ten दस

than से

thank you! मेहरबानी, धन्यवाद

that वह, कि

then तब, तब तो, फिर

just then तभी

there वहां, वहीं

therefore इसलिए

thing, f. चीज़, बात

think सोचना, मानना

think of विचार करना,
विचार होना

third तीसरा

thirteen तेरह

thirty तीस

  31 इकतीस

  32 बत्तीस

  33 तेंतीस

  34 चौंतीस

  35 पैंतीस

  36 छत्तीस

  37 सैंतीस

  38 अड़तीस

  39 उनतालीस

this यह, यही

thought, m. ख़्याल, विचार

thousand, m. हज़ार

three तीन

throw डालना

  allow to throw डलवाना

  throw colored water

    रंग खेलना, रंग डालना

Thursday गुरुवार, बृहस्पतिवार

ticket, m. टिकट

time, m. समय, वक़्त

  on time समय से (पर),

    वक़्त से (पर)

times, m. बार

to तक, को

today आज

tomorrow कल

too भी

tour, m. दौरा

town, m. नगर

train, f. गाड़ी, रेलगाड़ी

transfer, m. तबादला

trip, f. यात्रा

trouble, f. मुसीबत

      m. कष्ट

trousers, m. पैंट

true सच

try कोशिश करना

Tuesday मंगलवार

twelve बारह

twenty बीस

  21 इक्कीस

  22 बाइस

  23 तेइस

  24 चौबीस

  25 पच्चीस

  26 छब्बीस

  27 सत्ताइस

  28 अट्ठाइस

  29 उनतीस

two दो

  two and a half ढाई

U

undershirt, f. बनियाइन

understand समझना

unemployed बेकार

union, f. यूनियन

universal विश्व

university, m. विश्वविद्यालय

until तक

uselessly बेकार में

usually आम तौर पर,
  अक्सर

## V

vacation, f. छुट्टी

(in) vain बेकार में

very बहुत

vicinity, m. आसपास

village, m. गांव

## W

wages, f. मज़दूरी

wait इंतज़ार करना, इंतज़ार
  होना, प्रतीक्षा करना, प्रतीक्षा
  होना, रुकना

waiting, f. प्रतीक्षा
  m. इंतज़ार

walk घूमना

wall, f. दीवाल

want इच्छा करना, इच्छा
  होना, चाहना

washerman, m. धोबी

washerwoman, f. धोबिन

waste बरबाद करना

  be wasted बरबाद होना

water, m. पानी

way, m. रास्ता

weather, m. मौसम

Wednesday बुधवार

week, m. सप्ताह, हफ़्ता

weekly साप्ताहिक

welfare, m. हालचाल

west, m. पश्चिम

western पश्चिमी

what क्या, कौन

  what kind of कौन सा,
  कैसा

when कब, जब

where कहां, किधर

which कौन, जो

white सफ़ेद

who कौन, जो

whole सारा

why क्यों

wife, f. पत्नी

wind, f. हवा

  hot wind, f. लू

window, f. खिड़की

with के साथ, के पास, से

woman, f. औरत

wood, f. लकड़ी

woolen ऊनी

word, m. शब्द

work, m. काम

  work काम करना

worker, m. मज़दूर

  female worker, f.

    मज़दूरिन

worth seeing दर्शनीय

write लिखना

  write down लिख लेना

  cause to write लिखाना,

  लिखवाना

Y

year, m. साल, वर्ष

yearly वार्षिक

yellow पीला

yes हां, जी हां

yesterday कल

you तुम, आप

younger छोटा

your तुम्हारा, आपका

468